The Glory Of The Coming

By

Irvin S. Cobb

Double 9
BOOKS

The Glory Of The Coming
by Irvin S. Cobb

ISBN: 978-93-61427-99-2

Published by

DOUBLE 9 BOOKS

2/13-B, Ansari Road
Daryaganj, New Delhi – 110002
info@double9books.com
www.double9books.com
Tel. 011-40042856

ABOUT THE AUTHOR

Shrewsbury, Irvin Cobb (June 23, 1876 – March 11, 1944) was a Paducah, Kentucky-born author, humorist, editor, and columnist who moved to New York in 1904 and lived there for the rest of his life. As the highest-paid staff reporter in the United States, he worked for Joseph Pulitzer's newspaper, the New York World. Cobb also published almost 60 books and 300 short tales. Some of his works were made into silent films. Several of his Judge Priest short stories were adapted for two feature films directed by John Ford in the 1930s. Cobb was the second of four children born in Paducah, Kentucky, to Kentucky natives. Reuben Saunders, M.D., is credited with finding in 1873 that injections of morphine-atropine were effective in treating cholera. Cobb grew up in Paducah, and many of his later works were inspired by events and people from his upbringing. Cobb was afterwards dubbed the "Duke of Paducah." Cobb attended public and private elementary schools before enrolling in William A. Cade's Academy to study law. Cobb's father became an alcoholic when he was 16, following the death of his grandfather. Cobb began his writing career after being forced to drop out of school and find jobs.

CONTENTS

"Mine eyes have seen the glory of the coming of the Lord; He is trampling out the vintage where the grapes of wrath are stored; He hath loosed the fateful lightning of His terrible swift sword, His Truth is marching on."

—*Battle Hymn of the Republic*

This book is made up of articles written abroad in the spring and summer of 1918 and cabled or mailed back for publication at home. For convenience in arrangement, a few of these papers have been broken up into sectional subdivisions with new chapter headings inserted; otherwise the matter is here presented practically in its original form.

It has been given to the writer to behold widely dissimilar aspects of the Great War. As a neutral observer, hailing from a neutral country, I was a witness, in Belgium, in northern France, in Germany and in England, to some of its first stages. That was back in 1914 when I was for awhile with the British, then for a period with the Belgian forces afield, then for a much longer period with the German armies and finally with the British again. I was of like mind then with all my professional brethren serving publications in non-belligerent countries, excepting one or two or three of a more discerning vision than the rest. Behind the perfection of the German fighting machine I did not see the hideous malignant brutality which was there.

In the first half of this present year, as a partisan on the side of my country and its federated associates, I visited England and for a space of months travelled about over France, with two incursions into that small corner of Flanders which at this time remained in the hands of the Allies.

I have seen the Glory of the Coming. I have watched the American Expeditionary Force grow from a small thing into a mighty thing—the mightiest thing, I veritably believe, that since conscious time began, has been undertaken by a free people entering upon a war on foreign shores with nothing personally to gain except a principle, with nothing to maintain except honour, with nothing to keep except their national self-respect. In this war our only spoils out of the victory will be the establishment of the rights of other peoples to rule themselves, our only territorial enlargements will be the graves where our fallen dead sleep on alien soil, our only tangible reward for all that we are giving in blood and treasure and effort and self-denial, will be the knowledge that in a world crisis, when the liberties of the world were imperilled, we, as a world-power and as perhaps the most conspicuous example in the world, of a democracy, did our duty by ourselves, by our republican neighbours overseas and by our children and their children and their children's children.

No longer ago than last March, it was a small thing we had done, as viewed in the light of our then visible performances in France and an even smaller thing as viewed in the light of what our public men, many of them, and our newspapers, some of them, had promised on our behalf nearly a year earlier when we came into the war. At the beginning there was an army to be created; there was a navy to be built up; there was a continent to be crossed and an ocean to be traversed if we meant to link up all the States of our Union with all our plans; there was a military establishment to be started from the grass roots; there were ninety millions of us to be set from the ways of peace into the ways of war. But because some of our politicians professed to believe that by virtue of our resources, our energy and our so-called business efficiency we could do the impossible in an impossibly brief time, and more especially because, among the masses of Continental Europe there was a tendency to look upon us as a race of miracle-workers living in a magic-land and accomplishing unutterable wonders at will, and finally because these same masses accepted the words of our self-appointed, self-anointed prophets as they might accept Gospel-writ, a profound disappointment over the seeming failure of America to produce her legions on European soil, followed hard upon the exaltation which had prevailed among our Allies immediately after we broke with the common enemy of mankind. In France I know this to have been true; in other countries I have reason to believe it was true. As month after month passed until nearly a twelvemonth had gone by and still the armed millions from America did not materialise, I think it only natural and inevitable that, behind their hands and under their breaths, the Poilus called our soldiers "Boy Scouts" and spoke of our effort as "The Second Children's Crusade." For thanks be to a few men among us who worked with their mouths rather than with their hands, the French populace had been led to expect so very much of us in so short a space of time and yet there now was presented before their eyes, so very little as the tangible proofs of our voiced determination to offer all that we had and all that we were, in the fight for decency and for humanity.

Do you remember when, on or about the beginning of the last week of March, General Pershing offered to the Allied command the available mobile strength of the army under him, for service to aid the British, the French, the Belgians and the Portuguese in stemming the great German offensive which had been launched on the twenty-first day of that month? Pershing made the offer in all good faith and in all good faith it was accepted. But at that moment all he could spare out of the trenches and send across France from the East to the West to go into the line in threatened Picardy was one division of considerably less than forty thousand men; a puny handful as they measure fighting forces these times; and that division was stayed in part on French rations, equipped in part with borrowed French ordnance and provided in large part with French munitions. Without French aid it probably could not have gone forward at all; without French aid it could not have maintained itself after it had taken over the Normandy sectors to which Foch assigned it. It was not the fault of our military leaders abroad, perhaps it was not the fault of our people at home that, fifty weeks after entering the war, we were able to render only so small a share of immediate help in this most critical juncture of the entire war. But it was the fault of those who had boasted, those who had bragged, those who had preached at home what they did not practice, that the French people were beginning to think—and to whisper—that the United States had failed to live up to its pledges. These people had no way of knowing what we were accomplishing over here; they must judge by what they might see for themselves over there.

The great awakening came, though, before the first of June. Overnight, it almost seemed, our army began to function as an army. The sea became alive with our transports, the land became alive with our troops. Instead of two hundred and some odd thousands of men on French soil, we had half a million, then a million, then a million and a half. No longer were our forces without tanks of American manufacture, without machine-guns of American manufacture, without a proper and adequate equipment of heavy guns of American manufacture. There was even hope that our aeroplane production, up until then the most ghastly and pitiable failure of all, might by autumn, begin to measure up, in some degree at least, to the sanguine press-notices of the year before—1917. We who in France could see the growth of this thing came to feel that perhaps all of our dollar-a-year commercial giants were not being grossly overpaid and we came proudly to realise that our country now was responding with all its strength to the responsibilities it had assumed. The Yanks were no longer on the way; they were here—here in number sufficient to enable us to lend a strong and ever-strengthening hand in the turning-back of the enemy and in bringing closer the certainty of a complete triumph over him. It was the Glory of the Coming. Moreover it should not be forgotten in the reckoning-up of causes and results that the lodging of the allied command in the hands of one captain—the most powerful single factor in inspiring victory—was brought about largely through American insistence upon the election of a single leader and a unified leadership for all the forces of the confederated nations in the field of the western theatre of the war.

I sometimes think the most splendid thing I have seen in this war was not some individual act of heroism, or devotion, or resolution—glorious though it may have been. I sometimes think the most splendid thing I have seen was the making-over of nations, literally before my eyes, in the fiery furnace of this war. I have seen little Belgium wearing the marks of her transcendent sacrifice and her unutterable suffering, as the Redeemer of Man wore the nail-marks of His Crucifixion; I have seen Britain transformed from the fat, contented, slothful, old grandmother of the nations, sitting by the chimney-piece and feeding herself torpid on her plenty, into the militant Britain of yore that has put so many millions of her sons into khaki and so many of the ladies of Germany into mourning; I have seen France become an incomparably glorious model, before all the world for all time, of the heights to which a free people may rise in defence of national pledges, national integrity and national existence; and I have seen my own country taking her proper place, in the most desperate emergency that ever confronted civilisation, as a people united, determined, valiant and steadfast—the spirit of the New World binding herself with steel grapples to the best that is in the Old World and inevitably taking the first steps in the long-delayed campaign of understanding and conciliation and renewed affection with our kinspeople and our brethren of the British Isles who speak the same mother-tongue which we speak and with whom we are joint inheritors of Runnymede and Agincourt.

As I write these lines, victory appears to be very near. Seemingly, it is coming one year sooner than we, who were in France and Belgium in the first months of 1918, thought it would come. And speaking for my fellow-American correspondents as well as for myself, I make so bold as to say that all of us are devoutly hopeful that our leaders will make it a complete, not a conditional victory. For surely those who are without mercy themselves cannot appreciate and do not deserve mercy from others. To our way of thinking, the vanquished must be made to drink the cup of defeat to its bitterest lees, not because of any vengeful desire on our part to inflict unnecessary punishment and humiliation upon him, but because he who had no other argument than force, can be cured of his madness only by force. We who have seen what he has wrought by the work of his hands among his helpless victims in other lands believe this with all our hearts.

I. S. C.

New York, November, 1918.

CHAPTER I
WHEN THE SEA-ASP STINGS

BECAUSE she was camouflaged with streaky marks and mottlings into the likeness of a painted Jezebel of the seas, because she rode high out of the water, and wallowed as she rode, because during all those days of our crossing she hugged up close to our ship, splashing through the foam of our wake as though craving the comfort of our company, we called her things no self-respecting ship should have to bear. But when that night, we stood on the afterdeck of our ship, we running away as fast as our kicking screw would take us, and saw her going down, taking American soldier boys to death with her in alien waters, we drank toasts standing up to the poor old *Tuscania*.

I was one of those who were in at the death of the *Tuscania*. Her sinking was the climax of the most memorable voyage I ever expect to take. Five days have elapsed since she was torpedoed, and even though these words are being cabled across from London to the home side of the ocean, at least three weeks more must elapse before they can see printer's ink. So to some this will seem an old story; but the memory of what happened that night off the Irish coast is going to abide with me while I live. It was one of those big moments in a man's life that stick in a man's brain as long as he has a brain to think with.

Transatlantic journeys these days aren't what they used to be before America went into the war. Ours began to be different even before our ship pulled out from port. It is forbidden me now to tell her name, and anyhow her name doesn't in the least matter, but she was a big ship with a famous skipper, and in peacetimes her sailing would have made some small stir. There would have been crowds of relations and friends at the pier bidding farewell to departing travellers; and steamer baskets and steamer boxes would have been coming aboard in streams. Beforehand there would have been a pleasant and mildly exciting bustle, and as we drew away from the dock and headed out into midstream and down the river for our long hike overseas, the pierhead would have been alive with waving handkerchiefs, and all our decks would have been fringed with voyagers shouting back farewells to those they had left behind them. Instead we slipped away almost as if we had done something wrong. There was no waving of hands and handkerchiefs, no good-byes on the gang-planks, no rush to get back on land when the shore bell sounded. To reach the dock we passed through trochas of barbed-wire entanglements, past sentries standing with fixed bayonets at entryways. When we got inside the pier our people bade us farewell at a guarded gate. None but travellers whose passports read straight were allowed beyond that point. So alone and unescorted each one of us went soberly up the side of the ship, and then sundry hours later our journey began, as the ship, like a big grey ghost, slid away from land, as quietly as might be, into the congenial grey fog which instantly swallowed her up and left her in a little grey world of sea mist that was all her own. After this fashion, then, we started.

As for the first legs of the trip they were much like the first legs of almost any sea trip except that we travelled in a convoy with sundry other ships, with warcraft to guard us on our way. Our ship was quite full of soldiers—officers in the first cabin, and the steerage packed with khakied troopers—ninety per cent of whom had never smelled bilge water before they embarked upon their great adventure overseas. There were fewer civilians than one formerly might have found on a ship bound for Europe. In these times only those civilians who have urgent business in foreign climes venture to go abroad.

I sat at the purser's table. His table was fairly typical of the ship's personnel. With me there sat, of course, the purser, likewise two Canadian officers, two members of a British Commission returning from America, and an Irish brewer. There were not very many women on our passenger list. Of these women half a dozen or so were professional nurses, and two were pretty Canadian girls bound for England to be married on arrival there to young Canadian officers. There were only three children on board, and they were travelling with their parents in the second class.

Except for a touch of seriousness about the daily lifeboat drill, and except that regimental discipline went forward, with the troops drilling on the open deck spaces when the weather and the sea permitted, there was at first nothing about this voyage to distinguish it from any other midwinter voyage. Strangers got acquainted one with another and swapped views on politics, religion, symptoms and Germans; flirtations started and ripened furiously; concerts were organized and took place, proving to be what concerts at sea usually are. Twice a day the regimental band played, and once a day, up on the bridge, the second officer took the sun, squinting into his sextant with the deep absorption with which in happier times a certain type of tourist was wont to stare through an enlarging device at a certain type of Parisian photograph. At night, though, we were in a darkened ship, a gliding black shape upon black waters, with heavy shades over all the portholes and thick draperies over all the doors, and only dim lights burning in the passageways and cross halls, so that every odd corner on deck or within was as dark as a coal pocket. It took some time to get used to being in the state in which Moses was when the light went out; but then, we had time to get used to it, believe me! Ocean travel is slower these days, for obvious reasons. Personally, I retired from the ship's society during three days of the first week of the trip. I missed only two meals, missing them, I may add, shortly after having eaten them; but at the same time I felt safer in my berth than up on deck—not happier, particularly, but safer. The man who first said that you can't eat your cake and have it too had such cases as mine in mind, I am sure of that. I can't and I don't—at least not when I am taking an ocean voyage. I have been seasick on many waters, and I have never learned to care for the sensation yet.

When I emerged from semiretirement it was to learn that we had reached the so-called danger zone. The escort of warcraft for our transport had been augmented. Under orders the military men wore their life jackets, and during all their waking hours they went about with cork flaps hugging them about their necks fore and aft, so that they rather suggested Chinese malefactors with their heads incased in punishment casques. By request the civilian passengers were expected to carry their life preservers with them wherever they went; but some of them forgot the injunction. I know I did frequently. Also, a good many of them turned in at night with most of their outer clothing on their bodies; but I followed the old Southern custom and took most of mine off before going to bed.

Our captain no longer came to the saloon for his meals. He lived upon the bridge—ate there and, I think, slept there too—what sleeping he did. Standing there all muffled in his oilskins he looked even more of a squatty and unheroic figure than he had in his naval blue presiding at the head of the table; but by repute we knew him for a man who had gone through one torpedoing with great credit to himself and through numbers of narrow escapes, and we valued him accordingly and put our faith in him. It was faith well placed, as shall presently transpire.

I should not say that there was much fear aboard; at least if there was it did not manifest itself in the manner or the voice or the behaviour of a single passenger seen by me; but there was a sort of nagging, persistent sense of uneasiness betraying itself in various small ways. For one thing, all of us made more jokes about submarines, mines and other perils of the deep than was natural. There was something a little forced, artificial, about this gaiety—the laughs came from the lips, but not from points farther south.

We knew by hearsay that the *Tuscania* was a troopship bearing some of our soldiers over to do their share of the job of again making this world a fit place for human beings to live in. There was something pathetic in the fashion after which she so persistently and constantly strove to stick as closely under our stem as safety and the big waves would permit. It was as though her skipper placed all reliance in our skipper, looking to him to lead his ship out of peril should peril befall. Therefore, we of our little group watched her from our afterdecks, with her sharp nose forever half or wholly buried in the creaming white smother we kicked up behind us.

It was a crisp bright February day when we neared the coasts of the British Empire. At two o'clock in the afternoon we passed, some hundreds of yards to starboard, a round, dark, bobbing object which some observers thought was a floating mine. Others thought it might be the head and shoulders of a human body held upright in a life ring. Whatever it was, our ship gave it a wide berth, sheering off from the object in a sharp swing. Almost at the same moment upon our other bow, at a distance of not more than one hundred yards from the crooked course we were then pursuing, there appeared out through one of the swells a lifeboat, oarless, abandoned, empty, except for what looked like a woman's cloak lying across the thwarts. Rising and falling to the swing of the sea it drifted down alongside of us so that we could look almost straight down into it. We did not stop to investigate but kept going, zigzagging as we went, and that old painted-up copy cat of a *Tuscania* came zigzagging behind us. A good many persons decided to tie on their life preservers.

Winter twilight was drawing on when we sighted land—Northern Ireland it was. The wind was going down with the sun and the sharp crests of the waves were dulling off, and blunt oily rollers began to splash with greasy sounds against our plates. Far away somewhere we saw the revolving light of a lighthouse winking across the face of the waters like a drunken eye. That little beam coming and going gave me a feeling of security. I was one of a party of six who went below to the stateroom of a member of the group for a farewell card game.

Perhaps an hour later, as we sat there each intently engaged upon the favoured indoor American sport of trying to better two pairs, we heard against our side of the ship a queer knocking sound rapidly repeated—a sound that somehow suggested a boy dragging a stick along a picket fence.

"I suppose that's a torpedo rapping for admission," said one of us, looking up from his cards and listening with a cheerful grin on his face.

I think it was not more than five minutes after that when an American officer opened the stateroom door and poked his head in.

"Better come along, you fellows," he said; "but come quietly so as not to give alarm or frighten any of the women. Something has happened. It's the *Tuscania*—she's in trouble!"

Up we got and hurried aft down the decks, each one taking with him his cork jacket and adjusting it over his shoulders as he went. We came to the edge of the promenade deck aft. There were not many persons there, as well as we could tell in the thick darkness through which we felt our way, and not many more came afterward—in all I should say not more than seventy-five.

All the rest were in ignorance of what had occurred—a good many were at dinner. Accounts of the disaster which I have read since my arrival in London said that the torpedo from the U-boat thudded into the vitals of the *Tuscania*, disarranged her engines, and left her in utter darkness for a while until her crew could switch on the auxiliary dynamo. I think this must have been a mistake, for at the moment of our reaching the deck of our ship the *Tuscania* was lighted up all over. Her illumination seemed especially brilliant, but that, I suppose, was largely because we had become accustomed to seeing our fellow transports as dark bulks at night. I should say she was not more than a mile from us, almost due aft and a trifle to the left. But the distance between us visibly increased each passing moment, for we were running away from her as fast as our engines could drive us. We could feel our ship throb under our feet as she picked up speed. It made us feel like cowards. Near at hand a ship was in distress, a ship laden with a precious freightage of American soldier boys, and here were we legging it like a frightened rabbit, weaving in and out on sharp tacks.

We knew, of course, that we were under orders to get safely away if we could in case one of those sea adders, the submarines, should attack our convoy. We knew that guardian destroyers would even now be hurrying to the rescue, and we knew land was not many miles, away; but all the same, I think I never felt such an object of shame as I felt that first moment when the realisation dawned on me that we were fleeing from a stricken vessel instead of hastening back to give what succour we could.

As I stood there in the darkness, with silent, indistinct shapes all about me, it came upon me with almost the shock of a physical blow that the rows of lights I saw yonder through the murk were all slanting slightly downward toward what would be the bow of the disabled steamer. These oblique lines of light told the story. The *Tuscania* had been struck forward and was settling by the head.

Suddenly a little subdued "Ah! Ah!" burst like a chorus from us all A red rocket—a rocket as red as blood—sprang up high into the air above those rows of lights. It hung aloft for a moment, then burst into a score of red balls, which fell, dimming out as they descended. After a bit two more rockets followed in rapid succession. I always thought a rocket to be a beautiful thing. Probably this belief is a heritage from that time in my boyhood when first I saw Fourth-of-July fireworks. But never again will a red rocket fired at night be to me anything except a reminder of the most pitiable, the most heart-racking thing I have ever seen—that poor appeal for help from the sinking *Tuscania* flaming against that foreign sky.

There was silence among us as we watched. None of us, I take it, had words within him to express what he felt; so we said nothing at all, but just stared out across the Waters until our eyeballs ached in their sockets. So quiet were we that I jumped when right at my elbow a low, steady voice spoke. Turning my head I could make out that the speaker was one of the younger American officers.

"If what I heard before we sailed is true," he said, "my brother is in the outfit on that boat yonder. Well, if they get him it will only add a little more interest to the debt I already owe those damned Germans."

That was all he said, and to it I made no answer, for there was no answer to be made.

Fifteen minutes passed, then twenty, then twenty-five. Now instead of many small lights we could make out only a few faint pin pricks of light against the blackness to mark the spot where the foundering vessel must be. Presently we could distinguish but one speck of light. Alongside this one special gleam a red glow suddenly appeared—not a rocket this time, but a flare, undoubtedly. Together the two lights—the steady white one and the spreading red one—descended and together were extinguished. Without being told we knew, all of us—landsmen and seamen alike—what we had seen. We had seen the last of that poor ship, stung to death by a Hunnish sea-asp.

Still silent, we went below. Those of us who had not yet dined went and dined. Very solemnly, like men performing a rite, we ordered wine and we drank to the *Tuscania* and her British crew and her living cargo of American soldiers.

Next morning, after a night during which perilous things happened about us that may not be described here and now, we came out of our perils and into safety at an English port, and there it was that we heard what made us ask God to bless that valorous, vigilant little pot-bellied skipper of ours, may he live forever! We were told that the torpedo which pierced the *Tuscania* was meant for us, that the U-boat rising unseen in the twilight fired it at us, and that our captain up on the bridge saw it coming when it was yet some way off, and swinging the ship hard over to one side, dodged the flittering devil-thing by a margin that can be measured literally in inches. The call was a close one. The torpedo, it was said, actually grazed the plates of our vessel—it was that we heard as we sat at cards—and passing aft struck the bow of the *Tuscania* as she swung along not two hundred yards behind us. We heard, too, that twice within the next hour torpedoes were fired at us, and again a fourth one early in the hours of the morning. Each time chance or poor aim or sharp seamanship or a combination of all three saved us. We were lucky. For of the twelve ships in our transport two, including the *Tuscania*, were destroyed and two others, making four in all, were damaged by torpedoes before morning.

Next day, in London, I read that not a man aboard the *Tuscania*, whether sailor or soldier, showed weakness or fright. I read how those Yankee boys, many of them at sea for the first time in their lives, stood in ranks waiting for rescue or for death while the ship listed and yawed and settled under them; how the British sang "God Save the King," and the Americans sang to the same good Allied air, "My Country, 'Tis of Thee;" and how at last, descending over the side, some of them to be drowned but more of them to be saved, those American lads of ours sang what before then had been a meaningless, trivial jingle, but which is destined forevermore, I think, to mean a great deal to Americans. Perry said: "We have met the enemy, and they are ours." Lawrence said: "Don't give up the ship!" Farragut said: "Damn the torpedoes, go ahead." Dewey said: "You may fire, Gridley, when you are ready." Our history is full of splendid sea slogans, but I think there can never be a more splendid one that we Americans will cherish than the first line, which is also the title of the song now suddenly freighted with a meaning and a message to American hearts, which our boys sang that black February night in the Irish Sea when two hundred of them, first fruits of our national sacrifice in this war, went over the sides of the *Tuscania* to death: "Where do we go from here, boys; where do we go from here?"

CHAPTER II
"ALL AMURIKIN—OUT TO THEM WIRES"

IIE was curled up in a moist-mud cozy corner. His curved back fitted into a depression in the clay. His feet rested comfortably in an ankle-deep solution, very puttylike in its consistency, and compounded of the rains of heaven and the alluvials of France. His face was incredibly dirty, and the same might have been said for his hands. He had big buck teeth and sandy hair and a nice round inquisitive blue eye. His rifle, in good order, was balanced across his hunched knees. One end of a cigarette was pasted fast to his lower lip; the other end spilled tiny sparks down the front of his blouse.

Offhand you would figure his age to be halfpast nineteen. Just round the corner from him a machine gun at intervals spoke in stuttering accents. At more frequent intervals from somewhere up or down the line a rifle whanged where an ambitious amateur Yankee sniper tried for a professional and doubtlessly a bored German sniper across the way; or where the German tried back.

The youth in the cozy corner paid small heed. He was supposed to be getting his baptism of fire. In reality he was reading a two-months-old copy of a certain daily paper printed in a certain small city in a certain Middle Western state—to wit, the sovereign state of Ohio. He belonged to a volunteer regiment, and in a larger sense to the Rainbow Division. This was his first day in the front-line trenches and already he was as much at home there as though he had been cradled to the lullaby of those big guns grunting away in the distance. For a fact he was at home—reading home news out of the home paper and, as one might say, not caring a single dern whatsoever.

"Say, Tobe," he called in the husky half voice which is the prescribed and conventional conversational tone on the forward edges of No Man's Land; "Tobe, lissen!"

His mate, leaning against the slanted side of the trench ten feet away, blowing little smoke wisps up toward the pale-blue sky above him, half turned his head to answer.

"Well, what?"

"Whatter you know about this? It says here the New York Yanks is liable to buy Ty Cobb off of Detroit. Say, what'll them Detroits do without old Ty in there bustin' the fast ones on the nose, huh?"

"With all the money they'll get for that guy they should worry!"

The emphatic ker-blim of a rifle a hundred yards off furnished a vocal exclamation point to further accent the comment.

The reader shifted himself slightly in his scooped niche and turned over to another page. He was just the average kid private, but to me he was as typical as type can be. I figured him as a somewhat primitive, highly elemental creature, adaptable and simple-minded; appallingly green yet at this present trade, capable though of becoming amazingly competent at it if given experience and a chance; temperamentally gaited to do heroic things without any of the theatricalism of planned heroics—in short and in fine, the incarnated youthful spirit of the youthful land which bore him.

I came upon him with his cigarette and his favourite daily and his mud-boltered feet at the tail end of a trip along the front line of a segment of a sector held by our troops, and before I made his acquaintance sundry things befel. I had been in trenches before, but they were German trenches along the Aisne in the fall of the first year of this war business, and these trenches of our own people were quite different from those of 1914. French minds had devised them, with their queer twists, and windings, which seem so crazy and yet are so sanely ordained; and French hands had dug them out of the chalky soil and shored them up with timbers, but now Americans had taken them over and, in common with all things that Americans take over, they had become as much and as thoroughly American as though they had been Subway diggings in New York City, which indeed they rather resembled; or excavations for the foundations of the new Carnegie Library in Gallipolis. 'Tis a way our folks have. It may be a good way or a bad way—since I came over here I think the French neither understand it nor care deeply for it—but all the same it is our way.

At the beginning we quit a wrecked town that was a regimental headquarters. Its present population was all military, French and American. The villagers who had once lived there were gone to the last one of them, and had been gone for years probably. But more than by the shattered stone walls, or by the breached and empty church with its spire shorn away, or by the tiled roofs which were roofs no longer but sieves and colanders, its altered character was set forth and proved by the absence of any manure heaps against the house fronts. In this part of the world communal prosperity is measured, I think, by the size and richness of the manure heap. It is kept alongside the homes and daily it is turned over with spades and tormented with pitchforks, against the time when it is carried forth to be spread upon the tiny farm a mile or so away. The rank ammoniacal smell of the precious fertilizer which keeps the land rich is the surest information to the nose of the approaching traveller that thrifty folk abide in the hamlet he is about entering.

But this town smelled only of dust and decay and the peculiar odour of rough-cast plastering which has been churned by wheels and hoofs and feet into a fine white silt like powdered pumice, coating everything and everybody in sight when the weather is dry, and when the weather is wet turning into a slick and slimy paste underfoot.

We came out of a colonel's billet in a narrowshouldered old two-story house, my companion and I; and crossing the little square we passed through what once upon a time had been the front wall of the principal building in the place. The front wall still stood and the doorway was unscarred, but both were like parts of stage settings, for beyond them was nothing at all save nothingness — messed-about heaps of crumbled masonry and broken shards of tiling. From the inner side one might look through the doorway, as though it had been a frame for a picture, and see a fine scape beyond of marshland and winding road and mounting hills with pine trees growing in isolated groups like the dumpings in a gentleman's park.

In what had been the garden behind the principal house the colonel's automobile was waiting. We climbed into it and rode for upward of a mile along a seamed and rutted highway that wound up and over the abbreviated mountain of which we held one side and the Germans the other. For the preceding three days there had been a faint smell of spring in the air; now there was a taste of it. One might say that spring no longer was coming but had actually come. The rushes which grew in low places were showing green near their roots and the switchy limbs of the pollard willows bore successions of tiny green buds along their lengths. Also many birds were about. There were flocks of big corbie crows in their prim notarial black. Piebald French magpies were flickering along ahead of us, always in pairs, and numbers of a small starlinglike bird, very much like our field lark in look and habit, whose throat is yellowish and tawny without and lined with pure gold within, were singing their mating songs. Bursts of amorous pipings came from every side, and as the male birds mounted in the air their breast feathers shone in the clear soft afternoon sunshine like patches of burnished copper.

Undoubtedly spring was at hand — the spring which elsewhere, in the more favoured parts of this planet, meant reawakening life and fecundity, but which here meant only opportunity for renewed offensives and for more massacres, more suffering, more wastings of life and wealth and of all the manifold gifts of Nature. The constant sound of guns on ahead of us somewhere made one think of a half-dormant giant grunting as he roused. Indeed it was what it seemed — War emerging from his hibernation and waking up to kill again. But little more than a year before it had been their war; now it was our war too, and the realisation of this difference invested the whole thing for us with a deeper meaning. No longer were we onlookers but part proprietors in the grimmest, ghastliest proceeding that ever was since conscious time began.

We whizzed along the road for the better part of a mile, part of the time through dips, the contour of which kept us hidden from spying eyes in the hostile observation pits across the ridge to the eastward, and part of the time upon the backbone of this Vosges foothill. These latter places were shielded on their dangerous side by screens of marsh grasses woven in huge sheets ten feet high and swinging between tall poles set at six-yard intervals. There were rips and tears in these rude valances to show where chance shots from German guns had registered during the preceding few days of desultory artillery fire.

On the way we passed one full company of French infantry coming out of the front line for rest, and one contingent of our own soldiers. The Frenchmen were hampered, as French foot soldiers on the move always are, by enormous burdens draped upon them, back, flank and front; and under the dirt and dust their faces wore weary drawn lines. Laden like sumpter mules, they went by us at the heavy plodding gait of their kind, which is so different from the swaggering, swinging route step of the Yankee, and so different from the brisk clip at which the Britisher travels, even in heavy-marching order, but which all the same eats up the furlongs mighty fast.

The Americans were grouped on a little green breast of sod. At the peak of the small rounded elevation was a smaller terrace like a nipple, and from this rose one of those stone shrines so common in this corner of Europe — a stone base with a rusted iron cross bearing a figure of the Christ above it. There were a dozen or more of our boys lying or squatted here resting.

We came to a battalion headquarters, which seemed rather a high-sounding name for a collection of thatched dugouts under a bank. Here leaving the car we were turned over to a young intelligence officer, who agreed to pilot us through certain front-line defences, which our people only two days before had taken over from the French. But before we started each of us put on his iron helmet, which, next only to the derby hat of commerce, is the homeliest and the most uncomfortable design ever fashioned for wear in connection with the human head; and each one of us hung upon his breast, like a palmer's packet, his gas mask, inclosed in its square canvas case.

Single file then the three of us proceeded along a footpath that was dry where the sun had reached it and slimy with mud where it had lain in shadow, until we passed under an arbour of withered boughs and found ourselves in the mouth of the communication trench. It was wide enough in some places for two men to pass each other by scrouging, and in other places so narrow that a full-sized man bearing his accoutrements could barely wriggle his way through. Its sides were formed sometimes of shored planking set on end, but more often of withes cunningly wattled together. It is wonderful what a smooth fabric a French peasant can make with no material save bundles of pliant twigs and no tools save his two hands. Countless miles of trenches are lined with this osier work. Some of it has been there for years, but except where a shell strikes it stays put.

In depth the trench ranged from eight feet to less than six. In the deeper places we marched at ease, but in the shallow ones we went forward at a crouch, for if we had stood erect here our heads would have made fair targets for the enemy, who nowhere was more than a mile distant, and who generally was very much closer. Sometimes we trod on "duck boards" as the Americans call them, or "bath mats" in the Britisher's vernacular, laid end to end. A duck board is fabricated by putting down two scantlings parallel and eighteen inches apart and effecting a permanent union between them by means of many cross strips of wood securely nailed on, with narrow spaces between the strips so that the foothold is securer upon these corrugations than it would be on an uninterrupted expanse. It somewhat resembles the runway by which ducks advance from their duck pond up a steep bank; hence one of its names. It looks rather less the other thing for which it is named.

The duck board makes the going easier in miry places but it is a treacherous friend. Where it is not firmly imbedded fore and aft in the mud the far end of it has an unpleasant habit, when you tread with all your weight on the near end, of rising up and grievously smiting you as you pitch forward on your face. Likewise when you are in a hurry it dearly loves to teeter and slip and slosh round. However, to date no substitute for it has been found. Probably enough duck boards are in use on all the Fronts, in trenches and out of them, to make a board walk clear across our own continent. Beyond Ypres, where the British and Belgians are, I saw miles and miles of them the other day.

Here in Eastern France we sometimes footed it along these duck boards, but more often we dragged our feet in mud—sticky, clinging, affectionate yellowish-grey mud—which came up to the latchets of our boots and made each rod of progress a succession of violent struggles. It was through this muck, along the narrow twistywise passage, that food and munitions must be carried up to the front lines and the wounded must be carried back. Traversing it, men, as we saw, speedily became mired to the hair roots, and wearied beyond description. Now then, magnify and multiply by ten the conditions as we found them on this day after nearly a week of fair weather and you begin to have a faint and shadowy conception of trench conditions in the height of the rainy season in midwinter, when strong men grow so tired that they drop down and drown in the semiliquid streams.

The duck board is hard on human shins and human patience but it saves life and it saves time, which in war very frequently is more valuable than lives. It was the duck board, as much as the rifle and the big gun, which enabled the Canadians to win at Passchendaele last November. With its aid they laid a wooden pathway to victory across one of the most hideous loblollies in the flooded quagmires of Flanders. Somebody will yet write a tribute to the duck board, which now gets only curses and abuse.

We had come almost to the cross trench, meeting few soldiers on the way, when a sudden commotion overhead made us squat low and crane our necks. Almost above us a boche aëroplane was circling about droning like all the bees in the world. As we looked the antiaircraft guns, concealed all about us, began firing at it. Downy dainty pompons of smoke burst out in the heavens below it and above it and all about it.

As it fled back, seemingly uninjured, out of the danger zone I was reminded of the last time before this when I had seen such a sight from just such a vantage place. But then the scene had been the plateau before Laon in the fall of 1914, and then the sky spy had been a Frenchman and then the guns which chased him away had been German guns and for companion I had a German Staff-officer.

We went on, and round the next turn encountered half a dozen youngsters in khaki, faced with mud stripings, who barely had paused in whatever they were doing to watch the brief aerial bombardment. New as they were to this game they already were accustomed to the sight of air fighting. Half a dozen times a day or oftener merely by turning their faces upward they might see the hostile raider being harried back to its hangar by defending cannon or by French planes or by both at once. Later that same day we were to see a German plane stricken in its flight by a well-placed shot from an American battery. We saw how on the instant, like a duck shot on the wing, it changed from a living, sentient, perfectly controlled mechanism into a dishevelled, wounded thing, and how it went swirling in crazy disorganised spirals down inside its own lines.

For the trip through the cross trenches which marked the forward angle of our defences we were joined by a second chaperon in the person of an infantry captain—a man of German birth and German name, born in Cologne and brought to America as a child, who at the age of forty-three had given up a paying business and left a family to volunteer for this business, and who in all respects was just as good an American as you or I, reader, can ever hope to be. It was his company that held the trenches for the time, and he volunteered to let us see what they were doing.

The physical things he showed us are by now old stories to Americans. Reading descriptions of them would be stale business for people at home who read magazines—the little dirt burrows roofed with withes and leaves, where machine guns' crews squatted behind guns whose muzzles aimed out across the debatable territory; the observation posts, where the lads on duty grumbled at the narrow range of vision provided by the periscopes and much preferred to risk their lives peeping over the parapets; the tiny rifle pits, each harbouring a couple of youngsters; the gun steps, or scarps, on which men squatted to do sniper work and to try for hostile snipers across the way; the niches in the trench sides, where hand grenades—French and British models—lay in handy reach in case of a surprise attack; the stacks of rifle and machine-gun cartridges in their appointed places all along the inner sides of the low dirt parapets; the burrows, like the overgrown nests of bank martins, into which tired men might crawl to steal a bit of rest; the panels of thickly meshed barbed wire on light but strong metal frames so disposed that they might with instantaneous dispatch be thrust into place to block the way of invading raiders following along behind retreating defenders; the wire snares for the foes' feet, which might be dropped in the narrow footway after the retiring force had passed; and all the rest of the paraphernalia of trench warfare which the last three years and a half have produced.

Anyhow it was not these things that interested us; rather was it the bearing of our men, accustoming themselves to new duties in new surroundings; facing greater responsibilities than any of them perhaps had ever faced before in his days, amid an environment fraught with acute personal peril. And studying them I was prouder than ever of the land that bore them and sundry millions of others like unto them.

We halted at a spot where the trench was broken in somewhat and where the fresh new clods upon the dirt shelf halfway up it were all stained a strange, poisonous green colour. The afternoon before a shell had dropped there, killing one American and wounding four others. It was the fumes of the explosive which had corroded the earth to make it bear so curious a tint. This company then had had its first fatality under fire; its men had undergone the shock of seeing one of their comrades converted into a mangled fragment of a man, but they bore themselves as though they had been veterans.

In but one thing did they betray themselves as green hands, and this was in a common desire to expose themselves unnecessarily. As we went along their captain was constantly chiding them for poking their tin-hatted heads over the top, in the hope of spying out the German sharpshooters who continually shot in their direction from the coverts of a pine thicket, when they might have seen just as well through cunningly devised peepholes in the rifle pits.

"I know you aren't afraid," he said to two especially daring youngsters, "but the man who gets himself killed in this war without a reason for it is not a hero; he's just a plain damned fool, remember that."

Passing the spot where the soft damp loam was harried and the crumbs of it all dyed that diabolical greenish hue, I thought of a tale I had heard only the day before from a young Englishman who, having won his captaincy by two years of hard service, had then promptly secured a tranfer to the flying corps, where, as he innocently put it, "there was a chance o' having a bit of real fun," and who now wore the single wing of an observer upon the left breast of his tunic. I had asked him what was the most dramatic thing he personally had witnessed in this war, thinking to hear some tales of air craftsmanship. He considered for a moment with his brow puckered in a conscientious effort to remember, and then he said:

"I think perhaps 'twas something that happened last spring, just before I got out of the infantry into this bally outfit. My company had been in the trenches two days and nights, and had been rather knocked about. Really the place we were in was quite a bit exposed, you know, and after we had had rather an unhappy time of it we got orders to pull out. Just as the order reached us along came a whiz-bang and burst. It killed one of my chaps dead, and half a minute later another shell dropped in the same place and covered him under tons and tons of earth, all except his right hand, which stuck out of the dirt. Quite a decent sort he was too—a good fighter and cheerful and all that sort of thing; very well liked, he was. There was no time to dig him out even if we had been able to carry his body away with us; we had to leave him right there. So as the first man passed by where he was buried he bent over and took the dead hand in his hand and shook it and said 'Goodbye, old one!' like that. All the men followed the example.

Each one of us, officers included, shook the dead hand and said good-bye to the dead man; and this was the last we ever saw of him, or of that rotten old trench, either."

As nonchalantly as though he had been a paid postman going through a quiet street a volunteer mail distributor came along putting letters, papers and small mail parcels from the States into soiled eager hands. Each man, taking over what was given him, would promptly hunker down in some convenient cranny to read the news from home; news which was months old already. I saw one, a broad-faced, pale-haired youth, reading a Slavic paper; and another, a corporal, reading one that was printed in Italian. The other papers I noted were all printed in English.

It was from a begrimed and bespattered youngster who had got a paper printed in English that I heard the news about Ty Cobb; and when you appraised the character of the boy and his comrades a mud-lined hole in the ground in Eastern France, where a machine gun stammered round the corner and the snipers sniped away to the right of him and the left of him, seemed a perfectly natural place for the discussion of great tidings in baseball. If he had undertaken to discourse upon war or Germans I should have felt disappointed in him, because on his part it would not have been natural; and if he was anything at all he was natural.

At the end of perhaps a mile of windings about in torturous going we, following after our guides, turned into a shallower side trench which debouched off the main workings. Going almost upon all fours for about sixty or seventy yards we found ourselves in a blind ending. Here was a tiny ambuscade roofed over with sod and camouflaged on its one side with dead herbage, wherein two soldiers crouched. By a husky whisper floating back to us over the shoulder of the captain we learned that this was the most advanced of our listening posts. Having told us this he extended an invitation, which I accepted; and as he flattened back against the earth making himself small I wriggled past him and crawled into place to join its two silent occupants.

One of them nudging me in the side raised a finger and aimed it through a tiny peephole in the screening of dead bough and grasses. I looked where he pointed and this was what I saw:

At the level of my eyes the earth ran away at a gentle slope for a bit and then just as it reached a thicket of scrub pines, possibly two hundred feet away, rose sharply. Directly in front of me was our own tangle of rusted barbed wire. On beyond it, perhaps a hundred and sixty feet distant, where the rise began, was a second line of wire, and that was German wire, as I guessed without being told. In between, the soil was all harrowed and upturned into great cusps as though many swine had been rooting there for mast. A few straggly bushes still adhered to the sides of the shell holes, and the patches of grass upon the tortured sward displayed a greenish tinge where the saps of spring were beginning to rise from the roots.

Not far away and almost directly in front of me one of those yellow-breasted starling birds was trying his song with considerable success.

"How far away are they?" I inquired in the softest possible of whispers of the nearer-most of the hole's tenants.

"Right there in those little trees," he answered. "I ain't never been able to see any of them—they're purty smart about keepin' themselves out of sight—but there's times, 'specially toward night, when we kin hear 'em plain enough talking amongst themselves and movin' round over there. It's quiet as a graveyard now, but for a while this mornin' one of their sharpshooters got busy right over there in front of where you're lookin' now."

Involuntarily I drew my head down into my shoulders. The youth alongside laughed a noiseless laugh.

"Oh, you needn't worry," he said in my ear; "there ain't a chancet for him to see us; we're too well hid. At that, I think he must've suspected that this here lump of dirt was a shelter for our folks because twicet this mornin' he took a shot this way. One of his bullets lodged somewhere in the sods over your head but the other one hit that bush there. See where it cut the little twig off."

I peered where he indicated and made out a ragged stump almost within arm's reach of me, where a willow sprout had been shorn away. The sap was oozing from the top like blood from a fresh wound. My instructor went on:

"But after the second shot he quit. One of our fellers back behind us a piece took a crack at him and either he got him or else the Heinie found things gettin' too warm for him and pulled his freight back into them deep woods further up the hill. So it's been nice and quiet ever since."

The captain wormed into the burrow, filling it until it would hold no more.

"Is this your first close-up peep at No Man's Land?" he inquired in as small a voice as his vocal cords could make.

Before I could answer the private put in:

"It might a-been No Man's Land oncet, cap'n, but frum now on it's goin' to be all Amurikin clear out to them furtherest wires yonder."

So that was how and when I found the title for this chapter. Everything considered I think it makes a very good title, too. I only wish I had the power to put as much of the manifest spirit of our soldiers into what I have here written as is compassed in the caption I have borrowed.

What happened thereafter was largely personal so far as it related to my companion and me, but highly interesting from our viewpoint. We had emerged from the front-line trench on our way back. In order to avoid a particularly nasty bit of footing in the nearermost end of the communication work we climbed out of the trench and took a short cut across a stretch of long-abandoned meadowland. We thought we were well out of sight of the Germans, who at that point were probably half a mile away.

A cup of land formed a natural shield from any eyes except eyes in an aëroplane—so we thought—and besides there were no aëroplanes about. Once over the edge of the trench and down into the depression we felt quite safe; anyway the firing that was going on seemed very far away. We slowed up our gait. From dragging our feet through the mire we were dripping wet with sweat, so I hauled off my coat. This necessitated a readjustment of belt and gasmask straps. Accordingly all three of us—the young intelligence officer, my comrade and I—took advantage of the halt to smoke. The two others lit cigarettes but I preferred something stronger.

I was trying to light a practical cigar with a property match—which is a very common performance on the part of my countrymen in this part of the world—when a noise like the end of everything—a nasty, whiplike crash—sounded at the right of us, and simultaneously a German shell struck within a hundred feet of us, right on the rim of the little hollow in which we had stopped, throwing a yellow geyser of earth away up into the air and peppering our feet and legs with bits of gravel.

So then we came on away from there. I chucked away my box of matches, which were French and therefore futile, and I must have mislaid my cigar, which was American and therefore priceless, for I have never seen it since. Anyway I had for the time lost the desire for tobacco. There are times when one cares to smoke and times when one does not care to smoke. As we scuttled for the shelter of the trench four more shells fell in rapid succession and burst within a short distance of where the first one had gone off, and each time we felt the earth shake under our feet and out of the tails of our eyes saw the soil rising in a column to spread out mushroom fashion and descend in pattering showers.

So, using the trench as an avenue, we continued to go away from there; and as we went guns continued to bay behind us. An hour later, back at battalion headquarters, we learned that the enemy dropped seventy shells—five-inch shells—in the area that we had traversed. But unless one of them destroyed the cigar I left behind me it was all clear waste of powder and shrapnel, as I am pleased to be able to report.

That night just after dusk forty-five of our boys, with twice as many Frenchmen, went over the top at the very point we had visited, and next morning, true enough, and for quite a while after that, No Man's Land was "All Amurikin clear out to them furtherest wires."

CHAPTER III
HELL'S FIRE FOR THE HUNS

THE surroundings were as French as French could be, but the supper tasted of home. We sat at table, two of us being correspondents and the rest of us staff officers of a regiment of the Rainbow Division; and the orderlies brought us Hamburger steak richly perfumed with onion, and good hot soda biscuit, and canned tomatoes cooked with cracker crumbs and New Orleans molasses, and coffee, and fried potatoes; and to end up with there were genuine old-fashioned doughnuts—"fried holes," the Far Westerners call them.

The mingled aromas of these rose like familiar incense from strange altars, for the room wherein all of us, stout and willing trenchermen, sat and supped was the chief room of what once upon a time, before the war came along and cracked down upon the land, had been some prosperous burgher's home on the main street of a drowsy village cuddled up in a sweet and fertile valley under the shoulders of the Vosges Mountains.

From a niche in the corner a plaster saint, finished off in glaring Easter-egg colours, regarded us with one of his painted eyes, the other being gone. The stove had been carried away, either by the owner when he fled, away back in 1914, or by the invading Hun before he retreated to his present lines a few miles distant; but a segment of forgotten stovepipe protruded like a waterspout gone dry, from its hole above the mantelpiece. On the plastered wall of battered, broken blue cast, behind the seat where the colonel ruled the board, hung a family portrait of an elderly gentleman with placid features but fierce and indomitable whiskers. The picture was skewed at such an angle the whiskers appeared to be growing out into space sidewise. Generations of feet had worn grooves in the broad boards of the floor, which these times was never free of mud stains, no matter how often the orderlies might rid up the place. So far and so much the setting was French.

But stained trench coats of American workmanship dangled from pegs set in the plastering, each limply suggestive in its bulges and its curves of the shape of the man who wore it through most of his waking hours. The mantelshelf was burdened with gas masks and saucepan hats of pressed steel. A small trestle that was shoved up under one of the two grimed front windows bore a litter of American newspapers and American magazines.

As for the doughnuts, they were very crisp and spicy, as good Yankee doughnuts should be. I had finished my second one and was reaching for my third one when, without warning, a very creditable and realistic imitation of the crack o' doom transpired. Seemingly from within fifty yards of the building which sheltered us Gabriel's trumpet sounded forth in an ear-cracking, earth-racking,' hair-lifting blare calculated to raise goose flesh on iron statuary. The dishes danced upon the table; the coffee slopped out of the cups; and the stovepipe over the chimneypiece slobbered down a trickle of ancient soot that was, with age, turned brown and caky. Beneath our feet we could feel the old house rocking.

Through the valley and across to the foothill beyond, the obscenity of sound went ringing and screeching, vilely profaning the calm that had descended upon the country with the going-down of the sun.

As its last blasphemous echoes came back to us in a diminishing cadence one of our hosts, a major, leaned forward with a cheerful smile on his face and remarked as he glanced at the dial of his wrist watch: "There she goes — right on the minute!"

Sure enough, there she went. Right and left, before us and behind us, from the north of us and from the south of us, and from the east and the west of us, big guns and small ones, field pieces, howitzers, mortars and light batteries, both French and American but mostly French, joined in, like the wind, the wood and the brass of an orchestra obeying the baton of the leader. The coffee could not stay in the dancing cups at all. The venerable house was beset by an ague which ran up its shaken sides from the foundation stones to the roof rafters, where the loosened tiles clicked together like chattering teeth, and back down again to the foundations.

The thing which we had travelled upward of a hundred miles in one of Uncle Sam's automobiles to witness and afterward to write about was starting. The overture was on; the show would follow. And it was high time we claimed our reserved seats in the front row.

I use the word "show" advisedly, because in the glossary of phrases born out of this war anything in the nature of a thrust or a blow delivered against the enemy is a show. A great offensive on a wide front is a big show; a raid by night into hostile territory is a little show; a feint by infantry, undertaken with intent to deceive the other side at a given point while the real attack is being launched at a second given point, and accompanied by much vain banging of gunpowder and much squibbing-off of rockets and flares and star shells is a "Chinese show" — to quote the cant or trade name; I think the English first used the term, but our fellows have been borrowing ever since the first contingent came over last year.

This particular show to which we had been bidden as special guests was to be a foray by night over the tops preceded by artillery preparation. Now such things as these happen every night or every day somewhere on the Western Front; times are when they happen in different sectors at the rate of half a dozen within the twenty-four hours. In the dispatches each one means a line or so of type; in the field it means a few prisoners, a few fresh graves, a few yards of trench work blasted away, a few brier patches of barbed wire to be repatched; in the minds of most readers of the daily papers it means nothing but the tiresome reiteration of a phrase that is tiresome and staled. But to us it meant something. It was our boys who were going in and going over; and our guns were to be partners in the prior enterprise of blazing the way for them.

No matter how much one may read of the cost of war operations in dollars and in time and in labour, I am sure one does not really begin to appreciate the staggering expenditure of all three that is requisite to accomplish even the smallest of aggressive movements until one has opportunity, as we now had, to see with one's own eyes what necessarily had to be done by way of preliminary.

Take for instance the present case. The raid in hand was to be no great shakes of a raid. Forty-five Americans and three times their number of Frenchmen would participate in it. Within twenty minutes, if all went well—and it did—they would have returned from their excursion into hostile territory, with prisoners perhaps, or else with notes and letters taken from the bodies of dead enemies which might serve to give the Intelligence Department a correct appraisal of the character and numbers of the troops opposing us in this sector. In the vast general scheme of the campaign now about renewing itself it would be no more than an inconsequential pin prick in the foe's side—a thing to be done and mentioned briefly in the dispatches, and then forgotten.

But mark you how great and how costly the artillery accompaniment must be. More than a hundred guns, ranging in calibre from a nine-inch bore down to a three-inch bore, would join in the preparation and in the barrage fire. More than ten thousand rounds of ammunition would be fired, this not taking into account the supplies for the forty-three machine guns and for the batteries of trench mortars which were to cooperate. Many a great battle of our Civil War had been fought out with the expenditure on both sides of one-tenth or one-twentieth part the gross weight of metal that would be directed at the boche beyond the ridge. The cost for munitions alone, excluding every other item of a score of items, might run to a quarter of a million dollars; might conceivably run considerably beyond that figure.

And the toil performed and the pains taken beforehand to insure success—wowie!

For days past the French had been bringing up pieces and massing them here for the purpose of this one little stab at the Hun's armoured flank. As we travelled hither we had seen the motor-drawn guns labouring along the wide high roads; had seen the ammunition trucks crawling forward in long lines; had seen at every tiny village behind the Front the gun crews resting in bad streets named for good saints. By the same token, on the following day, which was Sunday, we were to see the same thing repeated, except that then the procession would be headed the other way—going back to repeat the same wearisome proceeding elsewhere.

Days, too, had been spent in planning the raid; in mapping out and plotting out the especial spot chosen for attack; in coordinating all the arms of the service which would be employed; in planning signals for the show and drilling its actors. And now all this preparation requisite and essential to the carrying out of the undertaking had been completed; and all the guns had been planted in their appointed places and craftily hidden; and all the shells had been brought up—thousands of tons of them—and properly bestowed; and the little handful of men who were to have a direct hand in the performance of the main job, for which all the jest would be purely preliminary, had been chosen and sent forward to ordained stations, there to await the word. And so up we got from table and went out across a threshold, which quaked like a living thing as we crossed it, to see the spectacular side of the show.

Inside the house the air had been churned up and down by the detonations. Outside literally it was being rent into fine bits. One had the feeling that the atmosphere was all shredded up fine, so that instead of lying in layers upon the earth it floated in torn and dishevelled strips; one had the feeling that the upper ether must be full of holes and voids and the rushing together of whipped and eddying wind currents. This may sound incoherent, but I find in my vocabulary no better terminology to convey a sense of the impression that possessed me as I stepped forth into the open.

We had known in advance that there were guns in great number disposed about the surrounding terrain. Walking about under military guidance in the afternoon we had seen sundry batteries ensconced under banks, in thickets and behind low natural parapets where the earth ridged up; and had noted how cunningly they had been concealed from aëroplanes scouting above and from the range of field glasses in the German workings on beyond.

The Glory Of The Coming | 33

But we had no notion until then that there were so many guns near by or that some of them were so close to the village where we had stopped to eat. We must almost have stepped on some of them without once suspecting their presence. The ability of the French so well to hide a group of five big pieces, each with a carriage as large as a two-ton truck and each with a snout projecting two or three yards beyond it, and with a limber projecting out behind it, shows what advances the gentle arts of ambuscade and camouflage have made since this war began. Seen upon the open road a big cannon painted as it is from muzzle to breach with splotchings of yellows and browns and ochres seems, for its size, the most conspicuous thing in the world. But once bedded down in its nest, with its gullet resting upon the ring back of earth that has been thrown up for it, and a miracle of protective colouration instantaneously is achieved. Its whole fabric seems to melt into and become a part of the soil and the withered herbage and the dirt-coloured sandbags which encompass it abaft, alongside and before. It is the difference between a mottled snake crawling across a brick sidewalk and the same snake coiled and motionless amid dried leaves and boulders in the woods. Nature always has protected her wild creatures thus; it took the greatest of wars for mankind to learn a lesson that is as old as creation is.

Standing there in the square of the wrecked village we could sense that in all manner of previously unsuspected coverts within the immediate vicinity guns were at work—guns which ranged from the French seventy-fives to big nine-inch howitzers. As yet twilight had not sufficiently advanced for us to see the flash of the firing, and of course' nowadays there is mighty little smoke to mark the single discharge of a single gun; but we could tell what went on by the testimony of a most vast tumult.

We were ringed about by detonations; by jars which impacted against the earth like blows of a mighty sledge on a yet mightier smithy; by demoniac screechings which tore the tortured welkin into still finer bits; by fierce clangings of metal; by thudding echoes floating back from where the charges had burst; by the more distant voices of certain German guns replying to our 'salvo as our gunners dedicated the dusk to all this unloosened hellishness and offered up to the evening star their sulphurous benedictions. It was Thor, Vulcan, Tubal Cain, Bertha Krupp and the Bethlehem Steel Works all going at full blast together; it was a thousand Walpurgis Nights rolled into one, with Dante's Inferno out-Infernoed on the side. And yet by a curious phenomenon we who stood there with this hand-made, man-made demonism unleashed and prevalent about us could hear plainly enough what a man five feet away who spoke in a fairly loud voice might be saying.

"You think this is brisk, eh?" asked our friend, the major. "Well, it's only the starter; the ball has just opened."

He tucked his thumbs into the girth harnessings of his Sam Browne and spraddled his legs wide apart.

"Wait," he promised; "just wait until all the guns get into action in twenty minutes or half an hour from now. Then you'll really hear something. Take it from me, you will. And in the meantime we might go along with these fellows yonder, don't you think so?"

Through the deepening twilight we followed a party of French infantrymen up a gentle slope to the crest of a little hill behind the shattered town, where the cemetery was. In this light the horizon-blue uniforms took on the colour tone of the uniforms worn by the Confederates in our Civil War, but their painted metal helmets looked like polished turtle shells. They slouched along, as the poilu loves to slouch along when not fully accoutred, their hands in their breeches pockets and their halfreefed putties flapping upon their shanks. We trailed them, and some of our soldiers, officers and enlisted men, trailed us.

Half an hour later I was to witness a curious and yet, I think, a characteristic thing. Most of the American privates grew tired of the spectacle that was spread out before them and slipped away to their billets to go to bed—this, too, in spite of the fact that scarcely one of them had ever witnessed cannonading on so extensive a scale or indeed on any scale before. Nevertheless, the bombardment speedily became to them a commonplace and rather tedious affair.

"Come on, you fellows," I heard one tall stripling say to a couple of his mates. "Me for the hay. If the Heinies would only slam a few big ones back in this direction there might be some fun, but as it is, there's nothin' doin' round here for me."

But the Frenchmen, all intent and alert, stayed until the show ended. Yet a thing like this was an old story to them, for they were veterans at the game whereat our men still were the greenest of novices. I suppose there was an element of theatricalism in the sight and in the fury of sound which appealed to the Gallic sense of drama that was in them. Be the cause what it was, the thing occurred just as I am telling it.

We mounted the hill and rounded the stone wall of the burying ground. The village in the hollow below had been quite battered out of its original contours, but strangely enough the cemetery, through the years of intermittent fighting and shell firing that had waged about it, was almost unscathed. It was a populous place, the cemetery was, as we had noted earlier in the day. Originally it had contained only the graves of the inhabitants, but now these were outnumbered twenty to one by mounds covering French soldiers who had fallen in action or had died of wounds or natural causes in this immediate vicinity. The same is true of hundreds of other graveyards in this country; is probably true of most of France's cemeteries.

I have seen places where the wooden crosses made hedge rows, line behind line for miles on a stretch, and so thick-set were the markers that, viewed from the distance, they conveyed the impression of paling fences.

France has become a land of these wooden crosses and these six-foot mounds. It is part of the toll—a small part of the toll—she has paid for the right of freedom and in the fight to make this world once more a fit place for decent beings to abide in.

On the knoll behind the cemetery we came to a halt. Night was creeping down from the foothills, making the earth black where before it had faded to a common grey; but overhead the sky still showed in the last faint traces of the afterglow, with the blue of an unflawed turquoise against which the stars stood out like crumbs of pure gold. The broken and snaggled roof lines of the clumped houses of the town were vanishing; the mountain beyond seemed creeping up nearer and nearer to us. More plainly than before we could mark out the positions of the nearmost batteries for now at each discharge of a gun a darting jab of red flame shot forth. Where all the guns of a battery were being served and fired in rapid succession the blazes ran together like hemstitches, making one think of a fiery needle plying in and out of a breadth of black velvet. Farther away the flashes were blurred into broader and paler flares so that on three sides of us the horizon was circled with constantly rising, constantly dying glows like heat lightning on a summer night.

The points where shells fell and burst were marked for us with red geysers, which uprose straight instead of slanting out at a slightly upward tilted angle, as did the spoutings from the mouths of the guns. As nearly as we might tell the enemy fire was comparatively light. Only we could see upon the far flanks of the little mountain in front of us a distant flickering illumination, which showed that his counter batteries were busy. On every hand white signal rockets rose frequently, and occasionally flares hung burning halfway up the walls of the sky.

Of a sudden all hell broke loose directly behind us. I use the term without desire to be profane and in a conscientious effort to give some notion of a physical occurrence. At any rate it seemed to us that all hell let loose. What really happened was that two guns of a French battery of nine-inch heavies, from their post directly in our rear and not more than an eighth of a mile distant from us, had fired simultaneously, and their shells had travelled directly over our heads, aiming for an unseen objective miles forward.

Then, and every time thereafter that one of the nine-inchers spewed its bellyful of high explosive forth, the sound of it dominated and overmastered all other sounds. First there was the crash—a crash so great that our inadequate tongue yields neither adjective nor noun fitly to comprehend it, the trouble being that the language has not kept step with the developments of artillery in this war. Our dictionary is going to need an overhauling when this job of licking Germany is finished.

Well, first off there was the crash that was like the great granddaddy of all the crashes in the world, making one feel that its vocal force must have folded up the heavens like a scroll. Then, as a part of it, would come the note of the projectile rushing through the ripped ether above us, and this might be likened to a long freight train travelling on an invisible aërial right of way at a speed a thousand times greater than any freight train ever has or ever will attain. Then there would float back a tremendous banshee wail, and finally, just before the roar of the shell's explosion, a whine as though a lost puppy of the size of ten elephants were wandering through the skies, complaining in a homesick key as it went—the whole transaction taking place in an infinitesimal part of the time which has here been required for me to set down my own auricular impressions of it, and incidentally creating an infinitely more vivid impression than possible can be suggested by my lame and inadequate metaphors.

Comparatively, there was a hush in the clamour and clangour succeeding this happening—not that the firing in any way abated, for rather was it augmented now—but only that it seemed so to me; and in the lull, away off on our left, I could for the first time make out the whirring, ripping sound of a machine gun or a row of machine guns.

The major consulted the luminous face of his wrist watch.

"I thought so," he vouchsafed. "It's time for the barrage to start and for the boys to go over the top. Now we ought to see some real fireworks that'll make what has gone on up to now seem puny and trifling and no account."

Which, all things considered, was an underestimation of what ensued hard on the heels of his announcement. Personally I shall not attempt to describe it; the size of the task leaves me abashed and mortified. But if the reader in the goodness of his heart and abundance of his patience will re-read what already I have written in an effort to tell him what I had heard and had seen and had felt, and will multiply it by five, adding, say, fifty per cent of the sum total for good measure, he will have, I trust, a measure of comprehension of the ensemble. But he must do the work; my founts are dry.

Furthermore, he must imagine the augmented hullabaloo—which should be pronounced hella-baloo—going on for twenty-five minutes at such rate that no longer might one distinguish separate reports—save only when the devil's fast freight aforementioned passed over our heads—but all were mingled and fused into one composite, continuous, screeching, whining, wailing, splitting chorus.

Twenty-five minutes thus, and then a green rocket went up from near the forward post of command where those directly in charge of the operation watched, and before it had descended in a spatter of emerald sparks which dimmed out and died as they neared the earth the firing from our batteries began to lessen in volume and in rapidity. Within those twenty-five minutes the real object of the operation had taken place. Either the raiders had gone over the top or they had been driven back in; either they had accomplished their design of penetrating the enemy's second line of defences or they had failed. In any event the movement, all carefully timed and all mathematically worked out, was as good as over. To learn better at firsthand exactly what results had been obtained we returned to the village and passed through it and picking our way in the inky darkness went along a road toward the post of command.

The road, though, was deserted, and after a bit we retraced the way back to the building where we had supped and made ourselves comfortable in the room of the colonel of the regiment holding the line at this particular point. An orderly brought us the last of the doughnuts to nibble on, and upon the ancient hearthstone we took turns at cracking French hazelnuts with a hammer while at intervals the building jarred to the thumpings of such guns as continued to fire.

Nearly an hour passed, and then in came the colonel and with him a French liaison officer, both of them with tired lines about their mouths. They had been under a strain, as their looks showed, and they flung themselves down on adjacent cots with little sighs of relief and told us the news. In a way the raid had been a success; in another way it had not. All the men who went over the top had returned again after penetrating up to the German secondary trenches. Several of the Frenchmen had been wounded, not seriously. None of the Americans had anything worse than barbed-wire cuts and bruised shins to show for his experience.

Returning, the raiders reported that our fire had completely obliterated the hostile front trench and had ripped its protecting wire jungle into broken ends. Likewise it had completely abolished such boches as had tarried too long in the enemy's forward pits and posts. Of these unfortunates only dismembered trunks had been found, with one exception. This exception was a body lying in a shell hole, and not badly mangled but completely nude. By some freak the shell which killed the German had stripped him stark naked down to his boots.

But the total of prisoners taken was zero, and likewise it was cipher. Forewarned by the preparatory volleying of the big guns playing on his counter batteries, the wily German, following his recently adopted custom, had, before the barrage began, drawn in his defending forces from the first line, leaving behind only a few, who fell victims to the first few direct hits scored by our side; and therein the raid had failed.

In the next sector on our right, where a daylight raid had been undertaken two hours before ours got under way, the raiders had suffered a few casualties but had brought back two wounded captives; and in another sector, on our left, yet a third raid had produced four prisoners. I saw the unhappy four the following day on their way back to a laager under guard. One of them was a middle-aged, sickly-looking man, and the remaining three were weedy, half-grown, bewildered boys; very different looking, all of them, from the prime sinewy material which formed the great armies I had seen pouring through Belgium in the late summer of 1914.

All four of them, moreover, were wall-eyed with apprehension, and flinchy and altogether most miserable looking. Not even a night of fair treatment and a decent breakfast had served to cure them of a delusion that Americans would take prisoners alive only for the pleasure of putting them to death at leisure afterward. What struck me as even more significant of the change in the personnel of the Kaiser's present army—conceding that these specimens might be accepted as average samples of the mass—was that not one of them wore an Iron Cross on his blouse. From personal observations in the first year of the war I had made up my mind that the decoration of the Iron Cross in the German Army was like vaccination in our own country, being, as one might say, compulsory. Here, though, was evidence either that the War Lord was running out of metal or that his system had slipped a cog. Likewise it was to develop later that the prisoners I saw wore paper underclothing.

But I am getting ahead of my story. The colonel, lying back on his cot with his head on a canvas pillow and his muddied legs crossed, said at the conclusion of his account:

"Well, we failed to bag any live game, but anyhow our boys behaved splendidly. They went over the top cheering and they came back in singing.

You'd never have guessed they were green hands at this game or that this was the first time they had ever crossed No Man's Land."

To the truth of a part of what he said I could testify personally, for late that afternoon I had seen the squad marching forward to the spot where they were to line up for the sally later. They had been like schoolboys on a lark. If any one of them was afraid he refused to betray it; if any one of them was nervous at the prospect before him he hid his nervousness splendidly well. Only, from them as they passed us, they radiated a great pride in having been chosen for the job, and a great confidence in its outcome, and a great joy that to them thus early in their soldiering had come the coveted chance to show the stuff that was in them. And while they passed, our friend the major, standing alongside watching them go by, had said with all the fervency of a man uttering a prayer:

"By Jove, aren't they bully! No officer could ask for finer men than that for his outfit. But they're leaving oodles of disappointment behind them at that."

"How's that?" I asked.

"I'll tell you how," he said: "Yesterday when the scheme for this thing was completed we were told that forty-five men out of our regiment were to be allowed to take part in tonight's doings. That meant fifteen men out of each battalion. So yesterday evening at parade I broke the glad tidings to my battalion and called for volunteers, first warning the men as a matter of routine that the work would be highly dangerous and no man need feel called upon to offer himself. Do you want to know how many men out of that battalion volunteered? Every single solitary last dog-goned one of them, that's all! They came at me like one man. So to save as much heartburning as possible I left the choice of fifteen out of nearly a thousand to the top sergeants of the companies. And in all your life you never saw fifteen fellows so tickled as the fifteen who were selected, and you never saw nine hundred and odd so downhearted as the lot who failed to get on the list.

"That wasn't all of it, either," he went on. "Naturally there were some men who had been off on detail of one sort or another and hadn't been at parade. When they came last night and found out what had happened in their absence—well, they simply raised merry blue hell, that's all. They figured somehow they'd been cheated. As a result I may say that my rest was somewhat broken. Every few minutes, all night long, some boy would break into my room, and in the doorway salute and say, in a broken-hearted way: 'Now look here, major, this ain't square. I got as much right to go over the top as any feller in this regiment has, and just because I happened to be away this evenin' here I am chiselled out of my chance to go along. Can't you please, sir, ask the adjutant or somebody to let me in on this?'

"That substantially was what every one of them said. And when I turned them down some of 'em went away crying like babies."

He glanced away across the blue hill. "I guess maybe I did a little crying myself."

I thought about what the major had said and what the colonel had said and what I myself had seen after I had climbed some shaky stairs to be bedded down for the night on a pallet of blankets upon the floor of a room where several tired-out officers already snored away, oblivious of the reverberations of the shelling from our guns and from the enemy's, which went on until nearly daybreak.

In the morning I got insight into another phase of the enlisted Yank's understanding. We came downstairs to breakfast—to a Sunday morning breakfast. For the moment a Sabbath calm hung over the wrecked town and over the country roundabout; all was as peaceful as a Quaker meeting. Red, the colonel's orderly, stood in the doorway picking his teeth. Red is six feet two inches tall, and disproportionately narrow. He is a member of a regiment recruited in the Middle West, but he hails from the Panhandle of Texas, and betrays the fact every time he opens his mouth. At the moment of our approach he was addressing an unseen and presumably a sympathetic listener beyond the threshold:

"Me, I'm, plum' outdone with these here French people," I heard him drawl. "Here we've been camped amongst 'em fer goin' on four months and they ain't learnt English yet. You'd think they'd want to know how to talk to people in a reg'lar honest-to-God language—but no, seein' seemin'ly not a-tall. I'd be ashamed to be so ignorunt and show it. Course oncet in a while you do run acrost one of 'em that's picked up a word here and there; but that's about all.

"Now frinstance you take that nice-lookin' little woman with the black eyes and the shiny teeth that runs that there little store in this here last town we stayed a spell in before we come on up here. I never could remember the name of that there town—it was so outlandish soundin'—but you remember the woman, don't you? Well, there's a case in p'int. She was bright enough lookin' but she was like all the rest—it seemed like she jest couldn't or jest wouldn't pick up enough reg'lar words to help her git around. Ef I went in her place and asked her fer sardines she'd know what I meant right off and hand 'em over, but ef I wanted some cheese she didn't have no idea whut I was talkin' about. Don't it jest beat all!"

CHAPTER IV
ON THE THRESHOLD OF BATTLE

WE left Paris at an early hour of March 25, which was the morning of the fourth day of perhaps the greatest battle in the history of this or any other war, and of the third day of the bombardment of Paris by the long-range steel monster which already had become famous as the latest creation of the Essen workshops.

There were three of us and no more—Raymond Carroll, Martin Green and I. To each of the three the present excursion was in the nature of a reunion. For more than six years we held down adjoining desks in the city room of a New York evening newspaper. Since we parted, Carroll and I to take other berths and Green to bide where he was, this had been the first time we had met on the same assignment.

I counted myself lucky to be in their company, for two better newspaper men never walked in shoe leather. Carroll among reporters is what Elihu Root is among corporation lawyers. There are plenty of men in the journalistic craft who know why certain facts pertinent to the proper telling of a tale in print may not be secured; he, better than almost any man I ever ran across in this business, knows how these facts may be had, regardless of intervening obstacles. In his own peculiar way, which is a calm, quiet, detached way, Green is just as effective. When it comes to figuring where unshirted Hades is going to break loose next and getting first upon the spot he is a regular Nathan Bedford Forrest. His North American sanity, which is his by birth, and his South of Ireland wit, which is his by inheritance, give strength and savour to what he writes once he has assembled the details in that card index of a mind of his.

We left Paris, heading north by east in the direction whence came in dim reverberations the never-ending sound of the big guns firing in the biggest of all big engagements. Through the courtesy of friends who are members of the French Government we bore special passes admitting us to the Soissons area. Later we were to learn that we were the only individuals not actively concerned in military operations who at particularly momentous time had been thus favoured, all other such passes having been cancelled; and by the same lucky token we are, I believe, the only three newspaper men of any nationality whatsoever who may lay claim to having witnessed at first-hand any part of the close-up fighting in the most critical period and at one of the most critical spots along the crest of the culminating German offensive of this present year of grace and gunpowder, 1918.

Indeed, so far as the available information goes, I think we were the only practitioners of the writing trade who actually got to the actual Front in the first week of the push. Whether any of our calling have got there in the succeeding weeks, I doubt. These times the war correspondent, so called, does not often enjoy such opportunities. After the army has dug itself in is another matter; then, within limitations, he may go pretty much where he pleases to go. But when the shove is on he stays behind, safely at the rear with the rest of the camp followers, and compiles his dispatches from the official communications, fatting them out with details out of the accounts of eyewitnesses and occasionally of participants.

For the three of us, though, was to be vouchsafed the chance which comes but once in the modern newspaperman's life, and sometimes not then. By a combination of rare luck and yet more rare luck we not only got to the Front but we got clear through it. As I write these lines I figuratively pat myself on the back at the thought of having seen what I never expected to see when I landed on French soil less than a month ago. At the same time it behooves me to disclaim for the members of our party that any special sagacity on our part figured in the transaction. Good fortune came flitting along and perched on our shoulders, that's all.

If our passes had shared the common fate of those other passes in being annulled, if any one charged with authority had seen fit to halt us, if any one of a half dozen other things had or had not befallen us—we never should have gone where we did go.

Except that we three were the only passengers on the train who did hot wear French uniforms, and except that the train ran very slowly, nothing happened on the journey to distinguish it from any other wartime journey on a railroad where always there is to be heard the distant booming of the guns mingling with the clickety-clank of the car wheels, and where always the sight of all manner of military activities is to be viewed from the car windows.

In a deep cut we halted. When we had waited there for perhaps twenty minutes a kindly officer volunteered the information in broken English that the station at Soissons was being shelled and that if we intended to enter the town it behooved us to walk in. So we took up our traps and walked.

Through old trenches where long-abandoned German defences once had run in zigzags across the flanks of the hills we laboured up to the top, to find the road along the crest cumbered and in places almost clogged with marching troops on their way back to rest billets, and with civilians fleeing southward from Soissons or from evacuated villages within the zone of active hostilities. We seemingly were the only civilians going in; all those we met on that three-mile hike were coming out. To me the spectacle was strikingly and pathetically reminiscent of Belgium in mid-August of 1914— old men trudging stolidly ahead with loads upon their bent backs; women, young and old, dragging carts or pushing shabby baby carriages that were piled high with their meagre belongings; grave-faced children trotting along at their elders' skirts; wearied soldiers falling out of the line to add to their already heavy burdens as they relieved some half-exhausted member of the exodus of an unwieldy pack. Over the lamentable procession hung a fog of gritty chalk particles that had been winnowed up by the plodding feet. Viewed through the cloaking dust the figures drifted past us like the unreal shapes of a dream. I saw one middle-aged sergeant, his whiskers powdered white and his face above the whiskers masked in a sweaty white paste like a circus clown's, who, for all that he was in heavy marching order, had a grimed mite of a baby snuggled up to the breast of his stained tunic, with its little feet dangling in the crisscross of his leather gear and its bobbing head on his shoulder. He carried the baby with one hand and with the other hand he dragged his rifle; and he looked down smiling at the bedraggled little mother who travelled alongside him shoving before her a barrow in which another child sat on a pillion of bed clothes.

I saw two infantrymen slide down a steep embankment to give aid to an old woman who struggled with a bundle almost as large as herself, and then, having accomplished the job, running with their accoutrements slapping against their legs to catch up with their company. I saw scores of sights such as this, and I did not hear one word of complaint uttered, nor did I look into one face that expressed aught save courage and patience. And seeing these things, multiplied over and over again, I said to myself then, as I say to myself now, that I do not believe Almighty God in His infinite mercy, designed that such people as these should ever be conquered.

Only one person spoke to us. A captain, grinning at us as he plodded by at the head of his company, said with a rearward flirt of his thumb over his shoulders: "No good, no good! much boom-boom!"

Much boom-boom was emphatically right. Over the clustered tops of the city the hostile shells were cracking, and frequently to our ears there came along with the smashing notes of the explosives the clatter of tumbling walls and smashing tiles. Drawing nearer we divined that the cannonading was directed mainly at the railroad station, so skirting to the left of the district under fire we made our way through almost deserted side streets to the centre of the town.

Hardly a house or a wall along our route but bore marks of punishment. Some were fallen into heaps of ruins; some merely were pecked-and scarred, with corners bitten out of the walls and chimneys broken into fantastic designs. Indeed we found out later that only one structure in Soissons had escaped damage in the shelling which went on intermittently in the earlier years of the war and which the Germans, with a sort of futile, savage fury, had lately renewed from their lines twelve miles away to the northward.

This sort of thing appears to be a favourite trick with our enemies. A village or a town may be abandoned by all save a few helpless citizens, living, God only knows how, in the litter of their homes; the place may be of absolutely no military value to the Allies; possibly no troop? are quartered there and no batteries or wagon trains are stationed within miles of it; but all the same when the frenzy of their madness descends upon them the Huns will level and loose their batteries upon the spot and make of the hideous hash which it has become a still more hideous hash. It is as though in sheer wantonness they kicked a corpse.

We skirted the sides of the wonderful old cathedral, which since 1914 has stood for the most part in ruins, with its beautiful stained windows— which never can be replaced, since the art of making such glass as this has been lost—lying underfoot in broken splinters of many colours. Just off the main square we secured quarters in a typical French inn of the second class, a small place with a grandiloquent name. Mainly the shops and houses in the neighbourhood were closed and their owners gone away, but the proprietor of the little hotel and his family and his help still abided under their belaboured roof. Plainly their motto was "Business as Usual."

Their only guests were a few American Red Cross workers, both men and women; a few American officers of the transport service; and a few French officers. But that day at noon, so we were told, the whole staff turned in and cooked and served, free of charge, a plentiful hot meal to two hundred refugees, who staggered in afoot from districts now overrun by the advancing Germans. These poor folk were all departed when we arrived; French camions and American motor trucks had carried them away to temporary asylums beyond the limit of the shelling, and for us there was abundant accommodation—seats at the common dining table, chambers on the second floor, and standing room in the deep wine cellars down below if we cared to occupy them when the bombardment became heavier or when hostile aëoplanes circled over to drop down bombs. The members of the ménage, as we learned later, slept regularly down among the casks and wine bottles, because nearly every night for a week past enemy airmen had been circling about doing what hurt they could to the town and its remaining inhabitants.

From the single shattered window of the bedroom to which I was assigned I could look out and down across the narrow roadway upon a smaller house which had caught the full force of a big shell. The thing must have happened within a day or two, for the splintered woodwork and caved-in masonry had not yet begun to wear the weathered, crumbly look that comes to débris after a few weeks of exposure in this rainy climate, and there was a fresh powdering of dust upon the mass of wreckage before the door. Curiously enough the explosive which had reduced the interior of the building to a jumble of ruination left most of the roof rafters intact, and to them still adhered tiles in a sort of ordered pattern, with gaps between the red squares, so that the effect might be likened to a kind of lacy architectural lingerie.

Any moment similar destruction might be visited upon the hotel opposite, but, despite the constant and the imminent danger, the big-bodied, broad-faced proprietor and his trim small wife were seemingly as tranquil as though they lived where the roar of guns was never heard. The man who looks upon the French as an excitable race has only to come here now, to this land, to learn his error and to realise that beneath their surface emotionalism they have splendid reserve forces of resolution and fortitude. By my way of reasoning, it is with these people not merely a case of getting used to a thing—it is something more than that, something deeper than that. It is a pure, clean courage cast in the matrix of a patient heroism which buoys them up to carry on the ordinary undertakings of life amid conditions abnormal and disordered to the point of being almost intolerable when endured for weeks and months and years on end.

Having established ourselves, we set about the task of securing the coveted transportation up to the vicinity of the planes of contact between the Allies and the enemy. The shelling had somewhat abated since our arrival, so we made so bold as to trudge across town to the railroad station, encountering but few persons on the way. In the immediate neighbourhood of the station the evidences of recent strafing were thicker even than in other parts of the old city. Where an hour before a shell had blown two loitering French soldiers to bits, a shattered stone gateway and a wide hole in the ground and a great smearing of moist red stains upon the upheaved earth spelled the tale of what had happened plainly enough. A withered old man was doing his feeble best to patch together the split and sundered planks of the gate; the bodies, what was left of them, had been removed by a burial squad.

At the railroad terminal there was pressing need for everything that went on wheels, and of a certainty there was nothing in the nature of a self-propelled vehicle available for the use of three men who came bearing no order that would give them the right to commandeer government equipment. So our next hope, and seemingly our last one, lay in the French. At a certain place we found numbers of kindly and sympathetic officers with staff markings on their collars, who professed to be glad to see us, at the same time expressing a polite surprise that a trio of unannounced American newspaper men should have dropped in upon them, seemingly out of the shell-harassed skies above.

But when we suggested we would appreciate the loan of an automobile and with the automobile an officer to escort us up to the battle front they lifted eyebrows, shoulder blades and arms toward heaven, all in the same movement signifying chagrin and regret. What we asked was quite impossible, considering the exigencies and emergencies of the moment. The most formidable engagement that ever had been or perhaps ever would be was in midblast. Every available bit of motive power was required; every available man was required.

Besides, the roads, as doubtless we knew, were blocked with reënforcements hurrying up to support the hard-pressed British north of the Aisne. Any other time, yes. But now—no, and once again, no. We were quite free to stay on in Soissons if we cared for a place temporarily so unhealthy. We might have free access to any of the maps or records on hand. We might visit any of the hospitals or rest camps in the immediate vicinity. But further than that our new friends could not go. They added, by way of advice, that our best course would be to return straightway to Paris and come again when the crisis had passed and the sector to the north had somewhat quieted.

There being nothing else to do, we took a walk to think things over. The walk ended at our stopping place just as the German guns north of us beyond the river resumed their afternoon serenade. More refugees were coming into the town in a long dismal procession from Chauny and Ham and Noyon and scores of smaller places. Some of them had been on the road for twenty-four hours, some for as long as forty-eight hours. They had rested a while in wrecked and empty villages during the preceding night, then had risen at daybreak and resumed their heart-breaking pilgrimage, with no goal in sight and no destination in view, and only knowing that what might lie ahead of them could never by any chance be half so bad as what the Germans were creating behind them.

At the beginning of this war, in Belgium and again in Northern France, not many miles from where we then were, I had seen on the edges of the vortex of battle and destruction many such eddying, aimless streams of human flotsam and jetsam of war; but to one who knew the facts of their case

The Glory Of The Coming | 47

the present plight of these poor wanderers had a special appeal. For this was the second time they had been dispossessed from their small holdings, the second time they had fled in huddles like frightened sheep before the path of the grey invader, the second time all that they owned had been swept away and smashed up and wasted beyond repairing.

Driven out of their homes in the first four weeks of the war, back in 1914, at the time of the great onslaught against Paris, they had been kept away from these homes for more than two years, all during the German occupation of their territory. After the great victory of the Allies over von Hindenburg in the Aisne country they had returned, tramping back in pairs and groups to the sites of their homesteads, filled with the tenacious impulse of the French peasant and the French villager to reroot himself in his native soil; had returned to find that before the Germans retreated beyond the Chemin des Dames they, in accordance with orders from the all-highest command, sawed down the fruit trees in the little orchards and burned the houses that had sheltered them, and tore up the vines and shovelled dung into the drinking wells.

Nevertheless, the repatriates had set to, working like beavers to restore a sorry semblance of the simple frugal communal system under which they and their fathers before them had existed since the Napoleonic wars. And now, just when they were beginning to patch together the broken ends of their lives, when with aid from the French Government and aid from Americans they had cleared and planted their devastated fields and had built new habitations for themselves out of the ruins of the old ones, again the enemy had come down upon them like a ravening wolf on a fold; and again they had run away, deserting all they could not carry in their arms or upon their backs, and knowing full well in the light of past experience that the Germans either would garner the work of their hands or else would make an utter end of it.

At a corner just above the hotel we came upon a mother and her family of nine. She was less than forty years old herself; her husband was a soldier at the Front. She wore wooden sabots on her feet, and upon her body a tattered, sleazy black frock. Her eldest child was fifteen years old, her youngest less than six months. For the ten of them to travel a distance of twelve miles had taken the better part of two days and two nights. The woman had contrived a sling of an old bed sheet, which passed over one of her shoulders and under the other; and in this hammock contrivance she had carried the youngest child against her bosom, with her bodice open at the breast so the baby might suckle while she pushed a crippled perambulator containing the two next youngest bairns. The rest of the brood had walked all the way. They were wearied beyond description; they were incredibly dirty and famishing for want of proper sustenance, but not a single one of the small wretches who was old enough to speak the word failed to murmur "*Merci, merci,*" when the neighbours brought them bowls of hot soup and gave them sups of warm milk and put big slices of bread smeared with jam into their dirty, clawlike little hands.

Having wolfed down the food they squatted, all of them, against a house front to wait for the camion which would take them to a refuge in a Red Cross station a dozen miles away. They had to wait a good while, since all the available wagons were engaged in performing similar merciful offices for earlier arrivals. The children curled up in little heaps like kittens and went to sleep, but the mother sat on a stone doorstep with her babe against her bare flesh, over her heart, to keep it warm, and stared ahead of her with eyes which expressed nothing save a dumb, numbed resignation.

An old priest in a black robe came along and he stopped, being minded, I think, to utter some message of comfort to this wife of a soldier of France, and in her way, I say, as valorous a soldier as her husband could be, did he wear twenty decorations for bravery. But either the priest could find no words to say or the words choked in his throat. Above her drooped head he made with his hand the sign of the cross in the air and went away. And as I stood looking on I did in my heart what any man with blood in his veins would have done had he been there in my stead—I consigned to the uttermost depths of perdition the soul of the Brute of Prussia whose diseased ambition brought to pass this thing and a million things like unto it.

CHAPTER V
SETTING A TRAP FOR OPPORTUNITY

HAD we waited that night for Opportunity to knock at our door I am inclined to think we might be waiting yet. We went out and we set a trap for Opportunity, and we caught her. No matter how or whence, the chance we coveted for a lift to the battle came to us before the night was many hours old. But before the design assumed shape we were to meet as blithe a young Britisher as ever I have seen, in the person of one Captain Pepper, a red-cheeked Yorkshireman in his early twenties, a fit and proper type of the men England has sent out to officer her forces overseas.

One of our Red Cross ambulances, while scouting out toward Noyon that afternoon, picked him up as he trudged up the road alone, with a fresh machine-gun wound through the palm of his right hand and his cap on the back of his head. His wound had been tied up at a casualty-dressing station and he had set out then to walk a distance of twenty-odd kilometres to Soissons, where he was told he might find a hospital to shelter him.

He dined with us, along with the ambulance driver who brought him in; and afterward he insisted on sitting a while with us, though he had been fighting, day and night almost continuously since the beginning of the battle and plainly was far spent from fatigue and lack of sleep. So far as I might judge, though, he did not have a nerve in his body. Gesturing with his swathed hand he told us not what he himself had done—somehow he managed in his self-effacing way to steer away from the personal note in his recital—but mainly about the stupendous tragedy in which he had played his part. Considering him as he sat there on a broken sofa with his long legs outstretched before a wood fire, one could not doubt that it had been a creditable part.

We gathered that in the second day of the fighting, as the English fell back before overwhelming odds but fighting for every inch, he became separated from his company. Next morning he found himself without a command in the heels of the orderly retreat and had offered himself for service to the first superior officer he met. Thereupon he was put in charge of a mixed detachment of two hundred men—gathered up anyhow and anywhere—and with his motley outfit had been told off to hold a strip of woods somewhere south of Chauny. Under him, he said, were stragglers cut off from half a dozen battered line regiments, and along with these, cooks, wagon drivers, engineers, officers' servants and stretcher bearers. In front of the squad, beyond the woods, was a strip of marsh, and this natural barrier gave them an advantage which, plus pluck, enabled them to beat off not one but several oncoming waves of Germans.

"We had machine guns, luckily enough," he said; "and, my word, but we gave the beggars a proper drubbing! We piled them up in heaps along the edges of that bally old bog. Everywhere along the Front—where we were and everywhere else, too, from what I can hear—they have outnumbered us four or five to one, but I'm quite sure we've killed or wounded ten of them for every man of ours that has been laid out since this show started four days ago.

"Well, that's all, except that this morning about ten o'clock I was hit and had to quit and come away, because you see I wouldn't be much use with one hand out of commission and bleeding all over the shop—would I now? I'm sorry to have to leave the chaps—they were a sporting lot; but since I had to stop a bullet I'm glad I've got a nice clean cushy wound. I shall be glad to get a taste of Blighty too; I'm a bit fagged, as you might say."

His head nodded forward on his chest when he got this far, and his limbs relaxed.

He protested, though, against being bundled off to bed, saying he was quite comfortable and that his hand scarcely pained him at all, but the man who had brought him took him away. As for Carroll and Green and me, we slept that night, what sleeping we did, with our clothes on us, ready to rise and hunt the wine cellar if anything of a violently unpleasant nature occurred over our heads. During the hours before daylight there was a spirited spell of banging and crashing somewhere in the town, and not so far away either, if one might judge by the volume of the tumult, which rattled the empty casement frame alongside my bed and made the ancient house to rock and creak; but when dawn came the gables above us were still intact and we were enjoying our beauty sleep in the calm which succeeded the gust of shelling or of bombing or whatever it was.

CHAPTER VI
THROUGH THE BATTLE'S FRONT DOOR

IMMEDIATELY after breakfast, in accordance with a plan already formulated, we quietly took possession of one of those small American-made cars, the existence of which has been responsible for the addition of an eighth joke to the original seven jokes in the world. We didn't know it then, but for us the real adventure was just starting. There were four of us in the flivver—the driver, a young American in uniform, whose duties were of such a nature that he travelled on a roving commission and need necessarily report to none concerning his daily movements; and for passengers, our own three selves. For warrant to fare abroad we had a small American flag painted on the glass wind shield, one extra tire, and an order authorising us to borrow gasoline—simply these and nothing more. Very unostentatiously we rode out of Soissons, steering a northwesterly course. We might not know exactly where we were going or when we should be back, but we were on our way.

At the same time, be it here said, there was method of a sort in our scheme of things, for we were aiming, as closely as we might, at the point where approximately the main French command jointed on to the right wing of the British, we figuring that at the junction place, where the overlapping and intermingled areas of control met, and more especially in a confused period when one army was falling back and the other bringing up its reserves, we stood a better chance in our credential-less and unaccredited state of wriggling on up from the back lines to the Front than would elsewhere be possible.

We reckoned the prospect after this fashion: If the French find us traversing the forbidden lands they may take it for granted that the British permitted us to pass. If we fall under the eyes of British guardians of the trail they are equally likely to assume that the French let us through. And so it turned out; which I claim is added proof that the standing luck of the American newspaper reporter on a difficult assignment is not to be discounted.

In stock we had one trump card, and only one, and we played it many a time during that somewhat crowded day. All of us were in khaki with tin helmets upon our heads and gas masks swung over our shoulders. The heavy trench coats in which we were bundled prevented betrayal to the casual eye of the fact that none of us wore badges denoting rank, upon our collars or shoulder straps. Outfitted thus we might have been major generals or we might have been second lieutenants of the American Expeditionary Forces. Who, on a cursory scrutiny of us, was to say?

So we decided among ourselves that ours must be a rôle suggestive of great personal importance and urgent business. Did any wayside sentinel, whether British or French, move out upon the crown of the road as though he meant to halt us, one of us, with an authoritative arm, would wave him clear of our path and we would go flitting imperiously by as though the officiousness of underlings roused in us only a passing annoyance. It proved a good trick. It may never work again in this war, but I bear witness that it has worked once.

In the very first leg of this expedition good old Madame Bonneaventure stood our friend. The River Aisne skirts the city of Soissons. At the far side of the bridge, spanning the stream, which bridge we must cross, stood a French noncom, charged, as we knew, with the duty of examining the passes of those outbound. If we disregarded his summons to halt, complications of a painful nature would undoubtedly ensue. But as the car slowed up, all of us with our fingers figuratively crossed, he either recognised the driver as one who passed him often or was impressed by our bogusly impressive mien, or possibly accepted the painted flag on Tin Lizzie's weather-beaten countenance as warrant of our authenticity.

As he waved to us to proceed and then came to a salute, we, returning the salute in due form, were uttering three silent but nonetheless vehement cheers. I think we also shook hands. We were past the first and by long side the most formidable barrier. The farther we proceeded toward the battle the greater would be our chances of proceeding, it being generally assumed that no one gets very deeply into the district of active hostilities unless he has a proper errand there and has proved it to the satisfaction of the highway warders behind.

Through several villages that were reduced by shell fire to litter heaps and tenanted only by detachments of French soldiers we passed. Next we skirted up the sides of a steep hill and rounded the crest to where, spread out before our eyes, was a glorious panorama of the terrain below and beyond.

We drew in our breaths. Each one of us had seen something of the panoply of warfare in the making, but nothing in my own experience since Belgium in 1914 had equalled this. All the world appeared to have put on cartridge belts and gone to war. As far as the eye could reach, away off yonder to where sky line and earth line met behind the dust screen, cavalry, artillery, infantry, supply trains, munition trains, and all imaginable branches of the portable machinery of an army were in sight and in motion. Their masses hid the earth with a shifting pattern as though a vast blue-grey carpet were magically weaving itself. Overhead, singly, in pairs and in formations, like flights of wild fowl, the scout planes, the observation planes and the battle planes went winging. They were like silver gulls escorting limitless schools of porpoise through placid waters.

Usually there is a seemingly interminable confusion in the vision of a great force upon the forward go. To the lay eye it appears that the whole movement has got itself inextricably snarled. This line travels one course, that line goes in exactly the opposite direction, a third one is bisecting the first two at cross angles. But here one great compelling influence was sending all the units forward along a common current. The heavy vehicles held to the roads which threaded the plain; the infantry took short cuts across lots, as it were; the cavalry traversed the fields and penetrated the occasional thickets; the sky craft trod the alleys of the air—but they all headed toward the same unseen goal. There was no doubt about it—France was hurrying up a most splendid army to reenforce the hard-pressed defenders of French soil, where the Hun pushed against the line of the inward-bending and battered but yet unbroken British battalions.

We coasted down off the heights into the plateau, and now as we came in among them we had opportunity for appraising the temper of those men hurrying on their forward march to the killing pits. Who says France is war wearied or that her sons are tired of fighting? No suggestion was there here of dumb oxen driven to slaughter. Why, these men were like bridegrooms bound for the marriage feast. They sang as they marched or as they rode. Usually what they sang was a snatch of some rollicking chanson, and through the dirt masks they grinned into our faces as we went slithering by.

There were hails and friendly gestures for us. It might be a boy private with a sprig of early spring wild flowers jauntily stuck in his cap who waved at us. It might be a cook balancing himself on the tailboard of a travelling field kitchen who raised a sweaty visage from his steaming soup caldron and made friendly circles in the air with a dripping iron instrument that was too big for a spoon and too small for a spade; or it might be a gunner on a bouncing ammunition truck with enough of potential death and disaster bestowed under his sprawled legs to blow him and, incidentally, us into ten million smithereens if ever it went off.

Kilometre after kilometre we skihooted through the press, and it was a comic thing to see how a plodding regiment would swing over or a battery would bounce and jolt off the fairway into the edges of the ditch at the insistent toot-toot of our penny whistle of a horn to let us by. It made one think of whales making room in a narrow tideway for an impudent black minnow to pass. And always there was the drone of the questing aëroplanes overhead and the thunderous roaring of the guns in front. We overtook one train of supply trucks with the markings of the U. S. A. and manned by dusty lads in the khaki fustian of Yankeeland—evidence that at least one arm of our service would have a hand in the epochal task confronting our allies. All the rest of it was French.

For us there was no halt until we reached Blérencourt. Now this place was a place having a particular interest for us, since it was at Blérencourt that the organisation known as the American Fund for French Wounded, which is headed by Miss Anne Morgan and which has for its field personnel American women exclusively, had during the past nine months centred its principal activities.

In the outskirts of the town, now evacuated of almost all its civilian residents, stand the massive stone gateways and the dried moat of the magnificent château of Blérencourt, which was destroyed by the peasants in the time of the Terror and never rebuilt. What remains constitutes one of the most picturesque physical reminders of the French Revolution that is to be found in the country to-day. We rode under the arched stone portals— and lo, it was almost as though we had come into the midst of a smart real-estate development somewhere on Long Island within easy communicating distance of New York City.

French francs, provided by the state, and American dollars, donated by the folks back home, had been used under American supervision to construct a model colony upon the exact site of the ancient castle of some vanished noble family of the old régime. There was a model barracks, a model dormitory, a model schoolhouse, two model cottages and an office building that was a model among models—all built of planking, all glistening and smart with fresh paint, all with neat doorsteps in front of them and trim flower plots and vegetable gardens about them. There was a chicken house and a chicken run, dotted with the shapes of plump fowls. There was a storeroom piled high with clothing and food sent over from America to the A. F. F. W. for distribution among destitute natives of the devastated districts, of which this, until a year ago, had been the centre.

These incongruously modern structures snuggled right up under the venerable walls of the battlements. Indeed several of the buildings were cunningly built into the ruins, so that on one side the composite edifice would show a withered stone face, with patches of furze growing in the chinks of the crumbled masonry like moles on the forehead of a withered crone, and on the other would present a view of a smart cottage with a varnished shingle roof and a painted front door which apparently had just arrived from some planing mill in the States. Underneath the floor was a cellar four hundred years old, but the curtains in the window had seemingly been cut and stitched only yesterday. Somehow, though, the blended effect was immensely effective. It made me think of Home-dale-on-the-Sound grafted upon a background of Louis the Grand; and for a fact that was exactly what it was.

This creation, representing as it did nine months of hard work on the part of devoted American women, had been closed only the day before. It stayed in operation until it seemed probable that the German legions might penetrate this far south in their effort to ford the River Oise. The little pupils of the kindergarten had been sent away in trucks, the main dormitory had been turned into a temporary resting place for refugees, and the American ranges in the kitchen had done valiant service in the cooking of hot meals for exhausted women and children tramping in from the north and west. Before the managers and teachers left at dusk of the preceding evening two crippled French soldiers, specially detailed for work here by the government, had been assigned to place vessels of kerosene in each building, with instructions to fire the oil at the first signs of approaching Germans.

The cans of inflammables were still in their places when we arrived and the maimed watchmen, one of them a one-armed man and the other a one-legged, had camped all night on the premises ready on warning to apply the torch and destroy this frontier outpost of American charity and American efficiency. But in the forenoon word was come that the enemy had been brought to bay seven miles away and that he might not break through the British-French line. He did break through, but that is another story. So Mrs. Dike, of New York, and Miss Blagden, of Philadelphia, two of Miss Morgan's assistants, had motored in from below, filled with thanksgiving that the patient work of their hands and their hearts would almost certainly be spared.

While Mrs. Dike, with tears in her eyes, was telling us of the things that had been accomplished here and while the troopers poured in unceasing streams along the main road beyond the gateway, a handful of belated refugees crept in under the weathered armorial bearings on the keystonp of the archway, to be fed and cared for and then sent along in the first empty truck that came by going toward Soissons.

In this group of newcomers was an elderly little man in a worn high hat and a long frock coat with facings of white dust upon its shiny seams, who looked as though he might be the mayor of some inconsequential village. He carried two bulging valises and a huge umbrella. With him was his wife, and she had in one hand a cage housing two frightened canaries and under the other arm a fat grey tabby cat which blinked its slitted eyes contentedly.

The most pitiable figure of them all to my way of thinking was an old woman—yes, a very old woman—she must have been all of eighty. Alongside one of the buildings I came upon her sitting in a huddle of her most treasured possessions. She was bent forward, with her gnarled hands folded in the lap of her dress, which was silk and shiny, for naturally when she fled from her home she had put on her back the best that she owned. Under the cope of a queer little old black bonnet with faded purple cloth flowers upon it her scanty hair lay in thin neat folds, as white and as soft as silk floss. Her feet in stiff, new, black shoes showed beneath her broad skirts. Her face, caving in about the mouth where her teeth were gone and all crosshatched with wrinkles, was a sweet, kindly, most gentle old face— the kind of face that we like to think our dead-and-gone grandmothers must have had.

She sat there ever so patiently in the soft sunlight, waiting for the truck which would carry her away to some strange place among stranger folk. When I drew near to her, wishing with all my heart that I knew enough of her tongue to express to her some of the thoughts I was thinking, she looked up at me and smiled a friendly little smile, and then raising her hands in a gesture of resignation dropped them again in her lap. But it was only with her lips that she smiled, for all the time her chin was quivering and her faded old blue eyes were brimming with a sorrow that was past telling in words.

She still sat there as we got into our car and drove off toward the battle. Looking back, the last thing I saw before we rounded the corner of the wall was her small black shape vivid in the sunshine. And I told myself that if I were an artist seeking to put upon canvas an image that would typify and sum up the spirit of embattled France to-day I would not paint a picture of a wounded boy soldier; nor yet one of a winged angel form bearing a naked sword; nor yet one of the full-throated cock of France, crowing his proud defiance. I would paint a picture of that brave little old withered woman, with the lips that smiled and the chin that quivered the while she smiled.

CHAPTER VII
AT THE FRONT OF THE FRONT

WHEN the last preceding chapter of mine ended I had reached a point in the narrative where our little party of four, travelling in our own little tin flivverette, were just leaving Blérincourt, being bound still farther west and aiming, if our abiding luck held out, to reach the front of the Front—which, I may add, we did.

To be exact we were leaving not one Blérincourt but three. First, Blérincourt, the town, with its huddle of villagers' homes, housing at this moment only French troopers and exhausted refugees; second, Blérincourt, the castle, a mouldering relic of a great house, testifying by its massive empty walls and its tottering ruin of a gateway to the fury which laid hold on the peasants of these parts in the days of the Terror; and, third, Blérincourt, the model colony of model cottages, which for us held the most personal interest, since it was here the American women of the American Fund for French Wounded had during the previous nine months centred their activities relating to the repopulating of districts in the Aisne country, now for the second time evacuated and given over again to the savage malice of the boche.

Behind us as we swung into the main highway lay this grouped composition of the wrecked château, the tiny old houses of weathered grey stone and the little frame domiciles, smart and glistening with fresh paint and fresh varnishing. Before us, within a space of time and distance to be spanned by not more than half an hour of steady riding, was somewhere the problematical doorway through which we hoped to pass into the forward lines of that battle which the historians of the future, I dare say, will call merely the Great Battle, knowing their readers require no added phraseology to distinguish it from the lesser engagements of this war—or in fact of any war.

We did not ask our way of any whom we met, either of those going ahead of us or those coming back in counter streams. To begin with, we deemed it inexpedient to halt long enough to give to any person in authority a chance for questioning the validity of present mission, since, as I already have explained, we carried no passes qualifying us to traverse this area; and besides there was no need to ask. The route was marked for us by signs and sounds without number, plainer than any mileposts could have been: By the columns of Frenchmen hurrying up to reenforce the decimated British who until now, at odds of one to five, had borne the buffets of the tremendous German onslaught; by the never-ending, never-slackening roar of the heavy guns; by the cloud of dust and powder, forming a wall against two sides of the horizon, which mounted upward to mingle its hazes with the hazes of the soft spring afternoon; by the thin trickling lines of light casualty cases, "walking wounded," in the vernacular of the Medical Corps—meaning by that men who, having had first-aid bandages applied to their hurts at forward casualty stations, were tramping rearward to find accommodations for themselves at field hospitals miles away.

At once we were in a maze of traffic to be likened to the conditions commonly prevalent on lower Fifth Avenue in the height of the Christmas-shopping season, but with two distinctions: Here on this chalk-white highroad the movement, nearly all of it, was in one direction; and instead of omnibuses, delivery vans, carriages and private automobiles, this vast caravansary was made up of soldiers afoot, soldiers mounted and soldiers riding; of batteries, horse drawn and motor drawn; of pontoon bridges in segments; of wagon trains, baggage trains, provision trains and munition trains; of field telephone, field telegraph and field wireless outfits upon wheels; of all the transportable impedimenta and all the myriad items of movable machinery pertaining to the largest army that has crossed a corner of France since the days of the first great invasion more than three and a half years before.

There were ambulances past counting; there were big covered camions in numbers sufficient to fit out a thousand circuses; there were horses and donkeys and mules of all the known sizes and colours; there were so many human shapes in uniforms of horizon blue that the eye grew weary and the brain rebelled at the task of trying, even approximately, to compute estimates of the total strength of the man power here focussed.

Through all this, weaving in and out, our impudent little black bug of a car scuttled along, with its puny horn honking a constant and insolent demand for clear passage. At a faster gait than anything in sight except the cruising aëroplanes above, we progressed upon our way, with none to halt us and none to turn us back. Where the dust hung especially thick at a crossroads set in the midst of the wide plain we almost struck three pedestrians who seemingly did not heed our hooted warning or take notice of it until we were right upon them. As they jumped nimbly for the ditch we could see that all these had staff markings at their throats, and that one, the eldest of the three, a stoutish gentleman with a short grizzled beard, wore three stars in a triangle upon his collar. Tin Lizzie had almost achieved the distinction for herself of having run down a major general of France.

We did not stop, though, to offer apologies or explanations. With rare sagacity our driver threw her wide open and darted into the fog, to take temporary shelter behind a huge supply wagon, which vehicle we followed for a while after the fashion of a new-foaled colt trailing its dam.

Proofs began to multiply that we were nearing the zone of live combat. Until now the only British soldiers we had seen were slightly wounded men bound afoot for the rear. All at once we found ourselves passing half a company of khaki-clad Britishers who travelled across a field over a course parallel to the one we were taking and who disappeared in a hazel copse beyond. Rifle firing could be heard somewhere on the far side of the thicket. At a barked command from an officer who clattered up on horseback a battery of those doughty little seventy-fives, which the French cherish so highly, and with such just cause, was leaving the road and taking station in a green meadow where the timid little wild flowers of a mild March showed purple and yellow in the rutted and trampled grass.

With marvellous haste the thing was accomplished almost instantly. The first gun of the five squatted in the field with its nozzle slanting toward the northwest, and behind it its four companions stood, all with their short noses pointing at precisely the same angle, like bird dogs on a back stand. Suddenly they did what well-broken bird dogs never do—they barked, one after the other. Almost before the whining whistle of the shells had died away the gunners were moving their pieces to a point closer up behind a screen of poplars and sending a second yelping salvo of shots toward an unseen target.

We became aware that the component units of the army were now quitting the roadway to take positions in the back lines. Indeed those back lines formed themselves while we watched. One battery after another swung off to the right or to the left and came into alignment, so that soon we rode between double rows of halted guns. With our canes we could have touched the artillerymen piling heaps of projectiles in convenient hollows in the earth close up to the edges of the road. Big covered wains discharged dusty infantrymen, who, pausing only long enough to unbuckle their packs from their shoulders and throw them under the hoods of the wagons, went at a shambling half-trot through the meadow. Cavalrymen, not dismounted, as they had mainly been during these dragging winter months of warfare that was stationary and static, but with their booted feet once more in their stirrups, cantered off, bound presumably for the thin woodlands which rimmed the plateau where the terrain broke away to the banks of the River Oise.

Here again at last was war in the open, as different from battle in the trenches as football is from trap shooting. The action of it was spread out before one's eyes, not masked in mud ambuscades. Each instant our eyes beheld some new and stirring picture, standing out by reason of its swift vigour from the vaster panorama of which it was a part. What I had seen of battle formations in the preceding three weeks had made me think mainly of subway diggin's or of construction work for a new railroad or of engineering operations in connection with a dam, say, or a dike. What I saw now most vividly suggested old-time battle pictures by Meissonier or Détaillé. War, for the moment at least, had gone back to the aspect which marked it before both sides dug themselves in to play the game of counterblasting with artillery and nibbling the foe's toes with raids and small forays.

Of another thing we were likewise aware, and the realisation of the fact cheered us mightily. Among the blue uniforms of the French the greenish buff of the British showed in patches of contrasting colour that steadily increased in size and frequency. By rare good luck we had entered the advanced positions at the identical place for which, blindly, we had been seeking—the place where the most westerly sector of the French left wing touched the most easterly sector of the British right wing; and better than that, the place where the French strength hurrying up to reënforce and if need be replace decimated divisions of their allies was joined on to and fused in with the retiring British Army, which, during the preceding three days, had sustained the main force of the German offensive. It was here if anywhere that we could count with the best prospects of success upon boring straight through to the Front, the reason being that the French might assume the British had given us passage and the British might assume the French had let us by.

There were perhaps three more miles of brisk travelling for us, during which I am sure that I saw more than ever I have seen in any three miles that ever I traversed in my life; and at the end of that stretch we could tell that we had well-nigh outrun the forward crest of the French ground swell and had come into the narrower backwash of the British retreat. A retreat of sorts it may have been, but a rout it most assuredly was not. We saw companies reduced to the strength of ten or twelve or twenty men under command of noncommissioned officers or possibly of a single lieutenant. We saw individual privates and we saw privates in squads of two or three or half a dozen men, who in the terrific fighting had become separated from a command, which possibly had been scattered but which it was more likely had been practically wiped out. Such men were not stragglers, nor were they malingerers; they were survivors, atoms flung backward out of the raging inferno which had swallowed up whole regiments and whole brigades.

And we took note that every single man of these broken and decimated detachments was in good humour, though dog tired; and that every single one of them had kept his accoutrements and his rifle; and that every single one of them, whether moving under orders or acting upon his own initiative, was intent upon just two things and two things only—to get back into the maelstrom from which temporarily he had been spewed forth, and pump more lead into the living tidal wave of grey coats. Some that we overtook were singing, and singing lustily too. Than this no man could ask to see a finer spectacle of fortitude, of pluck and of discipline, and I am sure that in his heart each one of us, while having no doubt of the outcome of the fiery test, prayed that our own soldiers, when their time of trial by battle came, might under reverses and under punishment acquit themselves as well as had these British veterans, Yorkshire and Bedfordshire and Canada, who came trudging along behind us, swallowing our dust. What impressed us as most significant of all was that only once that day did we see a scrap of personal equipment that had been cast aside. This was a cartridge belt of English make, with its pouches empty and its tough leather tom almost in two, lying like a broken-backed brown snake in a ditch.

Already from wounded English soldiers and from exhausted English hospital workers whom we had seen back in Soissons we comprehended a measure of appreciation of what these battered fragments of the forces had been called upon to endure during four days and five nights. We knew as surely as though we had stopped to take down the story of each one of the wearied, cheerful, resolute chaps, that they had their fill of killing the enemy and of seeing their mates about them blown to bits by high explosives or mowed down by rifle fire. I recalled what a bedraggled young surgeon, a Highlander by his accent, had said the night before:

"I crave never to pass through this experience again. I have seen so much of death since this battle started that I have in me now contempt not only for death but for life too. I thought last year on the Somme I saw real fighting. Man, it was but child's play to what I saw the day before yesterday!

"From the casualty dressing post where I was on duty I could see the fighting spread out before me like a cinema show. For our shelter—we were in a concrete dugout—was in the side of a hill with a wide sweep of lowland below and beyond us, and it was here in this valley that the Germans came at our people. Between jobs in the operating theatre—and God knows we had enough of them—I would slip out for a breath of air, and then I could watch through my glasses what went on.

"In wave after wave the Germans came on, marching close together in numbers incredible. They were like ants; they were like flies; like swarming grasshoppers. At first they tried a frontal attack against our trenches, but even the Germans, driven on as they must have been like cattle to the slaughter, couldn't stand what they got there. Within two hours they charged three times! Each time they fell back again, and each time they left their dead lying so thickly behind that finally the ground seemed as though it were covered with a grey carpet.

"That happened in the first day of their drive against our part of the line, which was the third line back, the two front lines having already been taken by them. So on the next day, which was the day before yesterday, they worked their way round to the south a bit and tried a flanking advance. Then it was I saw this, just as I'm telling it to you. I saw them caught by our machine-gun fire and piled up, heap on heap, until there was a windrow of them before the British trenches that must have been six feet high.

"They went back, but they came again and again, and they kept on coming. They climbed right over that wall of their own dead—I myself watched them scrambling up among the bodies—and they slid down on the other side and ran right into the wire entanglements, where those of them that were killed hung in the wires like garments drying on a line. They died there in such numbers that they fairly clogged the wires. And still they kept on coming.

"When our line began to bend in, farther away to the west, we got orders to evacuate the station; and the men in the trenches where I had seen the fighting got orders—what were left of them—to fall back too. They were Scotchmen, these laddies, and they were fairly mad with the fighting. They didn't want to go, and they refused to go. I'm told by reliable witnesses that their officers had almost to use force against them—not to make them keep on fighting but to make them quit fighting."

He looked into the coals of the wood fire and shivered.

"Man, it's not war any more; it's just plain slaughter. Mark my word—there'll never be another war such as this one has been or another battle such as the one that still goes on yonder. 'Tis not in flesh and blood to endure its repetition once the hate has been cooled by a taste of peace."

The men about us for the most part must have taken part as actors in scenes such as the young surgeon had described as an onlooker. But about them there was no sign of reluctance or of surcease. We realised as thoroughly as though we had been eyewitnesses to their conduct that they had carried on like brave men; and without being told we realised, too, that they were made of the stuff which keeps carrying on as long as there is life left in it. They were of the breed of the bulldog, and clean strain, at that.

Frenchmen grew fewer in number along the route we travelled; Britishers became more and more numerous. Where byways crossed the highroad and in wrecked villages the British already had posted military policemen to guide the traffic and point out the proper directions to bodies of men passing through. Those men stood in midroad giving their orders as calmly and as crisply as though they had been bobbies on the Strand. Even this emergency John Bull's military system did not disintegrate. As long as the organism lasted the organisation would last too. Nowhere was there any suggestion of confusion or conflict of will. I am prone to think that in the years to come the chief outstanding fact about the great spring offensive of 1918 will be not the way the Germans came forward but the way in which the British fell back.

Until now we had seen only British foot soldiers, and once or twice officers in motor cars or on horseback; but soon we came upon a battery of British light artillery. It was jolting across muddy pasture among the stumps of apple trees which the Germans with malignant thoroughness had felled before their big retreat of twelve months before. The place had been an orchard once. Now it was merely so much waste land, dedicated to uselessness by efficiency and kultur. The trees, as we could see, had not been blown down by shell fire or hewn down with axes. They had been neatly and painstakingly sawed through, clear down to the earth. Some of the butts measured a foot and a half across, and to have bolls of this size, fruit trees in this country must have attained great age.

The battery took position and went into immediate action behind a covert of willows and scrub at the far side of the ruined orchard. At the moment we did not know that the thicket was a screen along the southern bank of the Oise. At the left of where the guns were speaking was a group of empty and shattered cottages stretching along a single narrow street that ran almost due north and south. Coming opposite the foot of this street we glimpsed at the other end of it a glint of running water, and in the same instant, perhaps two or three miles away farther on across the river, we made out the twin spires of the cathedral of Noyon, for which, as we know, the contending armies had striven for forty-eight hours, and which the evening before had fallen into the enemy's hands. Literally we were at the front of the Front.

East of the clustered houses of the city a green hill rose above the tree tops. Across the flanks of this hill we saw grey-blue clumps moving. At that distance the sight was suggestive of a crawling mass of larvæ. Over it puffs of smoke, white for shrapnel and black for explosives, were bursting. We were too far away to observe the effect of this shelling, but knew that the crawling grey blanket meant Germans advancing in force down into the valley of the river, and we knew, too, that they were being punished by Allied guns as they came on to take up their new position.

CHAPTER VIII
A BRIDGE AND AN AUTOMOBILE TIRE

CURIOUSLY enough there was at this moment and at this place no return fire from the enemy. From this we deduced that the infantry in their impetuous onrush had so far outtravelled the heavy and more cumbersome arms of their service that the artillery had not caught up yet. However, a little later projectiles from hostile field pieces began to drop on our side of the stream.

Halfway of the length of the street our car halted. It did not seem the part of wisdom for the four of us to go ahead in a group, so I walked the rest of the way to spy out the land.

Behind the shattered stone and plaster houses French soldiers were squatted or lying. In the hope of finding some one who could speak the only language I knew I continued on until I came to the last two houses in the row. They overhung the riverbank. Beyond them were two bridges spanning the little river, one an old steel bridge with a concrete roadbed, and the other a sagging wooden structure, evidently built by soldier hands.

The mouth of the military bridge was stopped with a makeshift barricade thrown together any which way. The backbone of the barrier was formed of two tree trunks, but they were half hidden from sight beneath a miscellaneous riffle of upturned motor lorries, wheelbarrows and clustered household furniture, including many mattresses that plainly had been filched from the villagers' abandoned homes. Midway of the main bridge a handful of French engineers were pottering away, rather leisurely, I thought, at some job or other. Two Tommies were standing behind one of the farthermost buildings of the hamlet—a building which in happier days had been a café. Now it was a broken shell, foul inside with a litter of wreckage. The men wore the insignia of the Royal Lancers.

As I approached them they saluted, evidently mistaking me, in my trench coat and uniform cap, for an American officer. That an American officer should be in this place, so far away from any American troops, did not seem to surprise them in the least.

"What town is this?" was my first question.

"It's called Pontoise, sir," answered one of them, giving to the name a literal rendition very different from the French fashion of pronouncing this word.

"What's going on out yonder on the bridge?" I inquired next.

"The Frenchmen is minin' it to blow it up, sir. They mined it once already but the charge didn't explode, sir. Now they're goin' to give it another try. They'll be letting off the charge pretty soon, sir, I think—as soon as a few of their men and a few of ours who're over on the other bank in them bushes 'ave fallen back to this side 'ere."

"How close are the Germans?" I asked.

I figured they must be uncomfortably close. They were.

"Come along with me, sir, if you don't mind," quoth my informant.

Quite in the most casual way he led me out from behind the shelter of the ruined café. As we quitted its protection I could see over a broken garden wall the British battery down below at the left, firing as fast as the gunners could serve the pieces. Of all the men in sight these shirt-sleeved artillerymen were the only ones who seemed to have any urgent business in hand.

Together we advanced to the barricade, which at the spot where we halted came up to our middles. Across the top of it my guide extended a soiled hand.

"The beggars are right there, sir, in them bushes; about a 'undred and fifty yards away, sir, or two 'undred at the most," he said with the manner of a hired guide. "You carn't see them now, sir, but a bit ago I 'ad a peep at a couple of 'em movin' about. The reason they ain't firin' over 'ere is because they don't want us to locate 'em, I think, sir."

"Oh!" I said, like that. "Oh!"

By mutual but unspoken consent we then retired to our former position. The imperturbable Tommy fell back in good order, but I think possibly I may have hurried somewhat. I always was a fairly brisk walker, anyhow.

Inside the breached building my companions joined me, and while the shells from the battery and from the other batteries farther away went racketing over us toward Noyon we held a consultation of war. Any desire on the part of any one to stay and see what might happen after the bridge had been blown up was effectually squelched by the sudden appearance of two British officers coming through the village toward us. Did they choose to interrogate us regarding our mission in this parlous vicinity there might be embarrassment in the situation for us. So we went away from there.

As we departed from the place a certain thing impressed itself upon my consciousness. The men about me—the two Tommies certainly, the two officers presumably, and probably the Frenchmen—had but newly emerged from hard fighting. Of a surety they would very shortly be engaged in more hard fighting, striving to prevent the on-moving Germans from crossing the river. Over their head shells from their own guns were racking the air. Shells from hostile batteries were beginning to splatter down just beyond. This then was merely an interval, an interlude between acts of a most dire and tremendous tragedy.

And yet so firmly had the chance of death and the habit of war become a part of their daily and their hourly existence that in this brief resting spell they behaved exactly as men engaged in some wearing but peaceful labour might behave during a nooning in a harvest field. No one in sight was crouching in a posture of defence, with his rifle gripped in nervous hands and his face set and intent. Here were being exemplified none of the histrionic principles of applied heroics as we see them on the stage.

The Frenchmen were sprawled at ease behind the walls, their limbs relaxed, their faces betokening only a great weariness. One or two actually were asleep with their heads pillowed on their arms. Those who spoke did so in level, unexcited tones. They might have been discussing the veriest commonplaces of life. For all I knew to the contrary, they were discussing commonplaces. The two British privates leaned upon their rifles, with their tired legs sagging under them and with cigarette ends in their mouths. One of the officers was lighting a pipe as we drove past him. One of the Frenchmen was gnawing at a knuckle of bread.

Indeed there was nothing about the scene, except a knowledge of the immediate proximity of German skirmishers, which would serve to invest it with one-tenth of the drama that marked a hundred other sights we had that day witnessed. Later, though, we learned we had blundered by chance upon the very spot where the hinge of the greatest battle of history next day turned.

It was south of Noyon at the Pontoise ford and at other fords above and below Pontoise that the Germans designed to cross the river in their onslaught southward against the defences of Paris. But there they failed, thanks be to British desperation and French determination; and it was then, according to what students of strategy among the Allies say, that the hosts of the War Lord altered the plan of their campaign and faced about to the westward in their effort to take Amiens and sunder the line of communication between Paris and Calais—an effort which still is being made as I sit here in Paris writing these pages for the mail.

The day's journey was not over by any manner of means, but so far as I personally was concerned its culminating moment passed when I walked out on the bridge timbers with that matter-of-fact young Royal Lancer. What followed thereafter was in the nature of a series of anticlimaxes, and yet we saw a bookful before we rode back to Soissons for a second night under bombardment in that sorely beset and beleaguered old city. Before heading back we cruised for ten kilometres beyond Noyon, going west by south toward Compiègne.

On this side jaunt we mostly skirted the river, which on our bank was comparatively calm but which upon the farther bank was being contended for at the bayonet's point by British and French against Germans. The sound of the cannonading never ceased for a moment, and as dusk came on the northern horizon was lit up with flickering waves of a sullen dull red radiance. The nearer we came to Compiègne the more numerous were the British, not in squads and detachments and bits of companies but in regiments and brigades which preserved their formations even though some of them had been reduced to skeletons of their former proportions. In the fields alongside the way the artillerymen were throwing up earthen banks for the guns; the infantrymen were making low sod walls behind which they would sleep that night and fight on the morrow. From every hand came the smell of brewing tea, for, battle or no battle, the Tommy would have his national beverage. The troop horses were being properly bestowed in the shaggly thickets, and camp fires threw off pungent smells of wood burning. For the first time in a long time the campaign was outdoors, under the skies.

I saw one fagged trooper squatting at the roadside, with a minute scrap of looking-glass balanced before him in the twigs of a bare bush, while he painfully but painstakingly was shaving himself in cold ditch water. He had fought or marched all day, I imagine; his chances of being sent to eternity in piecemeal before another sunset were exceedingly good; but he would go, tidied and with scraped jowls, to whatever fate might await him. And that, except for one other small thing, was the most typically English thing I witnessed in the shank of this memorable evening.

The other incident occurred after we had faced about for our return. In a maze of byroads we got off our course. A lone soldier of the Bedfordshires—a man near forty, I should say at an offhand guess—was tramping along. Our driver halted our car and hailed him. He straightened his weary back and came smartly to a salute.

"We've lost our way," explained one of us.

He smiled at us whimsically.

"I'm afraid I can't help you, sirs," he said in the tones of an educated man. "I've lost my own way no less than six times to-day. I may add that I'm rather a stranger in these parts myself."

When we got to Blérincourt with an hour of daylight and another hour of twilight yet ahead of us we turned north toward Chauny, which the Germans now held and which the Allies were bombarding furiously. We had come to a crossroads just back of a small village, when with a low spiteful hiss of escaping air one of our rear tires went flat. We stopped to replace the damaged tube with a better one. Behind us, a quarter of a mile or so away, a British baggage train was making bivouac for the night. Just in front of us a British battery was firing over the housetops of the empty village toward Chauny.

We had the car jacked up and the old tire off the rim and the new one half on when—bang! the heavens and the world seemed to come together all about us. What happened was that a big shell of high explosives, fired from an enemy mortar miles away, had dropped within seventy, sixty yards of us in a field; what seemed to happen was that a great plug was pulled out of the air with a smiting and a crashing and a rending. The earth quivered as though it had taken a death wound. Our wind shield cracked across under the force of the concussion. Gravel and bits of clay descended about us in a pattering shower.

Speaking for myself, I may say that one of the most noticeable physical effects of having a nine shell exploding in one's immediate vicinity is a curious sinking sensation at the pit of the stomach, complicated with a dryness of the mouth and sudden chill in the feet.

Two more shells dropped within a hundred yards of us before we got that tire pumped up and departed. Even so, I believe the world's record for pumping up tires was broken on this occasion. I am in position to speak with authority on this detail, because I was doing the pumping.

CHAPTER IX
ACES UP!

INSIDE the German lines at the start of the war I met Ingold, then the first ace of the German aërial outfit; only the Germans did not call them aces in those days of the beginnings of things. The party to which I was attached spent the better part of a day as guests of Herr Hauptmann Ingold and his mates. Later we heard of his death in action aloft.

Coming over for this present excursion I crossed on the same steamer with Bishop of Canada—a major of His Britannic Majesty's forces at twenty-two, and at twenty-three the bearer of the Victoria Cross and of every other honour almost that King George bestows for valour and distinguished service, which means dangerous service. I have forgotten how many boche machines this young man had, to date, accounted for. Whether the number was forty-seven or fifty-seven I am not sure. I doubt if Bishop himself knew the exact figure.

At Paris, after my arrival, and at various places along the Front I have swapped talk and smoking tobacco with sundry more or less well-known members of the Lafayette Escadrille and with unattached aviators of repute and proved ability. From each of these men and from all of them— Belgians, Italians, Americans, Britishers and Frenchmen—I brought away an impression of the light-hearted gallantry, the modesty and the exceeding great competency which appear to be the outstanding characteristics of those who do their fighting—and, in a great many instances, their dying— in the air. It was almost as though the souls of these men had been made cleaner and as though their spirits had been made to burn with a whiter flame by reason of the purer element in which they carried on the bulk of their appointed share in this war business. You somehow felt that when they left the earth they shook off from their feet a good part of the dirt of the earth. I do not mean to imply that they had become superhuman, but that they had acquired, along with their training for a special and particularised calling, some touch of the romanticism that attached to the ancient and dutiful profession of knight-errantry.

Nor is this hard to understand. For a fact the flying men are to-day the knights-errant of the armies. To them are destined opportunities for individual achievement and for individual initiative and very often for individual sacrifice such as are denied the masses of performers in this war, which in so many respects is a clandestine war and which in nearly all respects is an anonymous war. I think sometimes that, more even than the abject stupidity of the enterprise, it is the entire taking-away of the drama — the colour of theatricalism, the pomp and the circumstance, the fuss and the feathers — that will make war an exceedingly unpopular institution for future generations, as it has been an exceedingly unprofitable if a highly necessary one for this present generation. When the planet has been purged of militarism, the parent sin of the whole sinful and monstrous thing, I am convinced that the sordid, physically filthy drabness that now envelops the machinery of it will be as potent an agency as the spreading of the doctrine of democracy in curing civilised mankind of any desire to make war for war's sake rather than for freedom and justice.

One has only to see it at first hand in this fourth year of conflict to realise how completely war has been translated out of its former elements. It is no longer an exciting outdoor sport for fox-chasing gentlemen in bright-red coats; no longer a seasonal diversion for crosscountry riders in buckskin breeches. It is a trade for expert accountants, for civil-engineering sharps, for rule of thumb, for pick and shovel and the land surveyor's instruments. As the outward romance of it has vanished away, in the same proportion the amount of manual labour necessary to accomplish any desired object has increased until it is nearly all work and mighty little play — a combination which makes Jack a dull boy and makes war a far duller game than it used to be. Of course the chances for heroic achievements, for the development and the exercise of the traits of courage and steadfastness and disciplined energy, are as frequent as ever they were, but generally speaking the picturesqueness with which mankind always has loved to invest its more heroic virtues has been obliterated — flattened under the steam roller.

To the average soldier is denied the prospect of ever meeting face to face the foe with whom he contends. For every man who with set jaw climbs the top to sink his teeth, figuratively or actually, in the embodied enemy, there are a dozen who toil and moil far back behind in manual labours of the most exacting and exhausting forms imaginable. A night raid is a variety of sublimated burglary, better adapted to the temperament of the prowler and the poacher than to the upstanding soldier man's instincts. If there be fear of gas he adds to the verisimilitude of the imitation by hiding his face behind a mask as though he were a footpad. If a battle be a massacre, which generally it is, then intermittent fighting is merely organised and systematised assassination.

By stealth, by trick and device, by artificial expedients smacking of the allied schools of the housebreaker and the highwayman, things are accomplished that once upon a bygone time eventuated from brawn, plus powder, plus chilled steel. Trench work means setting a man to dig in the mud a hole that may become his grave, and frequently does. He spends his days in a shallow crevice in the earth and his nights in a somewhat deeper one, called a dug-out. He combines in his customary life the habits of the boring grub and the habits of the blind worm, with a touch of the mine mule thrown in.

Once in a while he stings like a puff-adder, but not often. The infantryman plies a spade a week for every hour that he pumps a rifle. The cavalryman is more apt to be driving a truck or tramping long roads than riding a horse. The artilleryman sets up his pieces miles behind the line and fires at the indirect target of an invisible foe, without the poor satisfaction of being able to tell, with his eyes, whether he scored a hit or a miss. A sum in arithmetic is his guide and a telephone operator is his mentor. Mayhap some day a hostile shell descends out of a clear sky upon his battery; and then the men are mess and the guns are scrap and that is all there is to that small chapter of the great tale of the war.

The bomber who spends months learning how to cast the grenade may never get a chance to cast one except in practice. A man fights for his flag but doesn't see it when the action starts, for then it is furled. The regimental band plays him off to church service but not into the battle. When the battle begins the bandmen have exchanged their horns for the handles of a litter, becoming stretcher bearers. The general wears no epaulets. He wears a worried look brought on by dealing o' nights with strategic problems out of a book. The modern thin red line is a thing done in bookkeeper's ink on a ruled form. So it goes. The bubble reputation is won, not at the cannon's mouth, but across a desk top in a shell-proof fox den far from where the cannon are. The gallant six hundred do not ride into the jaws of death. Numbering many times six hundred, they advance afoot, creeping at a pallbearer's pace behind a barrage fire. So it keeps on going.

In only one wing of the service, and that the newest of all the wings, is there to be found a likeness to the chivalry and the showiness of these other times. The aviator is the one exception to a common rule. To him falls the great adventure. He goes jousting in the blue lists of the sky, helmeted and corseleted like a crusader of old. His lance is a spitting machine gun. His steed is a twentieth-century Pegasus, with wings of fine linen and guts of tried steel. Thousands of envying eyes follow him as he steers his single course to wage his single combat, and if he takes his death up there it is a clean, quick, merciful death high above the muck and more and jets of noxious laboratory fumes where the rest take theirs.

Even the surroundings of the birdman's nest are physically nore attractive than the habitat of his brother at arms who bides below. I can think of nothing homelier in outline or colour than the shelters—sometimes of planking, sometimes of corrugated iron, sometimes of earth—in which the soldiers hide here in France. The field hospital is apt to be a distressingly plain structure of unpainted boards with sandbags banked against it.

I have seen a general's headquarters in an underground tunnel that was like an overgrown badger's nest, with nothing outwardly to distinguish it from a similar row of tunnels except that it had a lettered sign over its damp and dripping mouth.

Tents, which have a certain picturesque quality when grouped, are rarely seen here in this closely settled Europe, where nearly always there are enough roofed and walled buildings to provide billets for the troops, however numerous. Instead of tents there are occasionally jumbles of makeshift barracks, and more often haphazard colonies of sheds serving as garages or as supply depots or as offices or as what not. War, which in itself is so ugly a thing, seems to possess the facility of making ugly its accessories before and after the fact.

But the quarters of the flying machines, through their vastness and isolation, acquire a certain quality of catching the eye that is entirely lacking for the rest of the picture—the big hangars in the background, suggesting by their shape and number the pitched encampment of a three-ring circus; the flappy canvas shields at the open side of the dromes, which being streaked and daubed with paint camouflage, enhance the carnival suggestion by looking, at a distance, like side-show banners; the caravans of trucks drawn up in lines; and in fine weather the flying craft resting in the landing field, all slick and groomed and polished, like a landed proprietor's blooded stock, giving off flashes from aluminum and varnish and steel and deft cabinetwork in answer to the caresses of the sunshine.

Right here I am reminded that the temperamental differences of the Allied nations are shown most aptly, I think, in the fashion in which the aviators decorate their gorgeous pets.

Upon its planes, of course, each bears the distinguishing mark of the country to which it belongs, but the bodies are the property, so to speak, of the individual flyers, to be treated according to the fancy of the individual.

Thus it befalls that an Italian machine generally carries a picture of a flower upon its sides. It is characteristic of the race that a French machine usually wears either a valorous, sonorous name or the name of a woman— perhaps the name of the aviator's sweetheart, or that of his mother or his sister possibly. But your average British airman is apt to christen his machine

Old Bill or Gaby or Our Little Nipper or The Walloping Window Blind—I have seen all of these cheery titles emblazoned upon splendid big aircraft in a British hangar—and just let it go at that.

I reckon the German, taking his morning hate along with his morning chicory, never will understand how it is the Britisher and the Yankee can make war and make jokes about it and be good sportsmen all at the same time. The German is very sentimental—I myself have heard him with tears in his voice singing his songs of the home place and the Christmas tree and the Rhine maiden as he marched past a burning orphan asylum in Belgium; but his sense of humour, if ever he really owned such a thing, was long ago smothered to death by the poisoned chemical processes of his own military machine. The man who was so bad that he was scared of himself must have been the original exemplar of the frightfulness doctrine. Anyhow he was born in Prussia—I'm sure of that much anyway.

But I am getting away from my subject—have been getting away from it for quite a spell, I fear; because in the first place I started out to tell about a meeting and a trip and a dinner and a song and divers other things. The affair dated from a certain spring noontime when two of us, writers by trade, were temporarily marooned for the day at the press headquarters of the American Expeditionary Force because we couldn't anywhere get hold of an automobile to take us for a scouting jaunt along the American sector. All of a sudden a big biplane came sailing into sight, glittering like a silver flying fish. It landed in a meadow behind the town and two persons, muffled in greatcoats, decanted themselves out of it and tramped across the half-flooded field toward us. When they drew near we perceived them to be two very young, very ruddy gentlemen, and both unmistakably English. My companion, it seemed, knew one of them, so there were introductions.

"What brings you over this way?" inquired my friend.

"Well, you see," said his acquaintance, "we were a bit thirsty—Bert and I—and we heard you had very good beer at the French officers' club here. So we just ran over for half an hour or so to get a drop of drink and then toddle along back again. Not a bad idea, eh, what?"

The speaker, I noted, wore the twin crowns of a captain on the shoulder straps of his overcoat. His age I should have put at twenty-one or thereabout, and his complexion was the complexion of a very new, very healthy cherub.

We showed the way toward beer and lunch, the latter being table d'hôte but good. En route my confrère was moved to ask more questions.

"Anything new happening at the squadron since I was over that way?" he inquired.

"Quiet enough to be a bore—weather hasn't suited for our sort these last few evenings," stated the taller one. "We got fed up on doin' nothin' at all, so night before last a squad started across the border to give Fritzie a taste of life. But just after we started the squadron commander decided the weather was too thickish and he signed us back—all but the Young-un, who claims he didn't see the flare and kept on goin' all by his little self." He favoured us with a tremendous wink.

"It seemed a rotten shame, really it did, to waste the whole evenin'." This was the Young-un, he of the pink cheeks, speaking. "So I just jogged across the jolly old Rhine until I come to a town, and I dropped my pills there and came back. Nice quiet trip it was—lonely rather, and not a bit excitin'."

Upon me a light dawned. I had heard of these bombing squadrons of the British outfits of young but seasoned flying men, who, now that reprisal in kind had been forced upon England and France by the continued German policy of aërial attacks on unprotected and unarmed cities, made journeys from French soil by sky line to enemy districts, there to spatter down retaliatory bombs upon such towns as Mainz, Stuttgart, Coblenz, Mannheim, Treves and Metz.

The which sounded simple enough in the bald telling, but entailed for each separate pair of flyers on each separate excursion enough of thrill, suspense and danger to last the average man through all his various reincarnations upon this earth. It meant a flight by darkness at sixty or seventy miles an hour, the pilot at the wheel and the observer at the guardian machine gun, above the tangled skeins of friendly trenches; and a little farther on above and past the hostile lines, beset for every rod of the way, both going and coming, by peril of attack from antiaircraft gun and from speedier, more agile German flyers, since the bombing airship is heavier and slower than scout planes commonly are. It meant finding the objective point of attack and loosing the explosive shells hanging like ripe plums from lever hooks in the frame of the engine body; and this done it meant winging back again—provided they got back—in time for late dinner at the home hangars.

Personally I craved to see more of men engaged upon such employment. Through lunch I studied the two present specimens of a new and special type of human being. Except that Bert was big and the Young-un was short, and except that the Young-un spoke of dropping pills when he meant to tell of spilling potential destruction upon the supply depots and railroad terminals of Germany, whereas Bert affectionately referred to his machine as The Red Hen and called the same process laying an egg or two, there was no great distinction to be drawn between them. Both made mention of the most incredibly daring things in the most commonplace and casual way imaginable; both had the inquisitive nose and the incurious eye of their breed; both professed a tremendous interest in things not one-thousandth part so interesting as what they themselves did; and both used the word "extraordinary" to express their convictions upon subjects not in the least extraordinary, but failed to use it when the topic dealt with their own duties and deserved to excess the adjectival treatment. In short, they were just two well-bred English boys.

CHAPTER X
HAPPY LANDINGS

OUT of the luncheon sprang an invitation, and out of the invitation was born a trip. On a day when the atmosphere was better fitted for automobiling in closed cars than for bombings we headed away from our billets, travelling in what I shall call a general direction, there being four of us besides the sergeant who drove. Things were stirring along the Front. Miles away we could hear the battery heavies thundering and drumming, and once in a lull we detected the hammering staccato of a machine gun tacking down the loose edges of a fight that will never be recorded in history, with the earnestness and briskness of a man laying a carpet in a hurry.

The Romans taught the French how to plan highroads, and the French never forgot the lesson. The particular road we travelled ran kilometre on kilometre straight as a lance up the hills and down again across the valleys, and only turned out to round the shoulders of a little mountain or when it flanked the shore line of one of the small brawling French rivers. The tall poplars in pairs, always in pairs, which edged it were like lean old gossips bending in toward the centre the better to exchange whispered scandal about the neighbours. Mainly the road pierced through fields, with infrequent villages to be passed and once a canal to be skirted; but also there were forests where wild boar were reputed to reside and where, as we know, the pheasant throve in numbers undreamed of in the ante-bellum days before all the powder in Europe was needed to kill off men, and while yet some of it might be spared for killing off birds.

Regarding the mountains a rule was prevalent. If one flank of a mountain was wooded we might be reasonably sure that the farther side would present a patchwork pattern of tiny farms, square sometimes, but more often oblong in shape, each plastered against the steep conformation and each so nearly perpendicular that we wondered how anybody except a retired paper hanger ever dared try to cultivate it. Let a husbandman's foot slip up there and he would be committing trespass in the plot of the next man below.

I shall not tell how far we rode, or whither, but dusk found us in a place which, atmospherically speaking, was very far removed from the French foothills, but geographically perhaps not so far. So far as its local colour was concerned the place in point more nearly than anything else I call to mind resembled the interior of a Greek-letter society's chapter house set amid somewhat primitive surroundings. In the centre of the low wide common room, mounted on a concrete box, was a big openwork basket of wrought iron. In this brazier burned fagots of wood, and the smoke went up a metal pipe which widened out to funnel shape at the bottom, four feet above the floor.

Such a device has three advantages over the ordinary fireplace: Folks may sit upon four sides of it, toasting their shins by direct contact with the heat, instead of upon only one, as is the case when your chimney goes up through the wall of your house. There were illustrations cut from papers upon the walls; there were sporting prints and London dailies on the chairs and trestles; there was a phonograph, which performed wheezily, as though it had asthma, and a piano, which by authority was mute until after dinner; there were sundry guitars and mandolins disposed in corners; there were sofa pillows upon the settees, plainly the handiwork of some fellow's best girl; there were clumsy, schoolboy decorative touches all about; there were glasses and bottles on tables; there were English non-coms, who in their gravity and promptness might have been club servants, bringing in more bottles and fresh glasses; and there were frolicking, boisterous groups and knots and clusters of youths who, except that they wore the khaki of junior officers of His Majesty's service instead of the ramping patterns affected by your average undergraduates, were for all the world just such a collection of resident inmates as you would find playing the goat and the colt and the skylark in any college fraternity hall on any pleasant evening anywhere among the English-speaking peoples.

For guests of honour there were our four, and for hosts there were sixty or seventy members of Night Bombing Squadron Number — —.

It so happened that this particular group of picked and sifted young daredevils represented every main division of the empire's domain. As we were told, there were present Englishmen, Cornishmen, Welshmen, Scots and Irishmen; also Canadians, Australians, New Zealanders, an Afrikander or two, and a dark youngster from India; as well as recruits gathered in from lesser lands and lesser colonies where the Union Jack floats in the seven seas that girdle this globe.

The ranking officer—a major by title, and he not yet twenty-four years old—bore the name of a Highland clan, the mere mention of which set me to thinking of whanging claymores and skirling pipes. His next in command was the nephew and namesake of a famous Home Ruler, and this one spoke with the soft-cultured brogue of the Dublin collegian. We were introduced to a flyer bred and reared in Japan, who had hurried to the mother isle as soon as he reached the volunteering age—a shy, quiet lad with a downy upper lip, who promptly effaced himself; and to a young Tasmanian of Celtic antecedents, who, curiously enough, spoke with an English accent richer and more pronounced than any native Englishman in the company used.

I took pains to ascertain the average age of the personnel of the squadron. I am giving no information to the enemy that he already does not know—to his cost—when I state it to be twenty-two and a half years. With perfect gravity veteran airmen of twenty-three or so will tell you that when a fellow reaches twenty-five he's getting rather a bit too old for the game— good enough for instructing green hands and all that sort of thing, perhaps, but generally past the age when he may be counted upon for effective work against the Hun aloft. And the wondrous part of it is that it is true as Gospel. 'Tis a man's game, if ever there was a man's game in this world; and it's boys with the peach-down of adolescence on their cheeks that play it best.

Well, we had dinner; and a very good dinner it was, served in the mess hall adjoining, with fowls and a noble green salad, and good honest-to-cow's butter on the table. But before we had dinner a thing befell which to me was as simply dramatic as anything possibly could be. What was more, it came at a moment made and fit for dramatics, being as deftly insinuated by chance into the proper spot as though a skilled playmaster had contrived it for the climax of his second act.

Glasses had been charged all round, and we were standing to drink the toast of the British aviator when, almost together, two small things happened: The electric lights flickered out, leaving us in the half glow of the crackling flames in the brazier, its tints bringing out here a ruddy young face and there a buckle of brass or a button of bronze but leaving all the rest of the picture in flickering shadows; right on top. of this a servant entered, saluted and handed to the squadron commander a slip of paper bearing a bulletin just received by telephone from the headquarters of a sister squadron in a near-by sector. The young major first read it through silently and then read it aloud:

"Eight machines of squadron ――― made a day-light raid this afternoon. The operation was successfully carried out." A little pause. "Three of the machines failed to return."

That was all. Three of the machines failed to return—six men, mates to these youngsters assembled here and friends to some of them, had gone down in the wreckage of their aircraft, probably to death or to what was hardly less terrible than death—to captivity in a German prison camp.

Well, it was all in the day's work. No one spoke, nor in my hearing did any one afterward refer to it. But the glasses came up with a jerk, and at that, as though on a signal from a stage manager, the lights flipped on, and then together we drank the airman's toast, which is:

"Happy landings!"

I do not profess to speak for the others, but for myself I know I drank to the memory of those six blithe boys—riders in the three machines that failed to return—and to a happy landing for them in the eternity to which they had been hurried long before their time.

The best part of the dinner came after the dinner was over, which was as a dinner party should be. We flanked ourselves on the four sides of the fire, and tobacco smoke rose in volume as an incense to good fellowship, and there were stories told and limericks offered without number. And if a story was new we all laughed at it, and if it was old we laughed just the same. Presently a protesting lad was dragooned for service at the piano. The official troubadour, a youth who seemed to be all legs and elbows, likewise detached himself from the background. Instead of taking station alongside the piano he climbed gravely up on top of it and perched there above our heads, with his legs dangling down below the keys. Touching on this, the Young-un, who sat alongside of me, made explanation:

"Old Bob likes to sit on the old jingle box when he sings, you know. He says that then he can feel the music going up through him and it makes him sing. He'll stay up there singing like a bloomin' bullfinch till some one drags him down. He seems to sort of get drunk on singin'—really he does. Extraordinary fancy, isn't it?"

I should have been the last to drag Old Bob down. For, employing a wonderful East Ender whine, Old Bob sang a gorgeous Cockney ballad dealing with the woeful case of a simple country maiden, and her smyle it was sublyme, but she met among others the village squire, and the rest of it may not be printed in a volume having a family circulation; but anyway it was a theme replete with incident and abounding in detail, with a hundred verses more or less and a chorus after every verse, for which said chorus we all joined in mightily.

From this beginning Old Bob, beating time with both hands, ranged far afield into his repertoire. Under cover of his singing I did my level best to draw out the Young-un—who it seemed was the Young-un more by reason of his size and boyish complexion than by reason of his age, since he was senior to half his outfit—to draw him out with particular reference to his experiences since the time, a year before, when he quit the line, being then a full captain, to take a berth as observer in the service of the air.

It was hard sledding, though. He was just as inarticulate and just as diffident as the average English gentleman is apt to be when he speaks in the hated terms of shop talk of his own share in any dangerous or unusual enterprise. Besides, our points of view were so different. He wanted to hear about the latest music-hall shows in London; he asked about the life in London with a touch in his voice of what I interpreted as homesickness. Whereas I wanted to know the sensations of a youth who flirts with death as a part of his daily vocation. Finally I got him under way, after this wise: "Oh, we just go over the line, you know, and drop our pills and come back. Occasionally a chap doesn't get back. And that's about all there is to tell about it.... Rummiest thing that has happened since I came into the squadron happened the other night. The boche came over to raid us, and when the alarm was given every one popped out of his bed and made for the dugout. All but Big Bill over yonder. Big Bill tumbled out half dressed and more than half asleep. It was a fine moonlight night and the boche was sailing about overhead bombing us like a good one, and Big Bill, who's a size to make a good target, couldn't find the entrance to either of the dugouts. So he ran for the woods just beyond here at the edge of the flying field, and no sooner had he got into the woods than a wild boar came charging at him and chased him out again into the open where the bombs were droppin'. Almost got him, too—the wild boar, I mean. The bombs didn't fall anywhere near him. Extraordinary, wasn't it, havin' a wild boar turn up like that just when he was particularly anxious not to meet any wild boar, not being dressed for it, as you might say? He was in a towerin' rage when the boche went away and we came out of the dugouts and only laughed at him instead of sympathisin' with him."

He puffed at his pipe.

"Fritz gets peevish and comes about to throw things at us quite frequently. You see, this camp isn't in a very good place. We took it over from the French and it stands out in the open instead of being in the edge of the forest where it should be. Makes it rather uncomfy for us sometimes—Fritzie does."

All of which rather prepared me for what occurred perhaps five minutes later when for the second time that night the electric lights winked out.

Old Bob ceased from his carolling, and the mess president, a little sandy Scotchman, spoke up:

"It may be that the boche is coming to call on us—the men douse the lights if we get a warning; or it may be that the battery has failed. At any rate I vote we have in some candles and carry on. This is too fine an evening to be spoiled before it's half over, eh?"

A failed battery it must have been, for no boche bombers came. So upon the candles being fetched in, Old Bob resumed at the point where he had left off. He sang straight through to midnight, nearly, never minding the story telling and the limerick matching and the laughter and the horse play going on below him, and rarely repeating a song except by request of the audience. If his accompanist at the piano knew the air, all very well and good; if not, 'Old Bob sang it without the music.

They didn't in the least want us to leave when the time came for us to leave, vowing that the fun was only just starting and that it would be getting better toward daylight. But ahead of us we had a long ride, without lights, over pitchy-dark roads, so we got into our car and departed. First, though, we must promise to come back again very soon, and must join them in a nightcap glass, they toasting us with their airmen's toast, which seemed so well to match in with their buoyant spirits.

When next I passed by that road the hangars were empty of life and the barracks had been tom down. The great offensive had started the week before, and on the third day of it, as we learned from other sources, our friends of Night Bombing Squadron Number — —, obeying an order, had climbed by pairs into their big planes and had gone winging away to do their share in the air fighting where the fighting lines were locked fast.

There was need just then for every available British aëroplane—the more need because each day showed a steadily mounting list of lost machines and lost airmen. I doubt whether many of those blithesome lads came out of that hell alive, and doubt very much, too, whether I shall ever see any of them again.

So always I shall think of them as I saw them last—their number being sixty or so and the average age twenty-two and a half—grouped at the doorway of their quarters, with the candlelight and the firelight shining behind them, and their glasses raised, wishing to us "Happy landings!"

CHAPTER XI
TRENCH ESSENCE

WHEN our soldiers arrive on foreign soil, almost invariably, so it has seemed to me watching them, they come ashore with serious faces and for the most part in silence. Their eyes are busy, but their tongues are taking vacation. For the time being they have lost that tremendous high-powered exuberance which marks them at home, in the camps and the cantonments, and which we think is as much a part of the organism of the optimistic American youth as his hands and his legs are.

I noticed this thing on the day our ship landed at an English port. We came under convoy in a fleet made up almost entirely of transports bearing troops—American volunteers, Canadian volunteers, and aliens recruited on American soil for service with the Allies. A Canadian battalion, newly organised, marched off its ship and out upon the same pier on which the soldiers who had crossed on the vessel upon which I was a passenger were disembarking. The Canadians behaved like schoolboys on a holiday.

It was not what the most consistent defender of the climate of Great Britain would call good holidaying weather either. A while that day it snowed, and a while it rained, and all the while a shrewish wind scolded shrilly in the wireless rig and rampaged along the damp and drafty decks. Nevertheless, the Canadians were not to be daunted by the inhospitable attitude of the elements.

One in three of them, about, carried a pennant bearing the name of his home town or his home province, or else he carried a little flag mounted on a walking stick. Nine out of ten, about, were whooping. They cheered for the ship they were leaving; they cheered for the sister ship that had borne us overseas along with them; they cheered to feel once more the solid earth beneath their feet; they cheered just to be cheerful, and, cheering so, they traversed the dock and took possession of the train that stood on a waterside track waiting to bear them to a rest camp. I imagine they were still cheering when they got there.

Now if you knew the types we had aboard our packet you might have been justified in advance for figuring that our outfit would be giving those joyous Canadian youngsters some spirited competition in the matter of making noises. We carried a full regiment of a Western division, largely made up, as to officers and as to men, of national guardsmen from the states of Colorado, Wyoming and Washington. They were cow-punchers, ranch hands, lumbermen, fruit growers, miners—outdoor men generally. Eighty men in the ranks, so I had learned during the voyage, were full-blooded Indians off of Northwestern reservations. We had men along who had won prizes for bronco-busting and bull-dogging at Frontier Day celebrations in Cheyenne and in California; also men who had travelled with the Wild West shows as champion ropers and experts at rough-riding. Never before, I am sure, had one vessel at one time borne in her decks so many wind-tanned, bow-legged, hawk-faced, wiry Western Americans as this vessel had borne.

But did one hear the lone-wolf howl as our fellows went filing down the gang-planks? Did one catch the exultant, shrill yip-yip-yip of the round-up or the far-carrying war yell of the Cheyenne buck? One most emphatically did not. If those three thousand and odd fellows had all been pallbearers officiating at the putting away of a dear departed friend they could not have deported themselves more soberly. Nobody carried a flag, unless you would except the colour bearers, who bore their colours furled about the staffs and protected inside of tarpaulin holsterings. Nobody waved a broad-brimmed hat either in salute to the Old World or in farewell to the ocean. Barring the snapped commands of the officers, the clinking in unison of hobbed and heavy boot soles, the shuffle of moving bodies, the creak of leather girthings put under strain, and occasionally the sharp clink and clatter of metal as some dangling side arm struck against a guard rail or some man shifted his piece, the march-off was accomplished without any noise whatsoever. It was interesting—and significant, too, I think—to spy upon those intent, set faces and those eager, steady eyes as the files went by and so away, bound, by successive stages of progress, with halts between at sessioning billets and at training barracks, for the battle fronts beyond the channel.

As between the Canadian and the United States soldiers I interpreted this striking difference in demeanour at the disembarking hour somewhat after this fashion: To a good many of the Dominion lads, no doubt, the thing was in the nature of a home-coming, for they had been born in England. A great many more of them could not be more than one generation removed from English birth. Anyhow and in either event, they as thoroughly belonged to and were as entirely part and parcel of the Empire as the islanders who greeted them upon the piers. One way or another they had always lived on British soil and under the shadow of the Union Jack. They were not strangers; neither were they aliens, even though they had come a far way; they were joint inheritors with native Englishmen of the glory that is England's. The men they would presently fight beside were their own blood kin. Quite naturally therefore and quite properly they commemorated the advent into the parent land according to the manner of the Anglo-Saxon when he strives to cover up, under a mien of boisterous enthusiasm, emotions of a purer sentiment. I could conceive some of them as laughing very loudly because inside of themselves they wanted to cry; as straining their vocal cords the better to ease the twitch-ings at their heart cockles.

But the Americans, even if they wore names bespeaking British ancestry—which I should say at an offhand guess at least seventy-five per cent of them did—were not moved by any such feelings. Such ties as might link their natures to the breed from which they remotely sprang were the thinnest of ties, only to be revealed in times of stress through the exhibition of certain characteristics shared by them in common with their very distant English and Scotch and Irish and Welsh kinsmen. For England as England they had no affectionate yearnings. England wasn't their mother; she was merely their great-great-grandmother, with whom their beloved Uncle Sam had had at least two serious misunderstandings. To all intents and purposes this was a strange land—certainly its physical characteristics had an alien look to them—and to it they had come as strangers.

I fancy, though, the chief reasons for their quiet seriousness went down to causes even deeper than this one. I believe that somehow the importance of the task to which they had dedicated themselves and the sense of the responsibility intrusted to them as armed representatives of their own country's honour were brought to a focal point of realisation in the minds of these American lads by the putting of foot on European soil. The training they had undergone, the distances they had travelled, the sea they had crossed—most of them, I gathered, had never smelt salt water before in their lives—the sight of this foreign city with its foreign aspect—all these things had chemically combined to produce among them a complete appreciation of the size of the job ahead of them; and the result made them dumb and sedate, and likewise it rendered them aloof to surface sensations, leaving them insulated by a sort of noncommittal pose not commonly found among young Americans in the mass—or among older Americans in the mass for that matter.

Perhaps a psychologist might prove me wrong in these amateur deductions of mine. For proof to bolster up my diagnosis I can only add that on three subsequent occasions, when I saw American troops ferrying ashore at French ports, they behaved in identically this same fashion, becoming for a period to be measured by hours practically inarticulate and incredibly earnest. Correspondents who chanced to be with me these three several times were impressed as I had been by the phenomenon.

But the condition does not last; you may be very sure of that. If there exists a more adaptable creature than the American soldier he has not yet been tagged, classified and marked Exhibit A for identification. Once the newly arrived Yank has lost his sea legs and regained his shore ones; once the solemnity and incidentally the novelty of the ceremony of his entrance into Europe has worn away; once he has learned how to think of dollars and cents in terms of francs and centimes and how to speak a few words in barbarous French—he reverts to type. His native irreverence for things that are stately and traditional rises up within him, renewed and sharpened; and from that moment forward he goes into this business of making war against the Hun with an impudent grin upon his face, and in his soul an incurable cheerfulness that neither discomfort nor danger can alloy, and a joke forever on his lips. That is the real essence of the trenches—the humour that is being secreted there with the grimmest and ghastliest of all possible tragedies for a background.

I wouldn't call it exactly a new type of humour, because always humour has needed the contrast of dismalness and suffering to set it off effectively, but personally I am of the opinion that it is a kind of humour that is going to affect our literature and our mode of living generally after the war is ended.

Bairnsfather, the English sketch artist, did not invent the particular phase of whimsicality—the essentially distinctive variety of seriocomic absurdity—which has made the world laugh at his pictures of Old Bill and Bert and Alf. He did a more wonderful thing: he had the wit and the genius to catch an illusive atmosphere which existed in the trenches before he got there and to put it down in black on white without losing any part of its savoury qualities. In slightly different words he practically told me this when I ran across him up near the Front the other day while he was setting about his new assignment of depicting the humour of the American soldier as already he had depicted that of the British Tommy. He had, he said, made one discovery already—that there was a tremendous difference between the two schools.

This is quite true, and if some talented Frenchman—it will take a Frenchman, of course—succeeds in making sketches that will reflect the wartime humour of the French soldier as cleverly as Bairnsfather has succeeded at the same job with the British high private for his model it will no doubt be found that the poilu's brand of humour is as distinctively his own as the American soldier's is or the English soldier's is.

There is an indefinable something, yet something structurally French, I think, in the fact that when Captain Hamilton Fish—called Ham Fish for short—arrived in France a few weeks before this was written the French soldiers with whom his command was brigaded immediately rechristened him Le Capitaine Jambon Poisson, and under this new Gallicised name he is to-day one of the best-known personages among the French in the country.

Likewise there is a certain African individuality, or rather an Afro-American individuality, in the story now being circulated through the expeditionary forces, of the private in one of our negro regiments who bragged at his company mess of having taken out a life-insurance policy for the full amount allowed a member of the Army, under the present governmental plan.

"Whut you wan' do dat fur?" demanded a comrade. "You ain't married an' you ain't got no fambly. Who you goin' leave all dat money to ef you gits killed?"

"I ain't aimin' to git killed," stated the first darky. "Dat's de very reason I taken out all dat insho'ence."

"How come you ain't liable to git killed jes' de same ez ary one of de rest of us is?"

"W'y, you pore ign'ant fool, does you s'pose w'en Gin'el Pershing finds out he's got a ten-thousand-dollar nigger in dis man's Army dat he's gwine take any chances on losin' all dat money by sendin' me up to de Front whar de trouble is? Naw suh-ree, he ain't!"

From a commingling of memories of recent events there stands out a thing of which I was an eye-and-ear-witness back in April, when the first of our divisions to go into the line of the great battle moved up and across France from a quieter area over in Lorraine, where it had been holding a sector during the early part of the spring. Each correspondent was assigned to a separate regiment for the period of the advance, being quartered in the headquarters mess of his particular regiment and permitted to accompany its columns as it moved forward toward the Picardy Front. That is to say, he was permitted to accompany its columns, but it devolved upon him to furnish his own motive power. Baggage trains and supply trains had been pared to the quick in order to expedite fast marching; no provision for transporting outsiders had been made, nor would any such provision have been permitted. A colonel was lucky if he had an automobile to himself and his adjutant; generally he had to carry a French liaison officer or two along with him in addition to his personal equipment.

I had been added to the personnel of an infantry regiment, which meant I could not steal an occasional ride while moving from one billet to another on the jolting limber of a field gun. Such boons were vouchsafed only to those more fortunate writers who belonged for the time being to the artillery wing.

One day I walked. I was lucky in that I did not have to carry my bedding roll and my haversack; these a kindly disposed ambulance driver smuggled into his wagon, rules and regulations to the contrary notwithstanding.

Another day the philanthropic lieutenant colonel rode his saddle horse and turned over to me his side car, the same being a sort of combination of tin bathtub and individual bootblack stand, hitched onto a three-wheeled motor cycle. What with impedimenta and all, rather overflowed its accommodations, but from the bottoms of my blistered feet to the topmost lock of my wind-tossed hair I was grateful to the donor as we went scudding along, the steersman and I, at twenty-five miles an hour.

On a third day I hired a venerable mare and an ancient two-wheeled covered cart, with a yet more ancient Norman farmer to drive the outfit, and under the vast poke-bonnet hood of the creaking vehicle the twain of us journeyed without stopping, from early breakfast time until nearly sunset time. The old man did not know a word of English, but mile after mile as we plodded along, now overtaking the troops who had started their hike at dawn, and now being overtaken by them as the antique mare lost power in her ponderous but rheumatic legs, he conversed at me—not with me, but steadily at me—in his provincial patois, which was the same as Attic Greek to me, or even more so, inasmuch as the only French I have is restaurant French, which begins with the hors d'oeuvres and ends just south of the fromages among the standard desserts.

Nevertheless, I deemed it the part of politeness to show interest by making a response from time to time when he was pausing to take a fresh breath. So about once in so often I would murmur "Yes," with the rising inflection, or "No," or "Is that so?" or "Can such things really be?" as the spirit moved me. And always he seemed perfectly satisfied with my observations, which he could not hear—I should have stated before now that among other things he was stone-deaf—and wouldn't have been able to understand even if he had heard them. And then he would go right on talking some more. From his standpoint, I am convinced, it was a most enjoyable journey and a highly instructive one besides.

Along toward sunset we ambled with the utmost possible deliberatio into our destination. It was like the average small town of Northwester France in certain regards. At a little distance it seemed to be all gab ends jumbled together haphazard and anyhow, as is the way of villa architecture in this corner of the world; and following an almost univer pattern the houses scraped sides with one another in a double file along twisting main street, only swinging back to form a sort of irregular squ in the centre.

Here, in the heart of things communal, the grey church reared its bulk above all lesser structures, with the school and the town hall facing it, flanked one side by the town pump and the town shrine and the other side by a public pond, where the horses and the cows watered, and grave, plump little French children played along the muddy brink. But this place had an air of antiquity which showed it antedated most of its fellows even in a land where everything goes back into bygone centuries.

Indeed, the guidebook in peace days, when people used guidebooks, gave it upward of a page of fine print—not so much for what it now was, but for what once upon a time it had been. Julius Cæsar had founded it and named it—and certain of the ruins of the original battlement still stood in massy but shapeless clumps, while other parts had been utilised to form the back ends of houses and barns and cowsheds. One of the first of those pitiable caravans of innocents that swelled the ranks of the Children's Crusade had been recruited here; and through the ages this town, inconsequential as it had become in these latter times, gave to France and to the world a great chronicler, a great churchman and at least one great warrior.

What a transformation the mere coming of our troops had made! In the public pond a squad of supply-trainsmen were sluicing down four huge motor trucks that stood hub deep in the yellow water—"bathing the elephants" our fellows called this job. Over rutted paving stones that once upon a time had bruised the bare feet of captured Frankish warriors Missouri mules were yanking along the baggage wagons, and their dangling trace chains clinked against the cobbles just as the fetters on the ankles of the prisoners must have clinked away back yonder.

In a courtyard where Roman soldiers may have played at knucklebones a portable army range sent up a cloud of pungent wood smoke from its abbreviated stack, and with the smell of the fire was mingled a satisfying odour of soldier-grub stewing. Plainly there would be something with onions in it—probably "Mulligan"—for supper this night.

Under a moss-hung wall against which, according to tradition, Peter the Hermit stood with the cross in his hand calling the crusaders to march with him to deliver the sepulchre of the Saviour out of the impious hands of the heathen, a line of tired Yankee lads were sprawled upon the scanty grass doing nothing at all except resting. There were wooden signs lettered in English—"Regimental Headquarters," and "Hospital," and "Intelligence Offices"—fastened to stone door lintels which time had seamed and scored with deep lines like the wrinkles in an old dame's face. Khaki-clad figures were to be seen wherever you looked.

Up the twisting and hilly street toiled a company belonging to my particular regiment, and as they came into the billeting place and I new the march was over, the wearied and burdened boys started singing the Doughboys' Song, which with divers variations is always sung in any infantry outfit that has a skeleton formation of old Regular Army men for its core, as this outfit had, and which to the extent of the first verse runs like this:

Here come the doughboys
With dirt behind their ears!
Here come the doughboys —
Their pay is in arrears.
The cavalree, artilleree, and the lousy engineers —
They couldn't lick the doughboys
In a hundred thousand years.

To the swinging lilt of the air the column angled past where my cart was halted; and as it passed, the official minstrel of the company was moved to deliver himself of another verse, evidently of his own composition and dealing in a commemorative fashion with recent sentimental experiences. As I caught the lines and set them down in my notebook they were:

Here go the doughboys —
Good-bye, you little dears!
Here go the doughboys —
The girls is all in tears!
The june ferns and the gossongs
And the jolly old mong peres —
Well, they wont fur git the doughboys
For at least a hundred years!

The troubadour with his mates rounded the outjutting corner of the church beyond the shrine, and I became aware of a highly muddied youngster who sat in a cottage doorway with his legs extending out across the curbing, engaged in literary labours. From the facts that he balanced a leather-backed book upon one knee and held a stub of a pencil poised above a fair clean page I deduced that he was posting his diary to date. Lots of the American privates keep war diaries — except when they forget to, which is oftener than not.

Three months before, or possibly six, the boy in the doorway would have been a strange figure in a strange setting. About him was scarce an object, save for the shifting figures of his own kind, to suggest the place whence he hailed. The broom that leaned against the wall alongside him was the only new thing in view. It was made of a sheaf of willow twigs bound about a staff. The stone well curb ten feet away was covered with the slow lichen growth of centuries. The house behind him, to judge by the thickness of its thatched and wattled roof and by the erosions in its three-foot walls of stone, had been standing for hundreds of years before the great-granddaddies of his generation fought the Indians for a right to a home site in the wilderness beyond the Alleghanies.

But now he was most thoroughly at home—and looked it. He spoke, addressing a companion stretched out upon the earth across the narrow way, and his voice carried the flat, slightly nasal accent of the midwestern corn-lands:

"Say, Murf, what's the name of this blamed town, anyhow?"

"Search me. Maybe they ain't never named it. I know you can't buy a decent cigarette in it, 'cause I've tried. The 'Y' ain't opened up yet and the local shops've got nothin' that a white man'd smoke, not if he never smoked again. What difference does the name make, anyway? All these towns are just alike, ain't they?"

With the sophisticated eyes of a potential citizen of, say, Weeping Willow, Nebraska, the first speaker considered the wonderfully quaint and picturesque vista of weathered, slant-ended cottages stretching away down the hill, and then, as he moistened the tip of his pencil with the tip of his tongue:

"You shore said a mouthful—they're all just alike, only some's funnier-lookin' than others. I wonder why they don't paint up and use a little whitewash once in a while. Take that little house yonder now!" He pointed his pencil toward a thatched cottage over whose crooked lines and mottled colours a painter would rave. "If you was to put a decent shingle roof on her and paint her white, with green trimmin's round the doors and winders, she wouldn't be half bad to look at. Now, would she? No cigarettes, huh? Nor nothin'!" Inspiration came to him as out of the skies and he grinned at his own conceit. "Tell you what—I'll jest put it down as 'Nowhere in France' and let it go at that."

On the following day my friend, the lieutenant colonel, brought to the noonday mess a tale which I thought carried a distinct flavour of the Yankee trench essence. There was a captain in the regiment, a last year's graduate of the Academy, who wore the shiniest boots in all the land round about and the smartest Sam Browne belt, and who owned the most ornate pair of riding trousers, and by other signs and portents showed he had done his best to make the world safe for some sporting-goods emporium back in the States. This captain, it seemed, had approached a sergeant who was in charge of a squad engaged in policing the village street, which is army talk for tidying up with shovel and wheelbarrow.

"See here, sergeant," demanded the young captain, "why don't you keep your men moving properly?"

"I'm tryin' to, sir," answered the sergeant.

"Well, look at that man yonder," said the captain, pointing toward a languid buck private who was leaning on his shovel. "I've been watching him and he hasn't moved an inch, except to scratch himself, for the last five minutes. Now go over there and stir him up! Shoot it into him good and proper! I want to hear what you say to him."

"Yes, sir," said the sergeant, saluting.

With no suspicion of a grin upon his face he charged down upon the delinquent.

"Here, you!" he shouted. "What do you mean, loafin' round here doin' nothin'? What do you think you are, anyhow—one of them dam' West Pointers?"

Floyd Gibbons, who was subsequently so badly wounded, rode one day into a battery of heavy artillery on the Montdidier Front. A begrimed battery man hailed him from a covert of green sods and camouflage where a six-inch gun squatted: "You're with the Chicago *Tribune*, ain't you?"

"Yes," answered Gibbons. "Why?"

"Well, I just thought I'd tell you that the fellows in this battery have got a favourite line of daily readin' matter of their own, these days."

"What do you call it?" inquired Gibbons. "We call it the Old Flannel Shirt," answered the gunner. "Almost any time you can see a fellow round here goin' through his copy of it for hours on a stretch. He's always sure to find something interestin' too. We may not be what you'd call bookworms in this bunch, but we certainly are the champion little cootie-chasers of the United States Army."

Body vermin or wet clothes or bad billets or the chance of a sudden and a violent taking-off—no matter what it is—the American soldier may be counted upon to make a joke of it.

This ability to distil a laugh out of what would cause many a civilian to swear or weep or quit in despair serves more objects than one in our expeditionary forces. For one thing it keeps the rank and file of the

Army in cheerful mood to have the mass leavened by so many youths of an unquenchable spirit. For another, it provides a common ground for fraternising when Americans and Britishers are brigaded together or when they hold adjoining sectors; for the Britisher in this regard is constituted very much as the American is, except that his humour is apt to assume the form of underestimation of a thing, whereas the American's fancy customarily runs to gorgeous hyperbole and arrant exaggeration.

In a certain Canadian battalion that has made a splendid record for itself—though for that matter you could say the same of every Canadian battalion that has crossed the sea since the war began—there is a young chap whom we will call Sergeant Fulton, because that is not his real name. This Sergeant Fulton comes from one of the states west of the Great Divide, and he elected on his own account and of his own accord to get into the fighting nearly two years before his country went to war. In addition to being a remarkably handsome and personable youth, Sergeant Fulton is probably the best rifle shot of his age in the Dominion forces. This gift of his, which is so valuable a gift in trench fighting, was made apparent to his superior officers immediately after he crossed the Canadian line in 1915 to enlist, whereupon he very promptly was promoted from the ranks to be a non-com, and when his command got into action in France he was detailed for sniper duty.

At that congenial employment the youngster has been distinguishing himself ever since. Into the rifle pits young Fulton took something besides his ability to hit whatever he shot at, and his marvellous eyesight—he took a most enormous distaste for the institution of royalty; and this, too, in spite of the fact that when he joined up he swore allegiance to His Gracious Majesty George the Fifth. His ideas of royalty seemingly were based upon things he read in school histories. His conception of the present occupant of the English throne was a person mentally gaited very much like Henry the Eighth or Richard the Third, except with a worse disposition than either of those historic characters had. Apparently he conceived of the incumbent as rising in the morning and putting on a gold crown and sending a batch of nobles to the Tower, after which he enacted a number of unjust laws and, unless he felt better toward evening, possibly had a few heads off.

Acquaintance with his comrades at arms served to rid Sergeant Fulton of some of these beliefs, but despite broadening influences he has never ceased to wonder—generally doing his wondering in a loud clear voice—how any man who loved the breath of freedom in his nostrils found it endurable to live under a king when he might if he chose live under a President named Woodrow Wilson.

One morning just at daybreak a Canadian captain—who, by the way, told me this tale—crawled into a shell hole near the German lines where Sergeant Fulton and two other expert riflemen had been lying all night, like big-game hunters at a water hole, waiting for dawn to bring them their chance. One of Fulton's mates was a Vancouver lad, the other a London Tommy—a typical East-ender, but a very smart sniper.

"Cap," whispered Fulton, from where he lay stretched on his belly in the herbage at the edge of the crater, "you've got here just in time. Ever since it began to get light a Fritzie has been digging over there in their front trench. I've had him spotted for half an hour. He has to squat down to dig; and that's telling on his back. Before long I figure he's going to straighten up to get the crick out of himself. When he does he'll show his head above the parapet, and that's when I'm going to part his hair in the middle with a bullet. Take a squint, Cap, through the periscope and you'll be able to locate him, dead easy. Then stay right there and you'll see the surprise party come off."

So the captain took a squint as informally requested. Sure enough, a hundred yards away, across the debatable territory, pocked with ragged shell pits and traversed by its two festering brown tangles of rusty barbed wire, he could see the flash of an uplifted shovel blade and see the brown clods flying over the lip of the enemy's parapet. He kept watching. Presently for just a tiny fraction of time the round cap of a German infantryman appeared above the earthen protection. The sergeant had guessed right, and the sergeant's gun spoke once. Once was enough—a greenhorn at this game would have known that much.

For there was a shriek over there, and a pair of empty outstretched hands were to be seen for one instant, with the fingers clutching at nothing; and then they disappeared, as their owner collapsed into the hole he had been digging.

Then, according to the captain, as the sergeant opened his rifle breach he turned toward the Cockney who crowded alongside him, and with a gratified grin on his face and a weight of sarcasm in his voice he said: "There goes another one, eh, bo, for King and Country?"

The Londoner answered on the instant, taking the same tone in the reply that the American had taken in the taunt. "My word," he said, "but Gawge will be pleased w'en 'e 'ears wot you done fur 'im!"

Three of us made a long trip by automobile to pay a visit to a coloured regiment, both trip and visit being described elsewhere in these writings. The results more than repaid us for the time and trouble. One of the main compensations was First Class Private Cooksey, who, because he used to be an elevator attendant in a Harlem apartment house, gave his occupation in his enlistment blank as "indoor chauffeur." It was to First Class Private Cooksey that the colonel of the regiment, seeing the expression on the other's face when a *Minenwerfer* from a German mortar fell near by on the day the command moved up to the Front, and made a hole in the earth deep enough and wide enough and long enough to hide the average smokehouse in—it was, I repeat, to First Class Private Cooksey that the colonel put this question:

"Cooksey, if one of those things drops right here alongside of us and goes off, are you going to stay by me?"

"Kurnal," stated Private Cooksey with sincerity, "I ain't goin' tell you no lie. Ef one of them things busts clost to me I'll jest natch-elly be obliged to go away frum here. But please, suh, don't you set me down as no deserter. Jest put it in de books as 'absent without leave,' 'cause I'll be due back jest ez soon ez I kin git my brakes to work."

"But what if the enemy suddenly appears in force without any preliminary bombardment?" pressed the colonel. "What do you think you and the rest of the boys will do then?"

"Kurnal," said Cooksey earnestly, "we may not stick by you but we'll shore render one service anyway: We'll spread de word all over France 'at de Germans is comin'!"

Nevertheless, when the Germans did advance it is of record that neither First Class Private Cooksey nor any of his black and brown mates showed the white feather or the yellow streak or the turned back. Those to whom the test came stayed and fought, and it was the Germans who went away.

It was a member of the Fifteenth who in all apparent seriousness suggested to his captain that it might be a good idea to cross the carrier pigeon with the poll parrot so that when a bird came back from the Front it would be able to talk its own message instead of bringing it along hitched to its shank.

Speaking of carrier pigeons reminds me of a yam that may or may not be true—it sounds almost too good to be true—that is being related at the Front. The version most frequently told has it that a half company of a regiment in the Rainbow Division going forward early one morning in a heavy fog for a raid across No Man's Land carried along with the rest of the customary equipment a homing pigeon. The pigeon in its wicker cage swung on the arm of a private, who likewise was burdened with his rifle, his extra rounds of ammunition, his trenching tool, his pair of wire cutters, his steel helmet, his gas mask, his emergency ration and quite a number of other more or less cumbersome items.

It was to be a surprise attack behind the cloak of the fog, so there was no artillery preparation beforehand nor barrage fire as the squads climbed over the top and advanced into the mist-hidden beyond. Behind, in the posts of observation and in the post of command—"P.O." and "P.C." these are called in the algebraic terminology of modern war—the colonel and his aids and his intelligence officers waited for the sound of firing, and when after some minutes the distant rattle of rifle fire came to their ears they began calculating how long reasonably it might be before word reached them by one or another medium of communication touching on the results of the foray. But the ground telephone remained mute, and no runner returned through the fog with tidings. The suspense tautened as time passed.

Suddenly a pigeon sped into view flying close to the earth. With scores of pairs of eager eyes following it in its course the winged messenger circled until it located its portable cote just behind the colonel's position, and fluttering down it entered its familiar shelter.

An athletic member of the staff hustled up the ladder. In half a minute he was tumbling down again, clutching in one hand the little scroll of paper that he had found fastened about the pigeon's leg. With fingers that trembled in anxiety the colonel unrolled the paper and read aloud what was written upon it.

What he read, in the hurried chirography of a kid private, was the following succinct statement: "I'm tired of carrying this derned bird." In London one night Don Martin, of the New York *Herald,* and I were crossing the Strand just above Trafalgar Square. In the murk of the unlighted street we bumped into a group of four uniformed figures. Looking close we made out that one was an American soldier, that one was a lanky Scot in kilts, slightly under the influence of something even more exhilarating than the music of the pipes, and that the remaining two were English privates. We gathered right away that an international discussion of some sort was under way. At the moment of our approach the American, a little dark fellow who spoke with an accent that betrayed his Italian nativity, had the floor, or rather he had the sidewalk. We halted in the half-darkness to listen.

"It's lika thees," expounded the Yanko-Italian, "w'en I say 'I should worry' it mean—it mean—why, it mean I shoulda not worry. You getta me, huh?"

He glanced about him, plainly pleased with the very clear and comprehensive explanation of this expressive bit of Americanism, which had come to him in a sudden burst of inspiration.

The others stared at him blankly. It was one of the Englishmen who broke the silence.

"You 'ave nothin' to worry habout hat all, and so you say that you hare worryin'—his that hit?" he inquired. The American nodded. "Well, then, hall Hi can say his hit sounds like barmy Yankee nonsense to me."

"Lusten here, laddie, to me," put in the Scotchman. "If you've naught to worry about, why speak of it at all? That's whut I would be pleased to know."

"Hoh, never mind," spoke up the second Englishman; "let's go get hanother drink at the pub."

"You're too late," stated his countryman in lachrymose tones. "While we've been chin-chinnin' 'ere the bloomin' pub 'as closed—it's arfter hours for a drink."

But the canny Scot already was feeling about with a huge paw in the back folds of his kilt. From some mysterious recess he slowly drew forth a flat flask.

"Lads," he stated happily, "in the language of our American friend here, we should worry, because as it happens, thanks to me own forethought, we ha' na need to concern ourselves wi' worryin' at all, d'ye ken? Ha' the furst nip, Yank!"

This recital would not be complete did I fail to include in it a paragraph or so touching on the humorous proclivities of—guess who!—the commander of a German submarine, no less; a person who operated last winter mainly off the southernmost tip of Ireland with occasional incursions into the British Channel. This facetious Teuton was known to the crews of the British and American destroyers that did their best to sink him—and finally, it is believed, did sink him—as Kelly. Indeed in the derisive messages that this deep-sea joker used to send over the wireless to our stations he customarily signed himself by that name.

One day shortly before Kelly's U-boat disappeared altogether a commander of an American destroyer was sending by radio to a French port a message giving what he believed to be the probable location of the pestiferous but cheerful foe. It must have been that the subject of his communication was listening in on the air waves and that he knew the code which the American was that day employing. For all at once he broke in with his own wireless, and this was what the astonished operator at the receiving station on shore got:

"Your longitude is fine, your latitude is rotten. This place is getting too warm for me. I'm going to beat it. Good-bye. Kelly."

Shortly after the first division of our new National Army reached France a group of fifty men were sent from it as replacements in the ranks of an old National Guard regiment which had been over for some time and which had suffered casualties and losses. When the squad went forward to their new assignment the general commanding the brigade from which the chosen fifty had been drawn sent to the commander of the regiment for which they were bound a letter reading somewhat after this style:

"There are not better men in our Army anywhere than the fifty I am giving you, in accordance with an order received by me from General Headquarters. Please see to it that no one in your regiment, whether officer or private, refers by word, look, deed or gesture to the circumstances under which these fifty men entered the service. Drafted men, regulars and volunteers are all on the same footing, and merely because my men came in with the draft and yours to a large extent came in a little earlier is no reason why any discrimination should be permitted in any quarter."

A few weeks after the transfer had been accomplished the brigadier met the colonel, and recalling to the latter the sense of the letter he had written inquired whether there had been any suggestion of superiority on the part of the former National Guardsmen toward the new arrivals.

"General," broke out the colonel, "do you know what those infernal cheeky scoundrels of yours have been doing ever since they joined? Well, I'm going to tell you. They've been walking to and fro in my regiment with their noses stuck up in the air, calling my boys 'draft-dodgers!'"

It's the essence of the trenches. And it's that—plus the courage they bring and the enthusiasm they have—which is winning this war sooner than some of the croakers at home expect it to be won.

CHAPTER XII
BEING BOMBED AND RE-BOMBED

AS I GO to and fro in the land I some-times wonder why the Germans keep a-picking on me. As heaven is my judge I tried to tell the truth about them and their armies when I was with them; but then, maybe that's the reason. At any rate I am here to testify that whenever I stop at a place in England or France either a battery of long-range guns shells it or else a hostile aëroplane happens along and bombs the town. The thing is more than a coincidence. It is getting to be a habit, an unhealthy habit at that. There must be method in it. And yet I have tried to bear myself in a modest and unostentatious way during this present trip. If in the reader's judgment the personal pronoun has occurred and recurred with considerable frequency in my writings I would say: Under the seemingly quaint but necessary rules of the censorship as conducted in these parts the only individual of American extraction at present connected in any way with war activities over here whom I may mention in my writings other than General Pershing is myself. Since the general to date has not figured to any extent in my personal experiences I am perforce driven to doing pieces largely about what I have seen and heard and felt.

Particularly is this true of these bombings and shellings. I repeat that I cannot imagine why the boche should single out a quiet, simple, private citizen for such attentions. It does not seem fair that I should ever be their target while shining marks move about the landscape with the utmost impunity. The German has a name for being efficient too. More than once in my readings I have seen his name coupled with the word efficiency. Take brigadier generals for example. Almost any colonel of our Expeditionary Forces in France, and particularly a senior colonel whose name is well up in the list, will tell you in confidence there are a number of brigadiers over here who could easily be spared and who would never be missed. Yet a brigadier general may move about from place to place in his automobile in comparative safety. But just let me go to the railroad station to buy a ticket for somewhere and immediately the news is transmitted by a mysterious occult influence to the Kaiser and he tells the Crown Prince and the Crown Prince calls up von Hindenburg or somebody, and inside of fifteen minutes the hands, August and Heinie, are either loading up the long-rangers or getting the most dependable bombing Gotha out of the sheds.

For nearly four weeks the raiders stayed away from London. I arrived in London sick with bronchitis and went to bed in a hotel. That night the Huns flew over the Channel and spattered down inflammables and explosives to their heart's content. One chunk of a shell fell in the street within a few yards of my bedroom window, gouging a hole in the roadway. A bomb made a mighty noise and did some superficial damage in a park close by. It was my first experience at being bombed from on high, and any other time I should have taken a lively interest in the proceedings; but I was too sick to get up and dress and too dopy from the potions I had taken to awaken thoroughly.

But the next night, when I was convalescent, and the following night, when I was well along the road toward recovery and able, in fact, to sit up in bed and dodge, back came Mister Boche and repeated the original performance with variations.

In order to get away from the London fogs, which weren't doing my still tender throat any good, I ran down to a certain peaceful little seaside resort on the east coast of England, reaching there in the gloaming. What did the enemy do but sprinkle bombs all about the neighbourhood within an hour after I got there? He went away at ten the same night, I the following morning at six-forty-five.

A delayed train was all that kept me from reaching Paris coincidentally with the first raiders who had attacked Paris in a period of months. The raiders covered up their disappointment by murdering a few helpless non-belligerents and departed, to return the next evening when I was present. I was domiciled in Paris on that memorable Saturday when the great long-distance gun began its bombardment of the city from the forest of Saint-Gobain nearly seventy miles distant. The first shell descended within two hundred yards of where I stood at a window and I saw the smoke of its explosion and saw the cloud of dust and pulverized débris that rose; the jar of the crash shook the building. Throughout the following day, which was Palm Sunday—only we called it Bomb Sunday—the shelling continued. I was there, naturally.

On Monday morning I started for Soissons. So the gunners of the long-distance gun playing on Paris took a vacation, which lasted until the day after my party returned from the north. We got into the Gare du Nord late one night; the big gun opened up again early the next morning. I am not exaggerating; merely reciting a sequence of facts.

For nearly two years the Germans had left poor battered Soissons pretty much alone, though it was within easy reach of their howitzers; moreover, one of their speedy flying machines could reach Soissons from the German lines south of Laon within five minutes. But, as I say, they rather left it alone. Perhaps in their kindly sentimental way they were satisfied with their previous handiwork there. They had pretty well destroyed the magnificent old cathedral. It was not quite so utter a ruin as the cathedral at Arras is, or the cathedral at Rheims, or the Cloth Hall at Ypres, or the University at Louvain; nevertheless, I assume that from the Prussian point of view the job was a fairly complete one.

The wonderful, venerable glass windows, which can never be replaced, had been shattered to the last one, and the lines of the splendid dome might now only be traced like the curves of tottering arches, swinging up and out like the ribs of a cadaver, and by a lacework of roofage where thousands of bickering ravens, those black devil birds of desolation, now fluttered and cawed, and befouled with their droppings the profaned sanctuary below. Altogether it was one of the most satisfactory monuments to Kultur to be found anywhere in Europe to-day.

Nor had the community at large been slighted. Everybody knows how thorough are the armies of the anointed War Lord. Relics which dated back to the days of Clovis had been battered out of all hope of restoration; things of antiquity and of inestimable historic value lay shattered in wreckage. Furthermore, from time to time, in 1914 and 1915 and even in 1916, when no military advantage was to be derived from visiting renewed affliction upon the vicinity and when no victims, save old men and women and innocent children, were likely to be added to the grand total of the grander tally which Satan, as chief bookkeeper, is keeping for the Kaiser, the guns had blasted away at the ancient city, leveling a homestead here and decimating a family there.

However, since the early part of 1916 they had somehow rather spared Soissons. But the train bearing us was halted within three miles of the station because, after keeping the peace for nearly two years, the enemy had picked upon that particular hour of that particular afternoon to renew his most insalubrious attentions per nine-inch mortars. Therefore we entered afoot, bearing our luggage, to the accompaniment of whistling projectiles and clattering chimney-pots and smashing walls.

In Soissons we spent two nights. Both nights the Germans shelled the town and on the second night, in addition, bombed it from aëroplanes. It may have been fancy, but as we came away in a car borrowed from a kindly French staff officer it seemed to us that the firing behind us was lessening.

From press headquarters near G. H. Q. of the Amex Forces we motored one day to Nancy for a good dinner at a locally famous café. Simultaneously with our advent the foe's airmen showed up and the *alerte* was sounded for a gas attack. As between the prospect of spending the evening in an *abri* and staying out in the open air upon the road we chose the latter, and so we turned tail and ran back to the comparative quiet of the front lines. A little later a cross-country journey necessitated our changing cars at Bar-le-Duc. The connecting train was hours behind its appointed minute, as is usual in these days of disordered time cards, and while we waited hostile airships appeared flying so high they looked like bright iridescent midges flitting in the sunshine. As they swung lower, to sow bombs about the place, antiaircraft guns opened on them and they departed.

That same night our train, travelling with darkened carriages, was held up outside of Châlons, while enemy aircraft spewed bombs at the tracks ahead of us and at a troop convoy passing through. The wreckage was afire when we crawled by on a snail's schedule an hour or so later.

Two of us went to pay a visit to a regimental mess in a sector held by our troops. The colonel's headquarters were in a small wrecked village close up to the frontier. This village had been pretty well smashed up in 1914 and in 1915, but during the trench warfare that succeeded in this district no German shells had scored a direct hit within the communal confines. Yet the enemy that night, without prior warning and without known provocation, elected to break the tacit agreement for localised immunity. The bombardment began with a shock and a jar of impact shortly after we had retired to bed on pallets upon the floor in the top story of what once, upon a happier time, had been the home of a prominent citizen. It continued for three hours, and I will state that our rest was more or less interrupted. It slackened and ceased, though, as we departed in the morning after breakfast, and thereafter for a period of weeks during which we remained away all was tranquil and unconcussive there in that cluster of shattered stone cottages.

Another time we made a two-day expedition to the zone round Verdun. The great spring offensive, off and away to the westward, was then in its second week and the Verdun area enjoyed comparative peace. Nevertheless, and to the contrary notwithstanding, seven big vociferous shells came pelting down upon an obscure hamlet well back behind the main defences within twenty minutes after we had stopped there. One burst in a courtyard outside a house where an American general was domiciled with his staff, and when we came in to pay our respects his aids still were gathering up fragments of the shell casing for souvenirs. The general said he couldn't imagine why the Him should have decided all of a sudden to pay him this compliment; but we knew why, or thought we knew: It was all a part of the German scheme to give us chronic cold feet.

At least, we so diagnosed the thing privately.

As a result of this sort of experience, continuing through a period of months, I feel that I have become an adept of sorts at figuring the sensations of a bombee. I flatter myself also that I have acquired some slight facility at appraising the psychology of towns and cities persistently and frequently under shell or aërial attack. In the main I believe it may be taken as an accepted fact that the inhabitants of a small place behave after rather a different fashion from the way in which the inhabitants of a great city may be counted upon to bear themselves. For example, there is a difference plainly to be distinguished, I think, between the people of London and the people of Paris; and a difference likewise between the people of Paris and the people of Nancy. Certainly I have witnessed a great number of sights that were humorous with the grim and perilous humour of wartimes, and by the same token I have witnessed a manifold number of others that were fraught with the very essence of tragedy.

All France to-day is one vast heart-breaking tragedy that is compounded of a million lesser tragedies. You note that the door-opener at your favourite café in Paris uses his left hand only, and then you see that his right arm, with the hand cased in a tight glove, swings in stiff uselessness from his shoulder. It is an artificial arm; the real one was shot away. The barber who shaves you, the waiter who serves you, the chauffeur who drives you about in his taxicab moves with a limping awkward gait that betrays the fact of a false leg harnessed to a mutilated stump.

In a sufficiently wide passage a couple coming toward you—a woman in nurse's garb and a splendid young boy soldier with decorations on his breast—bump into you, almost, it would seem, by intent. As mentally you start to execrate the careless pair for their inexcusable disregard of the common rights of pedestrians you see there is a deep, newly healed scar in the youth's temple and that his eyes stare straight ahead of him with an unwinking emptiness of expression, and that his fine young face is beginning to wear that look of blank, bleak resignation which is the mark of one who will walk for all the rest of his days on this earth in the black and utter void of blindness.

Behind the battle lines you often see long lines of men whose ages are anywhere between forty and fifty—tired, dirty, bewhiskered men worn frazzle-thin by what they have undergone; men who should be at home with their wives and bairns instead of toiling through wet and cold and misery for endless leagues over sodden roads.

Their backs are bent beneath great unwieldy burdens; their hands where they grip their rifles are blue from the chill; their sore and weary feet falter as they drag them, booted in stiff leather and bolstered with mud, from one cheerless billet to another. But they go on, uncomplainingly, as they have been going on uncomplainingly since the second year of this war, doing the thankless and unheroic labour at the back that the ranks at the front may be kept filled with those whom France has left of a suitable age for fighting.

You see that the highways are kept in repair by boys of twelve or thirteen and by grandsires in their seventies and their eighties, and by crippled soldiers, who work from daylight until dusk upon the rock piles and the earth heaps; that the fields are being tilled—and how well they are being tilled!—by young women and old women; that the shops in the smaller towns are minded by children, whose heads sometimes scarcely come above the counters.

You see where the tall shade trees along the roads and the small trees in the thickets are being shorn away in order that the furnaces and the hearthstones may not be altogether fireless, since the enemy holds most of the coal mines. I have come in one of the fine state forests upon a squad of American lumberjacks, big huskies from the logging camps of Northern Michigan, with their portable planing mill whining and their axes flashing, making the sawdust and the chips fly, in what once not long ago was a grove of splendid timber, where beeches and chestnuts, hundreds of years old, stood in close ranks; but which now is being turned into a wilderness of raw stumps and trodden earth and stacks of ugly planking.

You see an old woman, as fleshless as a fagot, helping a dog to drag a heavy cart up a rocky street, the two of them together straining and panting against the leather breast yokes. For every kilometre that the foe advances you see the refugees fleeing from their desolated steadings; indeed, you may very accurately gauge the rate of his progress by their number.

In one lonely little town in a territory as yet undefiled by actual hostilities I went one morning not long ago into a quaint thirteenth-century church. It was one of three churches in the place; and in point of membership, I think, the smallest of the three. But in the nave, upon a stone pillar, gnawed by time with furrows and runnels, I found a little framed placard containing the names, written in fine script, of those communicants who had died in service for their country in this war. The list plainly was incomplete. It included only those who had fallen up to the beginning of last year; the toll for 1917 and for 1918 was yet to be added; and yet of the names of the dead out of this one small obscure interior parish there were an even one hundred. I dare say the poll of the whole commune would have shown at least three times as many. France has shown the world how to fight. Now it shows the world how to die.

But of all the tragedies that multiply themselves so abundantly here in this bloodied land it sometimes seems to me there is none greater than the look of things that is implanted upon an unfortified town that has been subjected to frequent bombings. It is not so much the shattered, ragged ruins where bombs have scored direct downward hits that drive home the lesson of what this mode of reprisal, this type of punishment means; rather it is the echoing empty street, as yet undamaged, whence the dwellers all have fled—long stretches of streets, with the windows shuttered up and the shops locked and barred and the rank grass sprouting between the cobblestones, and the starveling tabby cats foraging like the gaunt ghosts of cats among forgotten ash barrels. And rather more than this it is the expression of those who through necessity or choice have stayed on.

I am thinking particularly of Nancy—Nancy which for environment, setting and architecture is one of the most beautiful little cities in the world; a city whose ancient walls and massy gateways still stand; whose squares and parks were famous; and whose people once led prosperous, contented and peaceful lives. Its Place Stanislaus, on a miniature scale, is, I think, as lovely as any plaza in Europe. Since it is so lovely one is moved to wonder why the Germans have so far spared it from the ruination they shower down without abatement upon the devoted city. It is well-nigh deserted now, along with all the other parts of the town. Those who could conveniently get away have gone; the state in the early part of this year transported thousands of women and children on special trains to safer territory in the south of France. Those who remain have in their eyes the haunting terror of a persistent and an unceasing fearsomeness.

To be in Nancy these times is to be in a stilled, half-deserted place of flinching and of danger, and of the death that comes by night, borne on whirring motors. I walked through its streets on a day following one of the frequent air raids and I had a conception of how these Old-World cities must have looked in the time of the plague. The citizens I passed were like people who dwelt beneath the shadow of an abiding pestilence, as indeed they did.

To them a clear still night with the placid stars showing in the heavens meant a terrible threat. It meant that they would lie quaking in their houses for the signal that would send them to the cellars and the dugouts, while high explosives and gas bombs and inflammable bombs came raining down. They knew full well what it meant to stay above ground during the dread passover of the Huns' planes, when hospitals had been turned into shambles and supply depots into craters of raging fire. Yet there remained traces of the racial temperament that has upbuoyed the French and helped them to endure what was unendurable.

A little waitress in a café said to three of us, with a smile: "Ah, but you should be in Nancy on a rainy night, for then the sound of snoring fills the place. We can sleep then—and how we do sleep!"

In Nancy they pray before the high altars for bad weather and yet more bad weather. And so do they in many another town in France that is within easy striking distance of the enemy's batteries and airdromes.

CHAPTER XIII
LONDON UNDER RAID-PUNISHMENT

OF all city dwellers I am sure the Londoner is the most orderly and the most capable of self-government, as he likewise is the most phlegmatic. Because of these common traits among the masses of the populace an air raid over London, considering its potential possibilities for destruction, is comparatively an unexciting episode everywhere in the metropolis, save and except only in those districts of the East End where the bulk of the foreign-born live. There, on the first wail of the shrieking sirens, before the warning "maroon" bombs go up or the barrage fire starts from protecting batteries in the suburbs and along the Thames, these frightened aliens, carrying their wives and children, flock pell-mell into the stations of the Underground. They spread out bedclothes on the platforms and camp in the Tube, which is the English name for what Americans call a subway, and sometimes refuse to budge until long after the danger has passed. At the height of the bombardment they pray and shriek, and the women often beat their breasts and tear at their hair in a very frenzy.

This is true only of the emotional Rus-and Rumanians. The native Londoners'ed in the most leisurely fashion walk to the subterranean shelters. Indeed, the chief task of the police is to keep them from exposing themselves in the open in efforts to get a sight the enemy. People who live on the lower floors of stoutly built houses mainly bide where they are, their argument—and a very sane one it is—being that since the chances of a man's being killed in his home at such a time are no greater than of his roof being pierced by lightning during a thunderstorm he is almost as safe and very much more comfortable staying in his bed than he would be squatting for hours in a damp Cellar.

No matter how intense the bombardment the busses keep on running, though they have few enough passengers. From one's window one may see the big double-deckers lumbering by like frightened elephants, empty of all but the drivers and the plucky women conductors, who invariably stick to their posts and carry on. The London bobby promenades at his usual deliberate pace no matter how thick the shrapnel from the defender guns may splash down about him in the darkened street; and the night postman calmly goes his rounds too.

One night in London after the alarm had been sounded I invaded the series of walled caverns and wine vaults known as the Adelphi Arches, which are just off the Strand, near Charing Cross. Several hundred men, women and children had already taken refuge there. Near one of the entrances a young mother was singing her baby to sleep; a little farther on a group of Australian soldiers were trying, rather unsuccessfully, to open beer bottles with their finger nails; and at the mouth of a side basement opening off a layer cave half a dozen typical Londoner civilians, of the sort who wear flat caps instead of hats and woollen neckerchiefs instead of collars, were warmly discussing politics in high nasal notes. Nowhere was there evident any concern or distress, or even any considerable amount of irritation at our enforced inconvenience.

Still, any man who figures that the Englishman is not stimulated to stouter resistance by these visitations from the German would be mistaken. Beneath the surface of his apparent indifference there is produced at each recurrent attack an enhanced current of hate ior the government that first inaugurated this system of barbaric warfare against unfortified communities. There is something so radically wrong in the Prussian propaganda it is inconceivable that any mind save a Prussian's mind could have conceived it. His imagination is on backward and he thinks hind part before. In the folly of his besetting madness he figures that he can subjugate a man by mangling that man's wife and baby to bits—the one thing that has always been potent to make a valiant fighter out of the veriest coward that lives.

They may not waste their rage in vain and vulgar mouthings—that would be the German, not the English way—but one may be sure that the people of London will never forgive the Kaiser for the hideous things his agents, in accordance with his policy of frightfulness, have wrought among innocent noncombatants in their city and in their island. They are entering up the balance in the ledgers of their righteous indignation against the day of final reckoning.

After I had seen personally some of the results of one of the nocturnal onslaughts I too could share in the feelings of those more directly affected, for I could realise that, given an opportunity now denied him by the mercy of distance and much intervening salt water, the Hun would be doing unto American cities what he had done to this English city; and I could picture the same unspeakable atrocities perpetrated upon New Haven or Asbury Park or Charleston as have been perpetrated upon London and Dover and Margate.

There was an old clergyman of the Established Church who lived in a rectory not far from Covent Garden, a man near seventy, who probably had never wittingly done an evil thing or a cruel thing in all his correct and godly life. He came to have the name of the Raid Preacher, because at every aerial attack he went forth fearlessly from his home, making the tour of all the shelters in the neighbourhood. At each place he would cheer and quiet the crowds there assembled, telling them there was no real danger, reading to them comforting passages of the Scriptures and encouraging them to sing homely and familiar songs. He had been doing this from the time when the Zeppelins first invaded the London district. He had held funeral services over the bodies of hundreds of raid victims, so they told me. Regardless of the religious affiliations of the dead, or the lack of church ties, their families almost invariably asked him to conduct the burials.

One night in the present year—I am forbidden to give the exact date or the exact place, though neither of them matters now—the raiders came. The old clergyman hurried to a cellar under a near-by business establishment, where a swarm of tenement dwellers of the quarter had congregated for safety. He was standing in their midst in the darkened place, bidding them to be of good and tranquil faith, when a two-hundred pound bomb of high explosives, sped from a Gotha eight thousand feet above and aimed by chance, came through the building, bringing the roof and the upper floors with it.

A great many persons were killed or wounded.

When the rescuers came almost the first body they brought out of the burning ruins was that of the Raid Preacher. They had found him, with torn flesh and broken bones, but with his face unmarred, lying on the floor. His thumbed leather Bible was under him, open at a certain page, and there was blood upon its leaves.

Men who saw his funeral cortège told me of it with tears in their eyes. They said that people of all faiths walked in the rain behind the hearse, and that the biggest of all the funeral wreaths was a gift from a little colony of poor Jewish folk in the district, and that one whole section of the sorrowful procession was made up of cripples and convalescents—pale, lame, halt men and women and children who limped on crutches or marched with bandaged heads or with twisted trunks; and these were the injured survivors of previous raids, to whom the dead man had ministered in their time of suffering.

In a hospital I saw a little girl who had been most terribly maimed by the same missile that killed the old rector. I am not going to dwell on the state of this child. When I think of her I have not the words to express the feelings that I have. But one of her hands was gone at the wrist, and the other hand was badly shattered; so she was just a wan little brutally abbreviated fragment of humanity, a living fraction, most grievously afflicted.

There was the pitiable wraith of a smile on her poor little pinched commonplace face, and to her breast, with the bandaged stump of one arm and with her remaining hand that was swarthed in a clump of wrapping, she cuddled up a painted china doll which somebody had brought her; and she was singing to it. The sight, I take it, would have been very gracious in the eyes of His Imperial Majesty of Prussia—except, of course, that the little girl still lived; that naturally would be a drawback to his complete enjoyment of the spectacle.

CHAPTER XIV
THE DAY OF BIG BERTHA

THERE was mingled comedy and woe in the scenes at Paris on the memorable day when the great long-distance gun—which the Parisians promptly christened "Big Bertha" in tribute to the titular mistress the Krupp works where it was produced—first opened upon the city from seventy-odd miles away and thereby established, among other records, a precedent for distance and scope in artillery bombardments. Paris was in a fit mood for emotion. The people were on edge; their nerves tensed, for there had been an alarm the evening before. The raiding planes had been turned back at the suburbs and driven off by the barrage fire, but the populace mainly had flocked into the *abris* and the underground stations of the Métropolitain.

At ten o'clock that night, after the danger was over, a funny thing occurred: The crew of a motor-drawn fire engine had fuddled themselves with wine, and for upward of half an hour the driver drove his red wagon at top speed up and down the Rue de Rivoli, past the Tuileries Gardens. With him he had four of his *confrères* in blue uniforms and brass helmets. These rode two on a side behind him, their helmets shining in the bright moonlight like pots of gold turned upside down; and as they rode the two on one side sounded the *alerte* signal on sirens, and the two on the other side sounded the "all clear" on bugles; and between blasts all four rocked in their places with joy over their little joke.

In London the thing would have constituted a public scandal; in New York there would have been a newspaper hullabaloo over it. It was typical of Paris, I think, that the street crowds became infected with the spirit which filled the roistering firemen and cheered them as they went merrily racketing back and forth. Nor, so far as I could ascertain, were the firemen disciplined; at least there was no mention in print of the incident, though a great many persons, the writer included, witnessed it.

At seven o'clock the following morning I was standing at the window of my bedchamber when something of a very violent and a highly startling nature went off just beyond the line of housetops and tree tops which hedged my horizon view to the northward. Another booming detonation, and yet another, followed in close succession. I figured to my own satisfaction that one of the enemy planes which were chased away the night before had taken advantage of the cloaking mists of the new day to slip back and pay his outrageous compliments to an unsuspecting municipality. Anyhow a fellow becomes accustomed to the sounds of loud noises in wartimes, and after a while ceases to concern himself greatly about their causes or even their effects unless the disturbances transpire in his immediate proximity. Life in wartime in a country where the war is consists largely in getting used to things that are abnormal and unusual. One takes as a matter of course occurrences that in peace would throw his entire scheme of existence out of gear. He is living, so to speak, in a world that is turned upside down, amid a jumble of acute and violent contradictions, both physical and metaphysical.

With two companions I set out for a certain large hotel which had the reputation of being able to produce genuine North American breakfasts for North American appetites. In the main grillroom we had just finished compiling an order, which included fried whiting, ham and eggs, country style, and fried potatoes, when a fire-department truck went shrieking through the street outside, its whistle blasting away as though it had a scared banshee locked up in its brazen throat.

There were not many persons in the room—to your average Frenchman his dinner is a holy rite, but his breakfast is a trifling incident—but most of these persons rose from their tables and straightway departed. The woman cashier hurried off with her hat on sidewise, which among women the world over is a thing betokening agitation.

The head waiter approached us with our bill in his tremulous hand, and bowing, wished to know whether messieurs would be so good as to settle the account now. By his manner lie sought to indicate that such was the custom of the house. We told him firmly that we would pay after we had eaten and not a minute sooner. He gave a despairing gesture and vanished, leaving the slip upon the tablecloth. Somebody hastily deposited within our reach the food we had ordered and withdrew.

Before we were half through eating a very short, very frightened-looking boy in buttons appeared at our elbows, pleading to know whether we were ready for our hats and canes. Since he appeared to be in some haste about it and since he was so small a small boy and so uneasy, we told him to bring them along. He did bring them along, practically instantaneously, in fact, and promptly was begone without waiting for a tip—an omission which up until this time had never marred the traditional ethics of hat-check boys either in France or anywhere else.

Presently it dawned upon us that as far as appearances went we were entirely alone in the heart of a great city. So when we were through eating we left the amount of the breakfast bill upon a plate and ourselves departed from there. The lobby of the hotel and the office and the main hallway were entirely deserted, there being neither guests nor functionaries in sight. But through a grating in the floor came up a gush of hot air, licking our legs as we passed. This may have been the flow from a unit of the heating plant, or then again it may have been the hot and feverish breathing of the habitués of that hotel, 'scaping upward through a vent in the subcellar's roof.

Outside, in the streets, the shopkeepers had put up their iron shutters. At intervals the plug-plug-blooie! of fresh explosions punctuated the hooting of fire engines racing with the alarm in adjacent quarters. Overhead, ranging and quartering the upper reaches of the sky, like pointer dogs in a sedge field, were scores of French aëroplanes searching, and searching vainly, for the unseen foeman.

The thing was uncanny; it was daunting and smacked of witchcraft. Here were the projectiles dropping down, apparently from directly above, and they were bursting in various sections, to the accompaniments of clattering débris and shattering glass; and yet there was neither sight nor sound of the agencies responsible for the attack. All sorts of rumours spread, each to find hundreds of earnest advocates and as many more vociferous purveyors.

One theory, often advanced and generally retailed, was that the Germans had produced a new type of aëroplane, with a noiseless motor, and capable of soaring at a height where it was invisible to the naked eye. Another possible solution for the enigma was that with the aid of spies and traitors the Germans had set up a gun fired by air compression upon a housetop in the environs and were bombarding the city from beneath the protection of a false roof. In the doorway of every *abri* the credulous and the incredulous held heated arguments, dodging back under shelter, like prairie dogs into their holes, at each recurring crash.

Presently it dawned upon the hearkening groups that the missiles were falling at stated and ordained periods. Twenty minutes regularly intervened between smashes. Appreciation of this circumstance injected a new element of surmise into a terrific and most profoundly puzzling affair. This was a mystery that grew momentarily more mysterious.

Business for the time being was pretty much suspended; anyhow nearly everybody appeared to be taking part in the debates. However, the taxicabs were still plying. A Parisian cabby may be trusted to take a chance on his life if there is a fare in sight and the prospect of a *pourboire* to follow. Two of us engaged a weather-beaten individual who apparently had no interest in the controversies raging about him or in the shelling either; and in his rig we drove to the scene of the first explosion, arriving there within a few minutes after the devilish cylinder fell.

There had been loss of life here—no great amount as loss of life is measured these times in this country, but attended by conditions that made the disaster hideous and distressing. The blood of victims still trickled in runlets between the paving stones where we walked, and there were mangled bodies stretched on the floor of an improvised morgue across the way—mainly bodies of poor working women, and one, I heard, the body of a widow with half a dozen children, who now would be doubly orphaned, since their father was dead at the Front.

Back again at my hotel after a forenoon packed with curious experiences, I found in my quarters a very badly scared chambermaid, trying to tidy a room with fingers that shook. In my best French, which I may state is the worst possible French, I was trying to explain to her that the bombardment had probably ended—and for a fact there had been a forty-minute lull in the new frightfulness—when one of the shells struck and went off among the trees and flowerbeds of a public breathing place not a hundred and fifty yards away. With a shriek the maid fell on her knees and buried her head, ostrich fashion, in a nest of sofa pillows.

I stepped through my bedroom window upon a little balcony in time to see the dust cloud rise in a column and to follow with my eyes the frenzied whirlings of a great flock of wood pigeons flighting high into the air from their roosting perches in the park plot. The next instant I felt a violent tugging at the back breadth of the leather harness that I wore. Unwittingly, in her panic the maid had struck upon the only possible use to which a Sam Browne belt may be put—other than the ornamental, and that is a moot point among fanciers of the purely decorative in the matter of military gearing for the human form. By accident she had divined its one utilitarian purpose. She had risen and with both hands had laid hold upon the crosspiece of my main surcingle and was striving to drag me inside. I rather gathered from the tenor of her contemporaneous remarks, which she uttered at the top of her voice and into which she interjected the names of several saints, that she feared the sight of me in plain view on that stone ledge might incite the invisible marauder to added excesses.

But I was the larger and stronger of the two, and my buckles held, and I had the advantage of an iron railing to cling to. After a short struggle my would-be rescuer lost. She turned loose of my kicking straps and breech bands, and making hurried reference to various names in the calendar of the canonised she fled from my presence. I heard her falling down the stairs to the floor below. The next day I had a new chambermaid; this one had tendered her resignation.

Not until the middle of the afternoon was the proper explanation for the phenomenon forthcoming. It came then from the Ministry of War, in the bald and unembroidered laconics of a formal communiqué. At the first time of hearing it the announcement seemed so inconceivable, so manifestly impossible that official sanction was needed to make men believe Teuton ingenuity had found a way to upset all the previously accepted principles touching on gravity and friction; on arcs and orbits; on aims and directions; on projectiles and projectives; on the resisting tensility of steel bores and on the carrying power of gun charges—by producing a cannon with a ranging scope of somewhere between sixty and ninety miles.

Days of bombardment followed—days which culminated on that never-to-be-forgotten Good Friday when malignant chance sped a shell to wreck one of the oldest churches in Paris and to kill seventy-five and wound ninety worshippers gathered beneath its roof.

After the first flurry of uncertainty the populace for the most part grew tranquil; now that they knew the origin of the far-flung punishment there was measurably less dread of the consequences among the masses of the people. On days when the shells exploded futilely the daily press and the comedians in the music halls made jokes at the expense of Big Bertha; as, for example, on a day when a fragment of shell took the razor out of the hand of a man who was shaving himself, without doing him the slightest injury; and again when a whole shell wrecked a butcher shop and strewed the neighbourhood with kidneys and livers and rib ends of beef, but spared the butcher and his family. On days when the colossal piece scored a murderous coup for its masters and took innocent life, the papers printed the true death lists without attempt at concealment of the ravages of the monster. And on all the bombardment days, women went shopping in the Rue de la Paix; children played in the parks; the flower women of the Madeleine sold their wares to customers with the reverberations of the explosions booming in their ears; the crowds that sat sipping coloured drinks at small tables in front of the boulevard cafés on fair afternoons were almost as numerous as they had been before the persistent thing started; and unless the sound was very loud indeed the average promenader barely lifted his or her head at each recurring report. In America we look upon the French as an excitable race, but here they offered to the world a pattern for the practice of fortitude.

A good many people departed from Paris to the southward. However, there was calmness under constant danger. Our own people, who were in Paris in numbers mounting up into the thousands, likewise set a fine example of sang-froid. On the evening of the opening day of the bombarding, when any one might have been pardoned for being a bit jumpy, an audience of enlisted men which packed the American Soldiers and Sailors' Club in the Rue Royale was gathered to hear a jazz band play Yankee tunes and afterward to hear an amateur speaker make an address. The cannon had suspended its annoying performances with the going down of the sun, but just as the speaker stood up by the piano the *alerte* for an air attack—which, by the way, proved to be a false alarm, after all—was heard outside.

There was a little pause, and a rustling of bodies.

Then the man, who was on his feet, spoke up. "I'll stay as long as any one else does," he said. "Anyhow, I don't know which is likely to be the worse of two evils—my poor attempts at entertaining you inside or the boche's threatened performances outside."

A great yell of approval went up and not a single person left the building until after the chairman announced that the programme for the evening had reached its conclusion. I know this to be a fact because I was among those present.

To be sure, the strain of the harassment got upon the nerves of some; that would be inevitable, human nature being what it is. Attendance at the theatres, especially for the matinées, fell off appreciably; this, though, being attributable, I think, more to fear of panic inside the buildings than to fear of what the missiles might do to the buildings themselves. And there was no record of any individual, whether man or woman, quitting a post of responsibility because of the personal peril to which all alike were exposed.

Likewise on those days when the great gun functioned promptly at twenty-minute intervals one would see men sitting in drinking places with their eyes glued to the faces of their wrist watches while they waited for the next crash. For those whose nerves lay close to their skins this damnable regularity of it was the worst phase of the thing.

There was something so characteristically and atrociously German, something so hellishly methodical in the tormenting certainty that each hour would be divided into three equal parts by three descending steel tubes of potential destruction.

Big Bertha operated on a perfect schedule. She opened up daily at seven a. m. sharp; she quit at six-twenty p. m. It was as though the crew that tended her carried union cards. They were never tardy. Neither did they work overtime. But if the Prussians counted upon bedeviling the people into panic and distracting the industrial and social economies of Paris they missed their guess. They made some people desperately unhappy, no doubt, and they frightened some; but the true organism of the community remained serene and unimpaired.

Some share of this, I figure might be attributed to the facts that in a city as great as Paris the chances of any one individual being killed were so greatly reduced that the very size of the town served to envelop its inhabitants with a sense of comparative immunity; the number of buildings, and their massiveness inspired a feeling of partial security. I know I felt safer than I have felt out in the open when the enemy's playful batteries were searching out the terrain round about. In a smaller city this condition probably would not have been manifest to the same degree. There almost everybody would be likely to know personally the latest victim or to be familiar with the latest scene of damage and this would serve doubtlessly to bring the apprehensive home to all households. Howsoever, be the underlying cause what it might, Paris weathered the brunt of the ordeal with splendid fortitude and an admirable coolness.

Being frequently in Paris between visits to one or another sector of the front, I was able to keep a fairly accurate score in the ravages of the bombardment and to get a fairly average appraisal of the effects upon the Parisian temper. Likewise by reading translated extracts out of German newspapers I got impressions of another phase of the tragedy which almost was as vivid as though I had been an eye witness to events which I knew of only at second-hand from the published descriptions of them.

I had the small advantage though on my side of being able to vizualise the setting in the Forest of St. Gobain, to the west of Laon for I was there once in German company. I could conjure up a presentiment of the scene there enacted on the day when Big Bertha's makers and masters sprang their well-guarded surprise, which so carefully and so secretly had been evolved during months of planning and constructing and experimentations. Behold then the vision: It is a fine spring morning. There is dew on the grass and there is song in the throats of the birds and young foliage is upon the trees. The great grey gun—it is nearly ninety feet long and according to inspired Teutonic chronicles resembles a vast metal crone—squats its misshapen mass upon a prepared concrete base in the edge of the woods, just on the timbered shoulder of a hill. Its long muzzle protrudes at an angle from the interlacing boughs of the thicket where it hides; at a very steep angle, too, since the charge it will fire must ascend twenty miles into the air in order to reach its objective. Behind it is a stenciling of white birdies and slender poplars flung up against the sky line; in front of it is a disused meadow where the newly minted coinage of a prodigal springtime—dandelions that are like gold coins and wild marguerites that are like silver ones—spangle the grass as though the profligate season had strewn its treasures broadcast there. The gunners make ready the monster for its dedication. They open its great navel and slide into its belly a steel shell nine inches thick and three feet long nearly and girthed with beltings of spun brass. The supreme moment is at hand.

From a group of staff officers advances a small man, grown old beyond his time; this man wears the field uniform of a Prussian field marshal. He has a sword at his side and spurs on his booted feet and a spiked helmet upon his head. He has a withered arm which dangles abortively, foreshortened out of its proper length. His hair is almost snow-white and his moustache with its fiercely upturned and tufted ends is white. From between slitted lids imbedded in his skull behind unhealthy dropical pouches of flesh his brooding, morbid eyes show as two blue dots, like touches of pale light glinting on twin disks of shallow polished agate. He bears himself with a mien that either is imperial or imperious, depending upon one's point of view.

While all about him bow almost in the manner of priests making obeisance before a shrine, he touches with one sacred finger the button of an electrical controller. The air is blasted and the earth rocks then to the loudest crash that ever issued from the mouth of a gun; for all its bulk and weight the cannon recoils on its carriage and shakes itself; the tree tops quiver in a palsy. The young grass is flattened as though by a sudden high wind blowing along the ground; the frightened birds flutter about and are mute.

The bellowing echoes die away in a fainter and yet fainter cadence. The-Anointed-of-God turns up his good wrist to consider the face of the watch strapped thereon; his staff follow his royal example. One minute passes in a sort of sacerdotal silence. There is drama in the pause; a fine theatricalism in the interlude. Two minutes, two minutes and a half pass. This is one part of the picture; there is another part of it:

Seventy miles away in a spot where a busy street opens out into a paved plaza all manner of common, ordinary work-a-day persons are busied about their puny affairs. In addition to being common and ordinary these folks do not believe in the divine right of kings; truly a high crime and misdemeanour. Moreover, they persist in the heretical practice of republicanism; they believe actually that all men were born free and equal; that all men have the grace and the authority within them to choose their own rulers; that all men have the right to live their own lives free from foreign dictation and alien despotism. But at this particular moment they are not concerned in the least with politics or policies. Their simple day is starting. A woman in a sidewalk kiosk is ranging morning papers on her narrow shelf. A half-grown girl in a small booth set in the middle of the square where the tracks of the tramway end, is selling street car tickets to working men in blouses and baggy corduroy trousers. Hucksters and barrow-men have established a small market along the curbing of the pavement. A waiter is mopping the metal tops of a row of little round tables under the glass markee of a café. Wains and wagons are passing with a rumble of wheels. Here there is no drama except the simple homely drama of applied industry.

Three minutes pass: Far away to the north, where the woods are quiet again and the birds have mustered up courage to sing once more, The Regal One drops his arm and looks about him at his officers, nodding and smiling. Smiling, they nod back in chorus, like well-trained automatons. There is a murmur of interchanged congratulations. The effort upon which so much invaluable time and so much scientific thought have been expended, stands unique and accomplished. Unless all calculations have failed the nine-inch shell has reached its mark, has scored its bull's eye, has done its predestined job.

It has; those calculations could not go wrong. Out of the kindly and smiling heavens, with no warning except the shriek of its clearing passage through the skies, the bolt descends in the busy square. The glass awning over the café front becomes a darting rain of sharp-edged javelins; the paving stones rise and spread in hurtling fragments from a smoking crater in the roadway. There are a few minutes of mad frenzy among those people assembled there. Then a measure of quiet succeeds to the tumult. The work of rescue starts. The woman who vended papers is a crushed mass under the wreckage of her kiosk; the girl who sold car tickets is dead and mangled beneath her flattened booth; the waiter who wiped the table-tops off lies among his tables now, the whole crown of his head sliced away by slivers of glass; here and there in the square are scattered small motionless clumps that resemble heaps of bloodied and torn rags. Wounded men and women are being carried away, groaning and screaming as they go. But in the edge of the woods at St. Gobain the Kaiser is climbing into his car to ride to his headquarters. It is his breakfast-time and past it and he has a fine appetite this morning. The picture is complete. The campaign for Kultur in the world has scored another triumph, the said score standing: Seven dead; fifteen injured.

CHAPTER XV
WANTED: A FOOL-PROOF WAR

THERE was a transportload of newly made officers coming over for service here in France. There was on board one gentleman in uniform who bore himself, as the saying goes, with an air. By reason of that air and by reason of a certain intangible atmospheric something about him difficult to define in words he seemed intent upon establishing himself upon a plane far remote from and inaccessible to these fellow voyagers of his who were crossing the sea to serve in the line, or to act as interpreters, or to go on staffs, or to work with the Red Cross or the Y. M. C. A. or the K. of C. or what not. He had what is called the superior manner, if you get what I mean—and you should get what I mean, reader, if ever you had lived, as I have, for a period of years hard by and adjacent to that particular stretch of the eastern seaboard of North America where, as nowhere else along the Atlantic Ocean or in the interior, are to be found in numbers those favoured beings who acquire merit unutterable by belonging to, or by being distantly related to, or by being socially acquainted with, the families that have nothing but.

Nevertheless, and to the contrary notwithstanding, divers of his brother travellers failed to keep their distance. Toward this distinguished gentleman they deported themselves with a familiarity and an offhandedness that must have been acutely distasteful to one unaccustomed to moving in a mixed and miscellaneous company.

Accordingly he took steps on the second day out to put them in their proper places. A list was being circulated to get up a subscription for something or other, and almost the very first person to whom this list came in its rounds of the first cabin was the person in question. He took out a gold-mounted fountain pen from his pocket and in a fair round hand inscribed himself thus:

"Bejones of Tuxedo"

There were no initials—royalty hath not need for initials—but just the family name and the name of the town so fortunate as to number among its residents this notable—which names for good reasons I have purposely changed. Otherwise the impressive incident occurred as here narrated.

But those others just naturally refused to be either abashed or abated. They must have been an irreverent, sacrilegious lot, by all accounts. The next man to whom the subscription was carried took note of the new fashion in signatures and then gravely wrote himself down as "Spirits of Niter"; and the next man called himself "Henri of Navarre"; and the third, it developed, was no other than "Cream of Tartar"; and the next was "Timon of Athens"; and the next "Mother of Vinegar" —and so on and so forth, while waves of ribald and raucous laughter shook the good ship from stem to stem.

However, the derisive ones reckoned without their host. For them the superior mortal had a yet more formidable shot in the locker. On the following day he approached three of the least impressed of his temporary associates as they stood upon the promenade deck, and apropos of nothing that was being said or done at the moment he, speaking in a clear voice, delivered himself of the following crushing remark:

"When I was born there were only two houses in the city of New York that had porte-cochères, and I—I was born in one of them."

Inconceivable though it may appear, the fact is to be recorded that even this disclosure failed to silence the tongues of ridicule aboard that packet boat. Rather did it enhance them, seeming but to spur the misguided vulgarians on and on to further evidences of disrespect. There are reasons for believing that Bejones of Tuxedo, who had been born in the drafty semipublicity of a porte-cochère, left the vessel upon its arrival with some passing sense of relief, though it should be stated that up until the moment of his debarkation he continued ever, while under the eye of the plebes and commoners about him, to bear himself after a mode and a port befitting the station to which Nature had called him. He vanished into the hinterland of France and was gone to take up his duties; but he left behind him, among those who had travelled hither in his company, a recollection which neither time nor vicissitude can efface. Presumably he is still in the service, unless it be that ere now the service has found out what was the matter with it.

I have taken the little story concerning him as a text for this article, not because Bejones of Tuxedo is in any way typical of any group or subgroup of men in our new Army—indeed I am sure that he, like the blooming of the century plant, is a thing which happens only once in a hundred years, and not then unless all the conditions are salubrious. I have chosen the little tale to keynote my narrative for the reason that I believe it may serve in illustration; of a situation that has arisen in Europe, and especially in France, these last few months—a condition that does not affect our Army so much as it affects sundry side issues connected more or less indirectly with the presence on European soil of an army from the United States, like most of the nations having representative forms of government that have gone into this war, we went in as an amateur nation so far as knowledge of the actual business of modern warfare was concerned. Like them, we have had to learn the same hard lessons that they learned, in the same hard school of experience. Our national amateurishness beforehand was not altogether to our discredit; neither was it altogether to our credit. Nobody now denies that we should have been better prepared for eventualities than we were. On the other hand it was hardly to be expected that a peaceful commercial country such as ours—which until lately had been politically remote as it was geographically aloof upon its own hemisphere from the political storm-centres of the Old World, and in which there was no taint of the militarism that has been Germany's curse, and will yet be her undoing—should in times of peace greatly concern itself with any save the broad general details of the game of war, except as a heart-moving spectacle enacted upon the stage of another continent and viewed by us with sympathetic and sorrowing eyes across three or four thousand miles of salt water. Prior to our advent into it the war had no great appeal upon the popular conscience of the United States. Out of the fulness of our hearts and out of the abundance of our prosperity we gave our dollars, and gave and gave and kept on giving them for the succour of the victims of the world catastrophe; but a sense of the impending peril for our own institutions came home to but few among us. Here and there were individuals who scented the danger; but they were as prophets crying in the wilderness; the masses either could not oc would not see it. They would not make ready against the evil days ahead.

So we went into this most highly specialised industry, which war has become, as amateurs mainly. Our Navy was no amateur navy, as very speedily developed, and before this year's fighting is over our enemy is going to realise that our Army is not an amateur army. We may have been greenhorns at the trade wherein Germans were experts by training and education; still we fancy ourselves as a reasonably adaptable breed. But if the truth is to be told it must be confessed that in certain of the Allied branches of the business we are yet behaving like amateurs. After more than a year of actual and potential participation in the conflict we even now are doing things and suffering things to be done which would make us the laughingstock of our allies if they had time or tempter for laughing. I am not speaking of the conduct of our operations in the field or in the camps or on the high seas. I am speaking with particular reference to what might be called some of the by-products.

None of us is apt to forget, or cease to remember with pride, the flood of patriotic sacrifice that swept our country in the spring of 1917. No other self-governing people ever adopted a universal draft before their shores had been invaded and before any of their manhood had fallen in battle. No other self-governing people ever accepted the restrictions of a food-rationing scheme before any of the actual provisions concerning that food-rationing scheme had been embodied into the written laws. Other countries did it under compulsion, after their resources showed signs of exhaustion. We did it voluntarily; and it was all the more wonderful that we should have done it voluntarily when all about us was human provender in a prodigal fullness. There was plenty for our own tables.

By self-imposed regulations we cut down our supplies so that our allies might be fed with the surplus thus made available. Outside of a few sorry creatures there was scarcely to be found in America an individual, great or small, who did not give, and give freely, of the work of his or her heart and hands to this or that phase of the mighty undertaking upon which our Government had embarked and to which our President, speaking for us all, had solemnly dedicated all that we were or had been or ever should be.

All sorts of commissions, some useful and important beyond telling, some unutterably unuseful and incredibly unimportant, sprang into being. And to and fro in the land, in numbers amounting to a vast multitude, went the woman who wanted to do her part, without having the least idea of what that part would be or how she would go about doing it. She knew nothing of nursing; kitchen work, a vulgar thing, was abhorrent to her nature and to her manicured nails; she could not cook, neither could she sew or sweep— but she must do her part.

She was not satisfied to stay on at home and by hard endeavour to fit herself for helping in the task confronting every rational and willing being between the two oceans. No, sir-ree, that would be too prosaic, too commonplace an employment for her. Besides, the working classes could attend to that job. She must do her part abroad—either in France within sound of the guns or in racked and desolated Belgium. Of course her intentions were good. The intentions of such persons are nearly always good, because they change them before they have a chance to go stale.

I think the average woman of this type had a mental conception of herself wearing a wimple and a coif of purest white, in a frock that was all crisp blue linen and big pearl buttons, with one red cross blazing upon her sleeve and another on her cap, sitting at the side of a spotless bed in a model hospital that was fragrant with flowers, and ministering daintily to a splendid wounded hero with the face of a demigod and the figure of a model for an underwear ad. Preferably this youth would be a gallant aviator, and his wound would be in the head so that from time to time she might adjust the spotless bandage about his brow.

I used to wish sometimes when I met such a lady that I might have drawn for her the picture of reality as I had seen it more times than once—tired, earnest, competent women who slept, what sleep they got, in lousy billets that were barren of the simplest comforts, sleeping with gas masks under their pillows, and who for ten or twelve or fifteen or eighteen hours on a stretch performed the most nauseating and the most necessary offices for poor suffering befouled men lying on blankets upon straw pallets in wrecked dirty houses or in half-ruined stables from which the dung had hurriedly been shoveled out in order to make room for suffering soldiers—stables that reeked with the smells of carbolic and iodoform and with much worse smells. It is an extreme case that I am describing, but then the picture is a true picture, whereas the idealistic fancy painted by the lady who just must do her part at the Front had no existence except in the movies or in her own imagination.

It never occurred to her that there would be slop jars to be emptied or filthy bodies, alive with crawling vermin, to be cleansed. It never occurred to her that she would take up room aboard ship that might better be filled with horse collars or hardtack or insect powder; nor that while over here she would consume food that otherwise would stay the stomach of a fighting man or a working woman; nor that if ever she reached the battle zone she would encounter living conditions appallingly bare and primitive beyond anything she could conceive; nor that she could not care for herself, and was fitted neither by training nor instinct to help care for any one else.

When I left America last winter a great flow of national sanity had already begun to rise above the remaining scourings of national hysteria; and the lady whose portrait I have tried in the foregoing paragraphs to sketch was not quite so numerous or so vociferous as she had been in those first few exalted weeks and months following our entrance into the war as a full partner in the greatest of enterprises. My surprise was all the greater therefore to find that she had beaten me across the water. She had pretty well disappeared at home.

One typical example of this strange species crossed in the same ship with me. Heaven alone knows what political or social influence had availed to secure her passport for her. But she had it, and with it credentials from an organisation that should have known better. She was a woman of independent wealth seemingly, and her motives undoubtedly were of the best; but as somebody might have said: Good motives butter no parsnips, and hell is paved with buttered parsnips. Her notion was to drive a car at the Front—an ambulance or a motor truck or a general's automobile or something. She had owned cars, but she had never driven one, as she confessed; but that was a mere detail. She would learn how, some day after she got to Europe, and then somebody or other would provide her with a car and she would start driving it; such was her intention. Unaided she could no more have wrested a busted tire off of a rusted rim than she could have marcelled her own back hair; and so far as her knowledge of practical mechanics went, I am sure no reasonably prudent person would have trusted her with a nutpick; but she had the serene confidence of an inspired and magnificent ignorance.

She had her uniform too. She had brought it with her and she wore it constantly. She said she designed it herself, but I think she fibbed there. No one but a Fifth Avenue mantuamaker of the sex which used to be the gentler sex before it got the vote could have thought up a vestment so ornate, so swagger and so complicated.

It was replete with shoulder straps and abounding in pleats and gores and gussets and things. Just one touch was needed to make it a finished confection: By rights it should have buttoned up the back.

The woman who had the cabin next to hers in confidence told a group of us that she had it from the stewardess that it took the lady a full hour each day to get herself properly harnessed into her caparisons. Still I must say the effect, visually speaking, was worthy of the effort; and besides, the woman who told us may have been exaggerating. She was a registered and qualified nurse who knew her trade and wore matter-of-fact garments and fiat-heeled, broad-soled shoes. She was not very exciting to look at, but she radiated efficiency. She knew exactly what she would do when she got over here and exactly how she would do it. We agreed among ourselves that if we were in quest of the ornamental we would search out the lady who meant to drive the car—provided there was any car; but that if anything serious ailed any of us we would rather have the services of one of the plain nursing sisterhood than a whole skating-rinkful of the other kind round.

In the latter part of 1917 there landed in France a young woman hailing from a Far Western city whose family is well known on the Pacific Slope. She brought with her letters of introduction signed by imposing names and a comfortable sum of money, which had been subscribed partly out of her own pocket and partly out of the pockets of well-meaning persons in her home state whom she had succeeded in interesting in her particular scheme of wartime endeavour. She was very fair to see and her uniform, by all accounts, was very sweet to look upon, it being a horizon-blue in colour with much braiding upon the sleeves and collar. It has been my observation since coming over that when in doubt regarding their vocations and their intentions these unattached lady zealots go in very strongly for striking effects in the matter of habiliments. Along the boulevards and in the tearooms I have encountered a considerable number who appeared to have nothing to do except to wear their uniforms.

However, this young person had no doubt whatever concerning her motives and her purposes. The whole thing was all mapped out in her head, as developed when she called upon a high official of our Expeditionary Forces at his headquarters in the southern part of France. She told him she had come hither for the express purpose of feeding our starving aviators. He might have told her that so long as there continued to be served fried potato chips free at the Crillon bar there was but little danger of any airman going hungry, in Paris at least. What he did tell her when he had rallied somewhat from the shock was that he saw no way to gratify her in her benevolent desire unless he could catch a few aviators and lock them up and starve them for two or three days, and he rather feared the young men might object to such treatment. As a matter of fact, I understand he so forgot himself as to laugh at the young woman.

At any rate his attitude was so unsympathetic that he practically spoiled the whole v war for her, and she gave him a piece of her mind and went away. She had departed out of the country before I arrived in it, and I learned of her and her uniform and her mission and her disappointment at its unfulfillment by hearsay only; but I have no doubt, in view of some of the things I have myself seen, that the account which reached me was substantially correct. Along this line I am now prepared to believe almost anything.

Here, on the other hand, is a case of which I have direct and first-hand knowledge. I encountered a group of young women attached to one of the larger American organisations engaged in systematised charities and mercies on this side of the water. Now, plainly these young women were inspired by the very highest ideals; that there was no discounting. They were full of the spirit of service and sacrifice. Mainly they were college graduates. Without exception they were well bred; almost without exception they were well educated.

The particular tasks for which they had been detailed were to care for pauperised repatriates returning to France through Switzerland from areas of their country occupied by the enemy, and to aid these poor folks in reestablishing their home life and to give them lessons in domestic science. To the success of their ministrations there was just one drawback: They were dealing with peasants mostly—furtive, shy, secretive folks who under ordinary circumstances would be bitterly resentful of any outside interference by aliens with their mode of life, and who in these cases had been rendered doubly suspicious by reason of the misfortunes they had endured while under the thumb of the Germans.

To understand them, to plumb diplomatically the underlying reasons for their prejudices, to get upon a basis of helpful sympathy with them, it was highly essential that those dealing with them not only should have infinite tact and finesse but should be able to fathom the meaning of a nod or a gesture, a sidelong glance of the eyes or the inflection of a muttered word. And yet of those zealous young women who had been assigned to this delicate task there was scarcely one in six who spoke any French at all. It inevitably followed that the bulk of their patient labours should go for naught; moreover, while they continued in this employment they were merely occupying space in an already crowded country and consuming food in an already needy country; the both of which—space and food—were needed for people who could accomplish effective things.

An American woman who is reputed to be a dietetic specialist came over not long ago, backed by funds donated in the States. Her instructions were to establish cafeterias at some of the larger French munition works. Probably her chagrin was equalled only by her astonishment when she learned that for reasons which seemed to it good and sufficient—and which no doubt were—the French Government did not want any American-plan cafeterias established at any of its munition works. Apparently it had not seemed feasible and proper to the sponsors of the diet specialist to find out before dispatching her overseas whether the plan would be agreeable to the authorities here; or whether there already were eating places suitable to the desires of the working people at these munition plants; or how long it would take, given the most favourable conditions, to cure the workers of their tenacious instinct for eating the kind of midday meal they have been eating for some hundreds of years and accustom them and their palates and their stomachs to the Yankee quick lunch with its baked pork and beans, its buckwheat cakes with maple sirup and its four kinds of pie. In their zeal the promoters, it would seem, had entirely overlooked those essential details. It is just such omissions as this one that the fine frenzy of helping out in wartime appears to develop in a nation that is given to boasting of its business efficiency and that vaunts itself that it knows how to give generously without wasting foolishly.

The field manager of an organisation that is doing a great deal for the comfort of our soldiers and the soldiers of our allies told me of one of his experiences. He had a sense of humour and he could laugh over it, but I think I noted a suggestion of resentment behind the laughter. He said that some months before lie set up and assumed charge of a plant well up toward the trenches in a sector that had been taken over by the American troops. It was a large and elaborate concern, as these concerns are rated in the field. The men were pleased with its accommodations and facilities, and the field manager was proud of it.

One day there appeared a businesslike young woman who introduced herself as belonging to a kindred organisation that was charged with the work of decorating the interiors of such establishments as the one over which he presided. Somewhat puzzled, he showed her, first of all, his canteen. It was as most such places are: There were boxes of edibles upon counters, in open boxes, so that the soldier customers might appraise the wares before investing; upon the shelves there were soft drinks and smoking materials and all manner of small articles of wearing apparel; likewise baseballs and safety razors and soap, toilet kits and the rest of it. Altogether the manager and his two assistants were rather pleased with the arrangement.

The newly arrived young woman swept the scene with a cold professional eye.

"On the whole this will do fairly well," she said with a certain briskness, in her tone. "Yes, I may say it will do very well indeed—with certain changes, certain touches."

"As for example, what, please?" inquired the superintendent.

"Well," she said, "for one thing we must put up some bright curtains at the windows; and to lighten up the background I think we'll run a stenciled pattern in some cheerful colour round the walls at the top."

It was not for the manager to inquire how the decorator meant to get her curtains and her stencils and her wall paints up over a road that was being alternately gassed and shelled at nights and on which the traffic capacity was already taxed to the utmost by the business of bringing up supplies, munitions and rations from the base some fifteen miles in the rear. He merely bowed and awaited the lady's further commands. "And now," she said, "where is the rest room?"

"The rest room, did you say?"

"Certainly, the rest room—the recreation hall, the place where these poor men may go for privacy and innocent amusement?"

"Well, you see, thus close up near the Front we haven't been able to make provision for a regular rest room," explained the manager. "Besides, in case of a withdrawal or an attack we might have to pull out in a hurry and leave behind everything that is not readily portable on wagons or trucks. The nearest approach that we have to a rest room is here at the rear." He led the way to a room at the back. It contained such plenishings as one generally finds in improvised quarters in the field—that is to say, it contained a curious equipment made up partly of crude bits of furniture collected on the spot out of villagers' abandoned homes and partly of makeshift stools and tables coopered together from barrels and boxes and stray bits of planking. Also it contained at this time as many soldiers as could crowd into it. A phonograph was grinding out popular airs, and divers games of checkers and cards were in progress, each with its fringe of interested onlookers ringing in the players.

"Oh, but this will never do—never!" stated the inspecting lady. "It is too bare, too cheerless! It lacks atmosphere. It lacks coziness; it lacks any appeal to the senses—in short it lacks everything! We must have some immediate improvements here by all means."

The man was beginning to lose his temper. By an effort he retained it.

"The men seem fairly well satisfied; at least I have heard no complaint," he said. "What would you suggest in the way of changes?"

As she answered, the visitor ticked off the items of her mental inventory of essentials on her fingers.

"Well, to begin with we must clear all this litter out of here," she said. "Then we must install some really comfortable chairs and at least two or three roomy sofas and some simple couches where the men may lie down. I should also like to see a piano here. That, with the addition of some curtains at the windows and some simple treatment of the walls and a few appropriate pictures properly spaced and properly hung, will be different, I think."

"Yes," demurred the manager, "but admitting that we could get the things you have enumerated up here, another problem would arise: This room, which, as you see, is not large, would be so crowded with the furnishings that there would be room in it for very many less men than usually come here. There are probably fifty men in it now. If it were filled up with sofas and couches and a piano I doubt whether we could crowd twenty men inside of it."

"Very well, then," stated the lady decorator calmly, "you must admit only twenty men at a time."

"Quite so; but how," he demanded—"how am I going to select the twenty?"

The young woman considered the question for a moment. Then a solution came to her.

"I should select the twenty neatest ones," she said.

Whereupon the manager excused himself and went out to frame a dispatch to headquarters embodying an ultimatum, which ultimatum was that the lady decorator went away from there forthwith or his resignation must take effect, coincident with his immediate departure from his present post. The home office must have called the lady off, because when I saw him he was still in harness, and swinging a man-size job in a competent way.

I would not have the reader believe that I am casting discredit upon either the patriotic impulses or the honest motives of the bulk of the lay workers who have journeyed to Europe, paying their own way and their own living expenses. Often they arrive, many of them, to strike hands with the military authorities in the task which faces our nation on Continental soil. There is room and a welcome in France, in Italy, in England and in Flanders for every civilian recruit who really knows how to do something helpful and who has the strength, the self-reliance and the hardihood to perform that particular function under difficult and complicated conditions, which nearly always are physically uncomfortable and which may become physically dangerous.

Nor would I wish any one to assume that I am deprecating by inference or by frontal attack the very fine things that are being accomplished every day by fine American women and girls who answered the first call for trained helpers, to serve in hospitals or canteens or huts, in settlement work or at telephone exchanges. It will make any American thrill with pride to enter a ward where the American Red Cross is in charge, or where a medical unit from one of the great hospitals or one of our great universities back home has control. The French and the British are quick enough to speak in terms of highest praise of the achievements of American surgeons, American nurses and American ambulance drivers. They say, and with good reason for saying it, that our people have pluck and that they have skill and that they above all are amazingly resourceful.

Personally I know of no smarter exhibition of native wit and courage that the war has produced than was shown by that group of Smith College girls who had been organising and directing colonisation work among the peasants in the reclaimed districts of Northern France and who were driven out by the great spring advance of the Germans. I met some of those young women. They were modest enough in describing their adventure. It was by gathering a shred of a story there and a scrap of an anecdote here that I was able to piece together a fairly accurate estimate of the self-imposed discipline, the clean-strained grit and the initiative which marked their conduct through three trying weeks.

Perhaps it was a mistake in their instance, as in the instances of divers similar organisations, that the work of resettling the wasted lands above the Aisne and the Oise should have been undertaken at points that would be menaced in the event of a quick onslaught by the Prussian high command. The British, I understand, privately objected to the undertakings on the ground that the presence of American women In villages which might fall again into the foe's hands—and which as it turned out did fall again into his hands—entailed an added burden and an added responsibility upon the fighting forces. The British were right. Practically all of the repatriated peasants had to flee for the second time, abandoning their rebuilt homes and their newly sowed fields.

On the heels of these, improvements which represented many thousands of American dollars and many months of painstaking labour on the part of devoted American women went up in flames. The torch was applied rather than that the little model houses and the tons of donated supplies on hand should go into hostile hands.

Those Smith College girls did not run away, though, until the Germans were almost upon them. Up to the very last minute they stayed at their posts, feeding and housing not only refugees but many exhausted soldiers, British and French, who staggered in, spent and sped after alternately fighting and retreating through a period of days and nights. When finally they did come away each one of them came driving her own truck and bearing in it a load of worn-out and helpless natives. One girl brought out a troop of frightened dwarfs from a stranded travelling caravan. Another ministered day and night to a blind woman nearly ninety years old and a family of orphaned babies. The passengers of a third were four inmates of a little communal blind asylum that happened to be in the invader's path.

On the way, in addition to tending their special charges, they cooked and served hundreds of meals for hungry soldiers and hungry civilians. They spent the nights in towns under shell fire, and when at length the German drive had been checked they assembled their forces in Beauvais. Thus and with characteristic adaptability some became drivers of ambulances and supply trucks plying along the lines of communication, and some opened a kitchen for the benefit of passing soldiers at the local railway station. If the faculty and the students and the alumnæ of Smith College did not hold a celebration when the true story of what happened in March and April reached them they were lacking in appreciation—that's all I have to say about it.

Right here seems a good-enough place for me to slip in a few words of approbation for the work which another 'organisation has accomplished in

France since we put our men into the field. Nobody asked me to speak in its favour because so far as I can find out it has no publicity department. I am referring to the Salvation Army—may it live forever for the service which, without price and without any boasting on the part of its personnel, it is rendering to our boys in France!

A good many of us who hadn't enough religion, and a good many more of us who mayhap had too much religion, look rather contemptuously upon the methods of the Salvationists. Some have gone so far as to intimate that the Salvation Army was vulgar in its methods and lacking in dignity and even in reverence. Some have intimated that converting a sinner to the tap of a bass drum or the tinkle of a tambourine was an improper process altogether. Never again, though, shall I hear the blare of the cornet as it cuts into the chorus of hallelujah whoops where a ring of blue-bonneted women and blue-capped men stand exhorting on a city street corner under the gas lights, without recalling what some of their enrolled brethren—and sisters—have done and are doing in Europe.

The American Salvation Army in France is small, but, believe me, it is powerfully busy! Its war delegation came over without any fanfare of the trumpets of publicity. It has no paid press agents here and no impressive headquarters. There are no well-known names, other than the names of its executive heads, on its rosters or on its advisory boards. None of its members is housed at an expensive hotel and none of them has handsome automobiles in which to travel about from place to place. No compaigns to raise nation-wide millions of dollars for the cost of its ministrations overseas were ever held at home. I imagine it is the pennies of the poor that mainly fill its war chest.

I imagine, too, that sometimes its finances are an uncertain quantity. Incidentally I am assured that not one of its male workers here is of draft age unless he holds exemption papers to prove his physical unfitness for military service. The Salvationists are taking care to purge themselves of any suspicion that potential slackers have joined their ranks in order to avoid the possibility of having to perform duties in khaki.

Among officers as well as among enlisted men one occasionally hears criticism—which may or may not be based on a fair judgment—for certain branches of certain activities of certain organisations. But I have yet to meet any soldier, whether a brigadier or a private, who, if he spoke at all of the Salvation Army, did not speak in terms of fervent gratitude for the aid that the Salvationists are rendering so unostentatiously and yet so very effectively. Let a sizable body of troops move from one station to another, and hard on its heels there came a squad of men and women of the Salvation Army. An army truck may bring them, or it may be they have a battered jitney to move them and their scanty outfits. Usually they do not ask for help from any one in reaching their destinations. They find lodgment in a wrecked shell of a house or in the corner of a barn. By main force and awkwardness they set up their equipment, and very soon the word has spread among the troopers that at such-and-such a place the Salvation Army is serving free hot drinks and free doughnuts and free pies. It specialises in doughnuts, the Salvation Army in the field does—the real old-fashioned homemade ones that taste of home to a homesick soldier boy.

I did not see this, but one of my associates did. He saw it last winter in a dismal place on the Toul sector. A file of our troops were finishing a long hike through rain and snow over roads knee-deep in half-thawed icy slush. Cold and wet and miserable, they came tramping into a cheerless, half-empty town within sound and range of the German guns. They found a reception committee awaiting them there—in the person of two Salvation Army lassies and a Salvation Army captain. The women had a fire going in the dilapidated oven of a vanished villager's kitchen. One of them was rolling out the batter on a plank with an old wine bottle for a rolling pin and using the top of a tin can to cut the dough into circular strips. The other woman was cooking the doughnuts, and as fast as they were cooked the man served them out, spitting hot, to hungry wet boys clamouring about the door, and nobody was asked to pay a cent.

At the risk of giving mortal affront to ultra-doctrinal practitioners of applied theology I am firmly committed to the belief that by the grace of God and the grease of doughnuts those three humble benefactors that day strengthened their right to a place in the Heavenly Kingdom.

As I said a bit ago, there is in France room and to spare and the heartiest sort of welcome for competent, sincere lay workers, both men and women. But there is no room, and if truth be known, there is no welcome for any other sort. These people over here long ago passed out of the experimental period in the handling of industrial and special problems that have grown up out of war. They have entirely emerged from the amateur stage of endeavour and direction. If any man doubts the truth of this he has only to see, as I have seen, the thousands of women who have taken men's jobs in the cities in order that the men might go to the colours; has only to see the overalled women in the big munition plants; has only to see how the peasant women of France are labouring in the fields and how the girls of the British auxiliary legions—the members of the W. A. A. C. for a conspicuous example—are carrying their share of the burden; has only to see women of high degree and low, each doing her part sanely, systematically and unflinchingly—to appreciate that, though Britain and France can find employment for every pair of willing and able hands somewhere behind the lines, they have no use whatsoever for the unorganised applicant or for the purely ornamental variety of volunteer or yet for the mere notoriety seeker.

I make so bold as to suggest that it is time we were taking the same lesson to heart; time to start the sifting process ourselves. I have seen in Paris a considerable number of American women who appeared to have no business here except to air their most becoming uniforms in public places and to tell in a vague broad way of the things they hope to do. The French, proverbially, are a polite race, and the French Government will endure a great deal of this kind of infliction rather than run the risk of engendering friction, even to the most minute extent, with the people or the administration of an Allied nation. But in wartime especially, too much patience becomes a dubious virtue, and if practiced for overlong may become a fault.

As yet there has been no intimation from any official source that the French would rather our State Department did not issue quite so many passports to Americans who have no set and definite purpose in making the journey to these shores, but even a superficial knowledge of the French language and the most casual acquaintance with the French nature enable one to get at what the French people are thinking. I am sure that had the prevalent condition been reversed our papers would have voiced the popular protest at the imposition long before now. Some of these days, unless we apply the preventive measures on our own side of the Atlantic, the perfectly justifiable resentment of the hard-pressed French is going to find utterance; and then quite a number of well-intentioned but utterly *inutile* persons will be going back home with their feelings all harrowed up.

CHAPTER XVI
CONDUCTING WAR BY DELEGATION

PLEASE do not think that because I have mainly dwelt thus far upon the women offenders that there are no American men in France who do not belong here, because that would be a wrong assumption. I merely have mentioned the women first because by reason of their military garbing—or what some of them fondly mistake for military garbing—they offer rather more conspicuous showing to the casual eye than the male civilian dress.

The men are abundantly on hand though; make no mistake about that! Some of them come burdened with frock-coated dignity as members of special commissions or special delegations; in certain quarters there appears to be a somewhat hazy but very lively inclination to try to run our share of this war by commission. Some, I am sure, came for the same reason that the young man in the limerick went to the stranger's funeral—because they are fond of a ride. Some I think came in the hope of enjoying an exciting sort of junketing expedition, and some because they were all dressed up and had nowhere to go.

As well as may be judged by one who has been away from home for going on five months now, the special-commission notion is being rather overdone. Individuals and groups of individuals bearing credentials from this fraternal organisation or that religious organisation or the other research society reach England on nearly every steamer that penetrates through the U-boat zone. Almost invariably these gentlemen carry letters of introduction testifying to their personal probity and their collective importance, which letters are signed by persons sitting in high places.

It may be that the English are thereby deceived into believing that the visitors are entitled to special consideration—as indeed some of them are, and indeed some of them most distinctly are not. Or then again it may be that the English are not aware of a device very common among our men of affairs for getting rid of a bore who is intent on going somewhere to see somebody and craves to be properly vouched for upon his arrival. In certain circles this habit is called passing the buck. In others it is known as writing letters of introduction.

At any rate the English take no chances on offending the right party, even at the risk of favouring the wrong one. When a half dozen Yankees appear at the Foreign Office laden with letters addressed "To Whom it May Concern" the Foreign Office immediately becomes concerned.

How is a guileless Britisher intrenched behind a flat-top desk to know that the August and Imperial Order of Supreme Potentates whose chosen emissaries are now present desirous of having a look at the war, and afterward to approve of it in a report to the Grand Lodge at its next annual convention, if so be they do see fit to approve of it—how, I repeat, is he to know that the August and Imperial Order of Supreme Potentates has a membership largely composed of class-C bartenders? Not knowing, he acts in accordance with the best dictates of his ignorance.

The commission or the delegation or the presentation, whatever it calls itself, is provided with White Passes all round. On the strength of these White Passes the investigators are at the public expense transferred across the Channel and housed temporarily at the American Visitors' Château. From there they are taken in automobiles and under escort of very bored officers on a kind of glorified Cook's tour behind the British Front. Thereafter they are turned over to the French Mission or to the American forces for similar treatment.

As a result they accumulate an assortment of soft-boiled and yolkless impressions which they incubate into the spoken or the written word on the way back home, after they have held a meeting to decide whether they like the way the war is going on or whether they do not like the way the war is going on. Always there is the possibility that as a result of the dissemination of underdone and undigested misinformations which they have managed to acquire these persons, though actuated by the best intentions in the world, may do considerable harm in shaping public opinion in America. And likewise one may be very sure a lot of pestered British and French functionaries are left to wonder what sort of folks the masses of American citizenship must be if these are typical samples of the thought-moulding class.

I am not exaggerating much when I touch on this particular phase of the topic now engaging me, for I have seen two delegations in Europe, of the variety I have sought briefly to describe in the lines immediately foregoing; and we are expecting more in on the next boat. There was no imaginable reason why those whom I saw should be in a country that is at war at such a time of crisis as this time is, but the main point was that they were here, eating three large rectangular meals a day apiece and taking up the valuable time of overworked military men who accompanied them while they week-ended at the war. How many more such delegations will sift through the State Department and seep by the passport bureau and journey hither during the latter half of 1918 unless the Administration at Washington shuts down on the game no man can with accuracy calculate.

Away down in the south of France I ran into a gentleman of a clerical aspect who lost no time in telling me about himself. He was tall and slender like a wand, and of a willowy suppleness of figure, and he was terribly serious touching on his mission. He represented a religious denomination that has several hundreds of thousands of communicants in the United States. He had been dispatched across, he said, by the governing body of his church. His purpose, he explained, was to inquire into the bodily and spiritual well-being of his coreligionists who were on foreign service in the Army and the Navy, with a view subsequently to suggesting reforms for any existing evil in the military and naval systems when he reported back to the main board of his church.

To an innocent bystander it appeared that this particular investigator had a considerable contract upon his hands. Scattered over land and sea on this hemisphere there must be a good many thousands of members of his faith who are wearing the khaki or the marine blue. It would be practically impossible, I figured, to recognise them in their uniforms for what, denominationally speaking, they were; and from what I had seen of our operations I doubted whether any commanding officer would be willing to suspend routine while the reverend tabulator went down the lines taking his census; besides, the latter process would invariably consume considerable time. I calculated offhand that if the war lasted three years longer it still would be over before he could complete his rounds of all the camps and all the ships and all the rest billets and bases and hospitals and lines of communication, and so on. So I ventured to ask him just how he meant to go about getting his compilations of testimony together.

He told me blandly that as yet he had not fully worked out that detail of the task. For the time being he would content himself with a general survey of the situation and with securing material for a lecture which he thought of giving upon his return to America.

I felt a strong inclination to speak to him after some such fashion as this:

"My dear sir, if I were you I would not greatly concern myself regarding the physical and the moral states of individuals composing our Expeditionary Forces. That job is already being competently attended to by experts. So far as my own observations go the chaplains are all conscientious, hard-working men. There are a large number of excellent and experienced chaplains over here—enough, in fact, to go round. They are doing everything that is humanly possible to be done to keep the men happy and amused in their leisure hours and to help them to continue to be decent, cleanminded, normal human beings. Almost without exception, to the best of my knowledge and belief, the officers are practically lending their personal influence and using the power and the weight of discipline to accomplish the same desirable ends.

"On the physical side our boys are in splendid condition. We may have bogged slightly down in some of the aspects of this undertaking, but there is plenty of healthful and nourishing food on hand for every American boy in foreign service. He is comfortably clothed and comfortably shod — his officers see to that; and he is housed in as comfortable a billet as it is possible to provide, the state of the country being what it is. While he is well and hearty he has his fill of victuals three times a day, and if he falls ill, is wounded or hurt he has as good medical attendance and as good nursing and as good hospital treatment as it is possible for our country to provide.

"Touching on the other side of the proposition I would say this: In England, where there are powerfully few dry areas, and here in France, which is a country where everybody drinks wine, I have seen a great many thousands of our enlisted men—soldiers, sailors and marines, engineers and members of battalions. I have seen them in all sorts of surroundings and under all sorts of circumstances. I have seen perhaps twenty who were slightly under the influence of alcoholic stimulant. As a sinner would put it, they were slightly jingled—not disorderly, not staggering, you understand, but somewhat jingled. I have yet to see one in such a state as the strictest police-court magistrate would call a state of outright intoxication. That has been my experience. I may add that it has been the common experience of the men of my profession who have had similar opportunities for observing the conduct of our fellows.

"It is true that the boys indulge in a good deal of miscellaneous cussing—which is deplorable, of course, and highly reprehensible. Still, in my humble opinion most of them use profanity as a matter of habit and not because there is any real lewdness or any real viciousness in their hearts. Mainly they cuss for the same reason that a parrot does. Anyhow, I could hardly blame a fellow sufferer for swearing occasionally, considering the kind of spring weather we have been having in these parts lately.

"As for their morals, I am firmly committed to the belief, as a result of what I have seen and heard, that man for man our soldiers have a higher moral standard than the men of any army of any other nation engaged in this war; and when in this connection I speak of our soldiers I mean the soldiers of Canada as well as the soldiers of the United States. Any man who tells you the contrary is a liar, and the truth is not in him. This is not an offhand alibi; statistics compiled by our own surgeons form the truth of it; and any man who stands up anywhere on our continent and says that the soldiers who have come from our side of the Atlantic to help lick Germany are contracting habits of drunkenness or that they are being ruined by the spreading of sexual diseases among them utters a deliberate and a cruel slander against North American manhood which should entitle him to a suit of tar-and-feather underwear and a free ride on a rail out of any community.

"There is absolutely nothing the matter with our boys except that they are average human beings, and it is going to take a long time to cure them of that. And please remember this—that, discipline being what it is and military restraint being what it is, it is very much harder for a man in the Army or the Navy to get drunk or to misconduct himself than it would be for him to indulge in such excesses were he out in civil life, as a free agent."

That in fact was what I wanted to pour into the ear of the ecclesiastical prober. But I did not. I saved it up to say it here, where it would enjoy a wider circulation. I left him engaged in generally surveying.

Officers and men alike are invariably ready and willing to voice their gratitude and their everlasting appreciation of the help and comfort provided by those who are attached to lay organisations having for the time being a more or less military complexion; they are equally ready to score the incompetents who infrequently turn up in these auxiliary branches of the service. A man who is fighting Fritz is apt to have a short temper anyhow, and meddlesome busybodies who want to aid without knowing any of the rudiments make him see red and swear blue.

A general of division told me that when he moved in with his command to the sector which he then was occupying he was tagged by an undoubtedly earnest but undeniably pestiferous person who wanted everything else suspended until his purposes in accompanying the expedition had been satisfied.

"I was a fairly busy person along about then," said the general. "We were within reach of the enemy's big guns and his aëroplanes were giving us considerable bother, and what with getting a sufficiency of dugouts and trench shelters provided for the troops and attending to about a million other things of more or less importance from a military standpoint I had mighty little time to spare for side issues; and my officers had less.

"But the person I am speaking of kept after me constantly. His idea was that the men needed recreation and needed it forthwith. He was there to provide this recreation without delay, and he couldn't understand why there should be any delay in attending to his wishes.

"Finally, to get rid of him, I gave orders that a noncommissioned officer and a squad of men should be taken away from whatever else they were doing and told off to aid our self-appointed amusement director in doing whatever it was he wanted done. It was the only way short of putting him under arrest that would relieve me of a common nuisance and leave my staff free to do their jobs.

"Well, it seemed that the young man had brought along with him a tent and a moving-picture outfit and a supply of knockdown seats. Under his direction the detail of men set up the tent on an open site which he selected upon the very top of a little hill, where it stood out against the sky line like a target; which, in a way of speaking, was exactly what it was. Then he installed his moving-picture machine and ranged his chairs in rows and announced that that evening there would be a free show. I may add that I knew nothing of this at the time, and inasmuch as the recreation man was known to be acting by my authority with a free hand no officer felt called upon to interfere, I suppose.

"The show started promptly on time, with a large and enthusiastic audience of enlisted men on hand and with the tent all lit up inside. In the midst of the darkness roundabout it must have loomed up like a lighthouse. Naturally there were immediate consequences.

"Before the first reel was halfway unrolled a boche flying man came sailing over, with the notion of making us unhappy in our underground shelters if he could. He found a shining mark waiting for him, so dropped a bomb at that tent. Luckily the bomb missed the tent, but it struck alongside of it and the concussion blew the canvas flat. The men came out from under the flattened folds and stampeded for the dugouts, wrecking the moving-picture machine in their flight. And the next day we were shy one amusement director. He had gone away from there."

In the Army itself there are exceedingly few members of the Bejones of Tuxedo family, and this, I take it, is a striking evidence of the average high intelligence of the men who have been chosen to officer our forces, considering that we started at scratch to mould millions of civilians into soldiers and considering also how necessary it was at the outset to issue a great number of commissions overnight, as it were. Howsomever, now and again a curious ornithological specimen does bob up, wearing shoulder straps.

A party of civilians, observers, were sent to France by a friendly power to have a look at our troops. When they reached General Headquarters they were being escorted by a beardless youth with the bars of a second lieutenant on his coat. He also wore two bracelets, one of gold and one of silver, on his right wrist. He also spoke with a fascinating lisp. He went straight to the office of the officer commanding the Intelligence Section.

"Colonel," he says, "I regard it as a great mistake to send me out here with this party. My work is really in Paris."

"Well," said the colonel, "you let Paris worry along without you as best it can while you toddle along and accompany these visiting gentlemen over such-and-such a sector. Oh, yes, there is one other thing: Kindly close the door behind you on your way out."

The braceleted one hid his petulance behind a salute, his jewelry meanwhile jingling pleasantly, and withdrew from the presence. For two days in an automobile he toured with his charge, at a safe distance behind the front lines. On the evening of the second day, when they reached the railroad station to await the train which would carry them back to Paris, he was heard to remark with a heartfelt but lispy sigh of relief: "Well, thank heaven for one thing anyhow—I have done my bit!"

Without being in possession of the exact facts I nevertheless hazard the guess that this young person either has been sent or shortly will be going back to his native land. Weeding-out is one of the best things this Army of our does. It would be well, in my humble judgment, if folks at home followed the Army's example in this regard, but conducted the weed-ing-out process over there.

For men and women who can be of real service, who can endure hardships without collapsing and without complaining, who can fend for themselves when emergencies arise, who are self-reliant, competent, well skilled in their vocations, there is need here in France in the Red Cross, in the Y. M. C. A., in the Y. M. H. A., in the K. of C., in the hospitals, in the telephone exchanges, the motor service, the ambulance service and in scores of other fields of departmental and allied activity. If these persons can speak a little French, so much the better.

But for the camouflaged malingerer, for the potential slacker, for the patriotic but unqualified zealot, for the incompetent one who mistakes enthusiasm for ability, and for the futile commission member there is no room whatsoever. This job of knocking the mania out of Germania is a big job, and the closer one gets to it the bigger it appears. We can't make it absolutely a fool-proof war, but by a proper discrimination exercised at home we can reduce the number of Americans in Europe for whose presence here there appears to be no valid excuse whatsoever.

P. S. I hope they read these few lines in Washington.

CHAPTER XVII
YOUNG BLACK JOE

YOU rode along a highroad that was built wide and ran straight, miles on, and through a birch forest that was very dense and yet somehow very orderly, as is the way with French highroads, and with French forests, too, and after a while you came to where the woods frazzled away from close-ranked white trunks into a fringing of lacy undergrowth, all giddy and all gaudy with wild flowers of many a colour.

Here, in a narrow clearing that traversed the thickets at right angles to the course you had been following, there disclosed himself a high-garbed North American mule, a little bit under weight, so that his backbone stood out sharply like the ridgepole of a roof pitched steep, with hollows by his hip joints to catch the rain water in. Viewing him astern or on the quarter you discerned that his prevalent architecture, though mixed, inclined to the mansard type. Viewing him bow-on you observed that he wore a gas mask upon his high and narrow temples and that from beneath this adornment, which would be startling elsewhere but which at the Front is both commonplace and customary, he contemplated the immediate foreground with half-closed, indolent eyes and altogether was as much at home as though his chin rested upon the hickory top rider of a snake fence in his native Ozarks instead of resting, as it did, athwart the crosspiece of a low signpost reading: "Danger Beyond—All Cars Halt Here! Proceed Afoot!"

You might be sure that never did any mule born in Missouri take his languid ease amid surroundings more unique for a mule to be in, inside or outside of that sovereign commonwealth. There was, to begin with, his gas mask, draped upon the spindled brow and ready, on warning, to be yanked down over the muzzle and latched fast beneath the throat; probably as a veteran mule he was used to that. But there were other things: High-velocity shells from a battery of six-inches somewhere in the woods to the west were going over his head at regular half-minute intervals, each in its passage making a sound as though everybody on earth in chorus had said "Whew-w-w-! "—like that. Merely by cocking an eyelid aloft he could have beheld, sundry thousands of feet up, three French combat planes hunting a German raider back to his own lines, the French motors humming steadily like honeybees but the German droning to a deeper note with sullen heavy rift tones breaking into its cadences, for all the world like one of those big noisy beetles that invade your bedchamber on a hot night. Merely by squinting straight ahead he could have seen at the farther edge of the little glade a triple row of white crosses, each set off by the wooden rosette device in red, white and blue with which the French, when given time, mark the graves of their fallen fighters. Merely by sniffing he could have caught from a mile distant the faint but unmistakable reek that hangs over battlefields when they are getting to be old battlefields but are not yet very old, and that nearly always distresses green work animals at the first time of taking it into their nostrils. None of these things he did though, but remained content and motionless save for his wagging ears and his switching tail and his uneasy lower lip. He was just standing there, letting the hot sunshine seep into him through all his pores.

Otherwise, however, his more adjacent settings were in a manner of speaking conventional and according to mules. For he was attached by virtue of an improvised gear of wire ropes and worn leather breeching to a small fiat car that bestraddled a rusty railroad track; and at his head stood a ginger-coloured youth of twenty years or thereabouts. In our own land you somehow expect, when you find a mule engaged in industry, to find an American of African antecedents managing him. So the combination was in keeping with the popular conception. Only in this instance the attendant youth wore part of a uniform and had a steel shrapnel helmet clamped down upon his skull.

Said youth caught a nod from a corporal of his own race who lounged against a broken wall, the wall being practically all that remained of what once had been the home of a crossings guard alongside a railroad that was a real railroad no longer; and at that he climbed nimbly on muleback.

He gathered up the guiding strings, and this then was the starting signal he gave as he showed all his teeth—he seemed to have fifty teeth at least—in a gorgeous and friendly grin: "All abo'd fur the Fifty-nint' Street crosstown line!"

By that you would have known, if you knew your New York at all, that this particular muleteer must hail from that nook of Li'l Ole Manhattan which since the days of the Yanko-Spanko war, when a certain group of black troopers did a certain valiant thing, has been called San Juan Hill, and that away off here where now he was, in the back edges of France, he had in his own mind at the moment a picture of West Fifty-ninth Street as it might look—and probably would—on this bright warm afternoon, stretching as a narrow band, biaswise, of the town from the Black Belt on the West Side with its abutting chop-suey parlours and its fragrant barber shops and its clubrooms for head and side waiters, on past Columbus Circle into the lighter coloured districts to the eastward; and likewise that since he did have the image in his mind he perhaps grinned his toothful grin to hide a pang of homesickness for the place where he belonged.

I figured that I knew these things, who had journeyed by motor with two more for a hundred and eighty miles across country to pay a visit to the first sector in our front lines that had been taken over by a regiment of negro volunteers—?-now by reason of departmental classifyings known as the Three Hundred and Somethingth of the American Expeditionary Forces. Because New York was where I also belonged, and this genial postilion was of a breed made familiar to me long time ago in surroundings vastly dissimilar to these present ones.

To the three of us word had come, no matter how, that negro troops of ours were in the line. No authoritative announcement to that effect having been forthcoming, we were at the first hearing of the news skeptical. To be sure the big movement overseas was at last definitely and audaciously under way; the current month's programme called for the landing on French soil of two hundred thousand Americans of fighting age and fighting dispositions, which contract, I might add, was carried out so thoroughly that not only the promised two hundred thousand but a good and heaping measure of nearly sixty thousand more on top of that arrived before the thirtieth. It is The Glory of the Coming all right, this great thing that has happened this summer over here, and I am glad that mine eyes have seen it. It is almost the finest thing that the eye of an American of this generation has yet seen or is likely to see before Germany herself is invaded.

But even though the sea lanes were streaky with the wakes of our convoys and the disembarkation ports cluttered with our transports, we doubted that coloured troops were as yet facing the enemy across the barbed-wire boundaries that separate him from us. Possibly this was because we had grown accustomed to thinking of our negroes as members of labour battalions working along the lines of communication—unloading ships and putting up warehouses and building depots and felling trees in the forests of France, which seem doomed to fall either through shelling or by the axes of the timbering crews of the Allies.

"You must be wrong," we said to him who brought us the report. "You must have seen an unusually big lot of negroes going up to work in the lumber camps in the woods at the north."

"No such thing," he said. "I tell you that we've got black soldiers on the job—at least two regiments of them. There's a draft regiment from somewhere down South, and another regiment from one of the Eastern

States—one of the old National Guard outfits I think it is—about fifteen miles to the east of the first lot. Here, I can show you about where they are—if anybody's got a map handy."

Everybody had a map handy. A correspondent no more thinks of moving about without a map than he thinks of moving about without a gas mask and a white paper, which is a pass. He wouldn't dare move without the mask; he couldn't move far without the pass, and the next to these two the map is the most needful part of his travelling equipment.

So that was how the quest started. As we came nearer to the somewhat indefinitely located spot for which we sought, the signs that we were on a true trail multiplied, in bits of evidence offered by supply-train drivers who told us they lately had met negro troopers on the march in considerable number. As a matter of fact there were then four black regiments instead of two taking up sector positions in our plan of defence. However, that fact was to develop later through a statement put forth with the approval of the censor at General Headquarters.

After some seven hours of reasonably swift travel in a high-powered car we had left behind the more peaceful districts back of the debatable areas and were entering into the edges of a village that had been shot to bits in the great offensive of 1914, which afterward had been partially rebuilt and which lately had been abandoned again, after the great offensive of 1918 started.

Right here from somewhere in the impending clutter of nondescript ruination we heard many voices singing all together. The song was a strange enough song for these surroundings. Once before in my life and only once I have heard it, and that was five years ago on an island off the coast of Georgia. I don't think it ever had a name and the author of it had somehow got the Crucifixion and the Discovery of America confused in his mind.

We halted the car behind the damaged wall of an abandoned garden, not wishing to come upon the unseen choristers until they had finished. Their voices rose with the true camp-meeting quaver, giving reverence to the lines:

> *In Fo'teen Hunnerd an' Ninety-one*
> *'Tuna den my Saviour's work begun.*

And next the chorus, long-drawn-out and mournful:

> *Oh, dey nailed my Saviour 'pen de cross,*
> *But he never spoke a mumblin' word.*

I was explaining to my companions, both of them Northern-born, that mumbling in the language of the tidewater darky means complaining and not what it means with us, but they bade me hush while we hearkened to the next two verses, each of two lines, with the chorus repeated after the second line:

In Fo'teen Hunnerd an' Ninety-two
My Lawd begin his work to do!

In F o'teen Hunnerd an' Ninety-three
Dey nailed my Saviour on de gallows tree.

And back to the first verse—there were only three verses, it seemed— and through to the third, over and over again.

An invisible choir leader broke in with a different song and the others caught it up. But this one we all knew—My Soul Bears Witness to de Lawd— so we started the machine and rode round from back of the wall. The singers, twenty or more of them, were lying at ease on the earth alongside a house in the bright, baking sunshine of a still young but very ardent summer. On beyond them everywhere the place swarmed with their fellows in khaki, some doing nothing at all and some doing the things that an American soldier, be he black or white, is apt to do when off duty in billets. Almost without exception they were big men, with broad shoulders and necks like bullocks, and their muscles bulged their sleeves almost to bursting. From the fact that nine out of ten were coal-black and from a certain intonation in their voices never found among up-country negroes, a man familiar with the dialects and the types of the Far South might know them for natives of the rice fields and the palmetto barrens of the coast. Lower Georgia and South Carolina—there was where they had come from plainly enough, with perhaps a sprinkling among them of Florida negroes. Our course, steered as it was by chance reckoning, had nevertheless been a true one.

We had found the draft outfit first. By the same token, if our original informant had been right, another negro regiment—of volunteers this time—would be found some fifteen miles to the eastward and northward of where we were; and this latter unit was the one whose whereabouts we mainly desired to discover, since, if it turned out to be the regiment we thought it must be, its colonel would be a personal friend of all three of us and his adjutant would be a former copy reader who had served on the staff of the same evening newspaper years before, with two of us.

We halted a while to pay our respects to the commander of these strapping big black men—a West Pointer, still in his thirties and inordinately proud of the outfit that was under him. He had cause to be. I used to think that sitting down was the natural gait of the tidewater darky; but here, as any one who looked might see, were soldiers who bore themselves as smartly, who were as snappy at the salute and as sharp set at the drill as any of their lighter-skinned fellow Americans in service anywhere. Most of the officers were Southern-born men, they having been purposely picked because of a belief that they would understand the negro temperament. That the choosing of Southern officers had been a sane choosing was proved already, I think, by what we saw as well as by things we heard that day. For example, one of the majors—a young Tennesseean—told us this tale, laughing while he told us:

"We've abolished two of our sentry posts in this town. Right over yonder, beyond what's left of the village church, is what's left of the village cemetery. I'll take you to see it if you care to go, though it's not a very pleasant sight. For a year or more back in 1914 and 1915 shells used to fall in it pretty regularly and rip open the graves and scatter the bones of those poor folks who were buried there—you know the sort of thing you're likely to find in any of these little places that have been under heavy bombardment. Well, when we moved here a week and a half ago and got settled a delegation from the ranks waited on the C. O. They told him that they had come over here to fight the Germans and that they were willing to fight the Germans and anxious to start the job right away, but that, discipline or no discipline, war or no war, orders or no orders, they just naturally couldn't be made to hang round a cemetery after dark.

"'Kernul, suh,' the spokesman said, 'ef you posts any of us cullud boys 'longside dat air buryin' ground, w'y long about midnight somethin'll happen an' you's sartain shore to be shy a couple of niggers when de mawnin' comes. Kernul, suh, we don't none of us wanter be shot fur runnin' 'way, but dat's perzactly whut's gwine happen ef ary one of us has to march back an' fo'th by dat place w'en de darkness of de night sets in.' And the colonel understood, and he took mercy on 'em, so that's why if the Germans should happen to arrive at night by way of the graveyard they could march right among us, probably without having a shot fired at them.

"But don't think our boys are afraid," the young major added with pride in his voice. "I'd take a chance on going anywhere with these black soldiers at my back. So would any of the rest of the officers. We haven't had any actual fighting experience yet—that'll come in a week or two when we relieve a French regiment that's just here in front of us holding the front lines—but we are not worrying about what'll happen when we get our baptism of fire. Only I'm afraid we're going to have a mighty disappointed regiment on our hands in about two months from now, when these black boys of ours find out that even in the middle of August watermelons don't grow in Northern France."

As we left the regimental headquarters, which was a half-shattered wine shop with breaches in the wall and less than half a roof to its top floor, the young major went along with us to our car to give our chauffeur better directions touching on a maze of cross roads along the last lap of the run.

En route he enriched my notebook with a lovely story, having the merit moreover—a merit that not all lovely stories have—of being true.

"Day before yesterday," so his narrative ran, "we began drilling the squads in grenade throwing—with live grenades. Up until then we'd exercised them only on dummy grenades, but now they were going to try out the real thing. We had batches of the new grenades—the kind that are exploded by striking the cap at the lower end upon something hard. You probably know how the drill is carried on: At the call of 'One' from the squad commander the men strike the cap ends against a stone or something; at 'Two' they draw back the thing full arm length, and at 'Three' they toss it with a stiff overhand swing. There's plenty of time of course for all this if nobody fumbles, because the way the fuses are timed five seconds elapse between the striking of the cap and the explosion. If you fling your grenade too soon a Heinie is liable to pick it up and throw it back at you before it goes off. If you hold it too long you're apt to lose an arm or your life. That's why we are so particular about timing the movements.

"Well, one squad lined up out here in a field with their eyes bulging out like china door knobs. They were game enough but they weren't very happy. The moment the word 'One' was given a little stumpy darky in my battalion that we call Sugar Foot flung his grenade as far as he could.

"When the rest of the grenades had been thrown the platoon commander jumped all over Sugar Foot. He said to him: 'Look here, what did you mean by throwing that grenade before these other boys threw theirs? Don't you know enough to wait for "Three" before you turn loose?'

"'Yas, suh, lieutenant,' says Sugar Foot; 'but I jes' natchelly had to th'ow it. W'y, lieutenant, I could feel dat thing a-swellin' in my hand.'"

It may have been the same Sugar Foot—assuredly it was the likes of him—who gave us the salute so briskly as we sped out of the village on the far side from the side on which we entered it. Followed then a swift coursing through a French-held sector wherein at each unfolding furlong of chalky-white highway we beheld sights which, being totted up, would have made enough to write a book about, say three years back. But three years back is ancient history in this war, and what once would have run into chapters is now worth no more than a paragraph, if that much.

At the end of this leg of the journey we were well out of the static zone and well into the active one. And so, after going near where sundry French batteries ding-donged away with six-inch shells—shrapnel, high explosives and gas in equal doses—at a German position five miles away, we emerged from the protecting screenage of forest after the fashion stated in the opening sentences of this chapter, and learned that we had landed where we had counted on landing when we started out.

It was the regiment we were looking for, sure enough. Its colonel, our friend, having been apprised by telephone from two miles rearward at one of his battalion headquarters that we were approaching, had sent word per runner that he waited to welcome us down at his present station just behind the forward observation posts.

So we climbed aboard the one piece of rolling stock that was left astride the metals of a road over which, until August of 1914, transcontinental trains had whizzed, and the ginger-colored humourist slapped the sloping withers of his steed and that patient brute flinched a protesting flinch that ran through his frame from neck to flanks, and we were off for the front trenches by way of the Fifty-ninth Street cross-town line on as unusual a journey as I, for one, have taken since coming over here to this war-worn country, where the unusual thing is the common thing these days. Off with an ex-apartment-house doorman from San Juan Hill, New York City, for our steersman; a creaking small flat car for a chariot; a homegrown mule for motive power; a Yankee second lieutenant and a French liaison officer for added passengers; and for special scenic touches alongside the bramble-grown cut through which we jogged, machine guns so mounted as to command aisles chopped through the thickets, and three-inch guns plying busily at an unseen objective. To this add the whewful remarks let fall in passing by the big ones from farther back as they conversed among themselves on their way over to annoy the Him, and at intervals aërial skirmishes occurring away up overhead—'twas a braw and a bonny day for aërial fighting, as a stage Scotchman might say—and you will have a fairly complete picture of the ensemble in your own mind, I trust. But don't forget to stir in the singing of birds and the buzzing of insects.

The negro troopers we encountered now, here in the copses, sometimes singly or oftener still in squads and details, were dissimilar physically as well as in certain temperamental respects to their fellows of the draft regiment we had seen a little while before. They were apt to be mulattoes or to have light-brown complexions instead of clear black; they were sophisticated and town wise in their bearing; their idioms differed from those others, and their accents too; for almost without exception they were city dwellers and many of them had been born North, whereas the negroes from Dixie were rural products drawn out of the heart of the Farther South. But for all of them might be said these things: They were soldiers who wore their uniforms with a smartened pride; who were jaunty and alert and prompt in their movements; and who expressed, as some did vocally in my hearing, and all did by their attitude, a sincere and heartfelt inclination to get a whack at the foe with the shortest possible delay. I am of the opinion personally—and I make the assertion with all the better grace, I think, seeing that I am a Southerner with all of the Southerner's inherited and acquired prejudices touching on the race question—that as a result of what our black soldiers are going to do in this war, a word that has been uttered billions of times in our country, sometimes in derision, sometimes in hate, sometimes in all kindliness—but which I am sure never fell on black ears but it left behind a sting for the heart—is going to have a new meaning for all of us, South and North too, and that hereafter n-i-g-g-e-r will merely be another way of spelling the word American.

However, that is getting in the moral of my tale before I am anywhere near its proper conclusion. The reader consenting, we'll go back to the place where we were just now, when we rode over the one-mule traffic line to the greeting that had been organised for us two miles away. By chance we had chosen a most auspicious moment for our arrival. For word had just been received touching on the honours which the French Government had been pleased to confer upon two members of the regiment, Henry Johnson and Needham Roberts, to wit, as follows: For each the War Cross and for each a special citation before the whole French Army, and in addition a golden palm, signifying extraordinary valour, across the red-and-green ribbon of Johnson's decoration. So it was shortly coming to pass that a negro, almost surely, would be the first private of the American Expeditionary Forces to get a golden palm along with his Croix de Guerre. It might be added, though the statement is quite superfluous in view of the attendant circumstances, that he earned it.

Through the cable dispatches which my companions straightway sent, they being correspondents for daily papers, America learned how Johnson and Roberts, two comparatively green recruits, were attacked at night in a front-line strong point by a raiding party estimated to number between twenty and twenty-five; and how after both had been badly wounded and after Roberts had gone down with a shattered leg he, lying on his back, flung hand grenades with such effect that he blew at least one of the raiders to bits of scrap meat; and how Johnson first with bullets, then with his clubbed rifle after he had emptied it, and finally with his bolo gave so valiant an account of himself that the attacking party fled back to their own lines, abandoning most of their equipment and carrying with them at least five of their number, who had been either killed outright or most despitefully misused by the valiant pair. If ever proof were needed, which it is not, that the colour of a man's skin has nothing to do with the colour of his soul these twain then and there offered it in abundance.

The word of what the French military authorities meant to do having been received, it had spread, and its lesson was bearing fruit.

So we found out when the colonel took us on a journey through the forward trenches. Every other private and every other noncom. we ran across had his rifle apart and was carefully oiling it. If they were including the coloured boys now when it came to passing round those crosses he meant to get one too, and along with it a mess of Germans—Bush-Germans, by his way of expression. The negro soldier in France insists on pronouncing boche as Bush, and on coupling the transmogrified word to the noun German, possibly because the African mind loves mouth-filling phrases or perhaps just to make all the clearer that, according to his concepts, every boche is a German and every German is a boche.

As we passed along we heard one short and stumpy private, with a complexion like the bottom of a coal mine and a smile like the sudden lifting of a piano lid, call out to a mate as he fitted his greased rifle together:

"Henry Johnson, he done right well, didn't he? But say, boy, effen they'll jes gimme a razor an' a armload of bricks an' one half pint of bust-haid licker I kin go plum to Berlin."

CHAPTER XVIII
"LET'S GO!"

THE most illuminating insight of all, into the strengthened ambition which animated the rank and file of the Old Fifteenth was vouchsafed to us as we three, following along behind the tall shape of the Colonel, rounded a corner of a trench and became aware of a soldier who sat cross-legged upon his knees with his back turned to us and was so deeply intent upon the task in hand that he never heeded our approach at all. On a silent signal from our guide we tiptoed near so we could look downward over the bent shoulders of the unconscious one and this, then, was what we saw:

A small, squarely built individual, of the colour of a bottle of good cider-vinegar, who balanced upon his knees a slab of whitish stone—it looked like a scrap of tombstone and I am inclined to think that is what it was—and in his two hands, held by the handle, a bolo with a nine-inch blade. First he would anoint the uppermost surface of the white slab after the ordained fashion of those who use whetstones, then industriously he would hone his blade; then he would try its edge upon his thumb and then anoint and whet some more. And all the while, under his breath, he crooned a little wordless, humming song which had in it some of the menace of a wasp's petulant buzzing. He was making war-medicine. A United States soldier whose remote ancestors by preference fought hand to hand with their enemies, was qualifying to see Henry Johnson and go him one better. The picture was too sweet a one to be spoiled by breaking in on it. We slipped back out of sight so quietly the knife-sharpener could never have suspected that spying eyes had looked in upon him as he engaged in these private devotions of his.

"They're all like that buddy with the bolo, and some of them are even more so," said the colonel after we had tramped back again to the dugout in a chalk cliff, which he temporarily occupied as a combination parlour, boudoir, office, breakfast room and headquarters. "We were a pretty green outfit when they brought us over here. Why, even after we got over to France some of my boys used to write me letters tendering their resignations, to take effect immediately. They had come into the service of their own free will—as volunteers in the National Guard—so when they got tired of soldiering, as a few of them did at first, they couldn't understand why they shouldn't go out of their own free wills.

"They used us on construction work down near one of the ports for a while after we landed. Then here a couple of weeks ago they sent us up to take over this sector. The men are fond of saying that all they had by way of preparation for the job was four days' drilling and a haircut.

"Did I say just now that we were green? Well, that doesn't half describe it, let me tell you. This sector was calm enough, as frontline sectors go, when we took it over. But the first night my fellows had hardly had time enough to learn to find their way about the trenches when from a forward rifle pit a rocket of a certain colour went up, 'signifying: 'We are being attacked by tanks.'

"It gave me quite a shock, especially as there had been no artillery preparation from Fritz's side of the wire, and besides there is a swamp between the lines right in front of where that rifle pit is, so I didn't exactly see how tanks were going to get across unless the Germans ferried them over in skiffs. So before calling out the regiment I decided to make a personal investigation. But before I had time to start on it two more rockets went up from another rifle pit at the left of the first one, and according to the code these rockets meant: 'Lift your barrage—we are about to attack in force.' Since we hadn't been putting down any barrage and there was no reason for an attack and no order for one this gave me another shock. So I put out hot-foot to find out what was the matter.

"It seemed a raw recruit in the first pit had found a box of rockets. Just for curiosity, I suppose, or possibly because he wished to show the Bush-Germans that he regarded the whole thing as being in the nature of a celebration, or maybe because he just wanted to see what would happen afterward, he touched off one of them. And then a fellow down the line seeing this rocket decided, I guess, that a national holiday of the French was being observed and so he touched off two. But it never will happen again.

"The very next night we had a gas alarm two miles back of here in the next village, where one of my battalions is billeted. It turned out to be a false alarm, but all through the camp the sentries were sounding their automobile horns as a warning for gas masks. But Major Blank's orderly didn't know the meaning of the signals, or if he did know he forgot it in the excitement of the moment. Still he didn't lose his head altogether. As he heard the sound of the tootings coming nearer and nearer he dashed into the major's billet—the major is a very sound sleeper—and grabbed him by the shoulder and shook him right out of his blankets. "'Wake up, major!' he yelled, trying to keep on shaking with one hand and to salute with the other. 'Fur Gawd's sake, suh, wake up. The Germans is comin'—in automobiles!'

"Oh yes, they were green at the start; but they are as game as any men in this man's Army are. You take it from me, because I know. They weren't afraid of the cold and the wet and the terrific labour when they worked last winter down near the coast of France on as mean a job of work as anybody ever tackled. They were up to their waists in cold water part of the time—yes, most of the time they were—but not a one of them flinched. And believe me there's no flinching among them now that we are up against the Huns! You don't need the case of Johnson and Roberts to prove it. It is proved by the attitude of every single man among them. It isn't hard to send them into danger—the hard part is to keep them from going into it on their own accord. They say the dark races can't stand the high explosives— that their nerves go to pieces under the strain of the terrific concussion. If that be so the representatives of the dark races that come from America are the exceptions to the rule. My boys are getting fat and sassy on a fare of bombings and bombardments, and we have to watch them like hawks to keep them from slipping off on little independent raiding parties without telling anybody about it in advance. Their real test hasn't come yet, but when it does come you take a tip from me and string your bets along with this minstrel troupe to win.

"My men have a catch phrase that has come to be their motto and their slogan. Tell any one of them to do a certain thing and as he gets up to go about it he invariably says, 'Let's go!' Tell a hundred of them to do a thing and they'll say the same thing. I hear it a thousand times a day. The mission may involve discomfort or the chance of a sudden and exceedingly violent death. No matter—'Let's go!' that's the invariable answer. Personally I think it makes a pretty good maxim for an outfit of fighting men, and I'll stake my life on it that they'll live up to it when the real trial comes."

Two days we stayed on there, and they were two days of a superior variety of continuous black-face vaudeville. There was the evening when for our benefit the men organised an impromptu concert featuring a quartet that would succeed on any man's burlesque circuit, and a troupe of buck-and-wing dancers whose equals it would be hard to find on the Big Time. There was the next evening when the band of forty pieces serenaded us. I think surely this must be the best regimental band in our Army. Certainly it is the best one I have heard in Europe during this war. On parade when it played the Memphis Blues the men did not march; the music poured in at their ears and ran down to their heels, and instead of marching they literally danced their way along. As for the dwellers of the French towns in which this regiment has from time to time been quartered, they, I am told, fairly go mad when some alluring, compelling, ragtime tune is played with that richness of syncopated melody in it which only the black man can achieve; and as the regiment has moved on, more than once it has been hard to keep the unattached inhabitants of the village that the band was quitting from moving on with it.

If I live to be a hundred and one I shall never forget the second night, which was a night of a splendid, flawless full moon. We stood with the regimental staff on the terraced lawn of the chief house in a half-deserted town five miles back from the trenches, and down below us in the main street the band played plantation airs and hundreds of negro soldiers joined in and sang the words. Behind the masses of upturned dark faces was a ring of white ones where the remaining natives of the place clustered, with their heads wagging in time to the tunes.

And when the band got to Way Down Upon the Swanee River I wanted to cry, and when the drum major, who likewise had a splendid barytone voice, sang, as an interpolated number, Joan of Arc, first in English and then in excellent French, the villagers openly cried; and an elderly peasant, heavily whiskered, with the tears of a joyous and thankful enthusiasm running down his bearded cheeks, was with difficulty restrained from throwing his arms about the soloist and kissing him. When this type of Frenchman feels emotion he expresses it moistly.

Those two days we heard stories without number, all of them true, I take it, and most of them good ones. We heard of the yellow youth who beseeched his officer to send him with a "dang'ous message" meaning by that that he craved to go on a perilous mission for the greater glory of the A. E. F. and incidentally of himself; and about the jaunty individual who pulled the firing wire of a French grenade and catching the hissing sound of the fulminator working its way toward the charge exclaimed: "That's it—fry, gosh dem you, fry!" before he threw it. And about how a sergeant on an emergency trench-digging job stuck to the task, standing hip-deep in icy water and icy mud, until from chill and exhaustion he dropped unconscious and was like to drown in the muck into which he had collapsed head downward, only his squad discovered him up-ended there and dragged him out; and about many other things small or great, bespeaking fortitude and courage and fidelity and naïve Afric waggery.

Likewise into my possession came copies of two documents, both of which I should say are typical just as each is distinctive of a different phase of the negro temperament. One of them, the first one, was humorous. Indeed to my way of thinking it was as fine an example of unconscious humour as this war is likely to produce. The other was—well, judge for yourself.

Before the regiment moved forward for its dedication to actual warfare it was impressed upon the personnel in the ranks that from now on, more even than before, a soldier in his communications with his superior officer must use the formal and precise language of military propriety. The lesson must have sunk in, because on the thrillsome occasion when a certain private found himself for the first time in a forward rifle pit and for the first time heard German rifle bullets whistling past his ears he called to him a runner and dispatched to the secondary lines this message, now quoted exactly as written except that the proper names have been changed:

"Lieutenant Sidney J. McClelland,

"Commanding Company B, —, A. E. F.,

U. S. A.

"Dear Sir: I am being fired on heavily from the left.
I await your instructions.

"Trusting these few lines will find you the same,

I remain, Yours truly,

"Jefferson Jones."

The other thing was an extract from a letter written by an eighteen-year-old private to his old mother in New York, with no idea in his head when he wrote it that any eyes other than those of his own people would read it after it had been censored and posted. The officer to whom it came for censoring copied from it one paragraph, and this paragraph ran like this:

"Mammy, these French people don't bother with no colour-line business. They treat us so good that the only time I ever knows I'm coloured is when I looks in the glass."

Coming away—and we came reluctantly—we skirted the edge of the billeting area where the regiment of Southern negroes was quartered, and again we heard them singing. But this time they sang no plaintive meeting-house air. They sang a ringing, triumphant, Glory-Glory-Hallelujah song. For—so we learned—to them the word had come that they were about to move up and perhaps come to grips with the Bush-Germans. Yes, most assuredly n-i-g-g-e-r is going to have a different meaning when this war ends.

CHAPTER XIX
WAR AS IT ISN'T

THREE of us, correspondents, had gone up with a division of ours that was taking over one of the Picardy sectors. The French, moved out by degrees as we by degrees moved in. On the night when we actually came into the front lines two of us slept—or tried to—in a house of a village perhaps a mile and a half behind the forward trenches. The third man went on perhaps a half mile nearer the trouble zone with a battalion of an infantry regiment that on the morrow would relieve some sorely battered poilus in the trenches. It is with an experience of this third man I now mean to deal.

He found lodgment in a château on the outskirts of a village the name of which does not matter—and probably never will matter again, seeing that it fairly was blasted out of the earth by its foundations the next time the Germans attempted to resume their advance toward the Channel. As for the château, which likewise must be quite gone by now, it was more of a château than some of the buildings that go by this high-sounding title in the edges of Normandy.

A château may mean a veritable castle of a place, with towers upon it and a moat and gardens and terraces and trout ponds round about it. Then again on the other hand it may mean merely a sizable private residence, standing somewhat aloof in its own plot from the close-huddled clustering of lesser folks' cottages that make up the town proper. The term is almost as elastic in its classifications as the word estate is in America. In this instance, though, the château was a structure of some pretensions and much consequence. Rather, it had been when its owner fled before the great spring advance, leaving behind him all that he owned except a few portable belongings. The neighbours had run away, too, and for months now the only tenants of the vicinity had been troops.

French officers and a few American officers were occupying the château. Every room and every hallway was crowded already, but space for the correspondent to spread down his bedding roll was provided in an inner chamber on the second floor. At two o'clock in the morning, by consent of the divisional commander, he was going out into the debatable land between the trenches with a wire-mending party. There is always a chance that a wire party will bump into a squad of enemies on the prowl or surprise a raiding outfit from Fritzie's trenches, and then there are doings to ensue.

Two o'clock was four hours off and the special guest hoped to get a little sleep in the 'tween times. It was a vain hope, because, to judge by their behaviour, the Germans had found out a relief division was on its way in. Since nightfall they had been shelling the back areas of the sector, and particularly the lines of communication, with might and main—and six-inch guns. For the most part the shells were passing entirely over and far beyond the château, but they made quite as much noise as though they had been dropping in the courtyard outside—more noise, as a matter of seeming, because the screech of a big shell in its flight overhead racks the eardrums as the crash of the explosion rarely does unless the explosion occurs within a few rods of one.

So for four hours or thereabouts our correspondent lay on his pallet, wide-eyed, and with every nerve in his body standing on end and wriggling. When the French liaison officer who had volunteered to escort him on the adventure rapped upon his door he was quite ready to start. He had taken off nothing except his trench helmet and his gas mask before turning in, anyhow.

"Walk very quietly, if you please," bade the Frenchman, leading the way out, with a pocket flashlight in his hand.

Obeying the request the correspondent tiptoed along behind his guide. To get outdoors they passed through two other rooms and down a flight of stairs and along a hallway opening into the wrecked garden. In the beds that were in the rooms and upon blankets on the floors of the rooms and also in the hallway French officers were stretched, exhaling the heavy breaths of men who have worked hard and who need the rest they are taking. Only one man stirred, and that was downstairs as the pair who were departing picked their way between the double rows of sleepers. A loose plank creaked sharply under the weight of the American, and a man stirred in his coverlids and opened his eyes for a moment; and then, turning over, was off again almost instantly.

At that, understanding came to the correspondent—he knew now why the thoughtful liaison officer had cautioned him to step lightly. To these men lying here about him the infernal clamour of the shells had become a customary part of their lives, whether waking or sleeping. To their natures, accustomed as they were to it, this hideous din was a lullaby song. But any small unusual sound, such as the noise of a booted foot falling upon a squeaky board, might rouse them, and two men clumping carelessly past them would have brought every one of them out of his slumbers, sitting up.

Paradoxes such as this are forever cropping up in one's wartime experiences. Indeed, war may be said to be made up of countless paradoxes, overlapping and piled one upon another. To me the most striking of the outstanding manifestations of war on its paradoxical side is the fact that in this war nothing, or almost nothing, actually turns out in accordance with what one's idea of it had been beforehand. Looking backward on what I myself have viewed of its physical and metaphysical aspects I can think of scarcely an element or a phase which accorded with my preconceived brain image of the thing. I do not mean by this that as a spectacle it has been disappointing, but that almost invariably it has been different from what I was expecting it would be. I found this to be true in 1914, back at the very beginning.

Take for example the fashion after which men bear themselves as they go into battle; and, for a more striking illustration than that, their customary deportment after they actually are in the battle. I figure that beforehand my own notion of what these two demonstrations would be like was based probably in part upon conceptions derived from old-time pictures of Civil War engagements, highly coloured, highly imaginative representations such as used to hang upon the parlour walls of every orthodox rural home in our country; and in part upon fiction stories with war for a background which I had read; and finally perhaps in some lesser part upon the moving-picture man's ideas as worked out with more or less artistic license in the pre-war films. I rather think the average stay-at-home's notions in these regards must be pretty much what mine were, because he probably derived them from the same sources. The utter dissimilarity of the actual thing as I have repeatedly viewed it in three countries of Europe astonished me at first, and in lessening degree continued to astonish me until the real picture of it had supplanted the conjured one in my mind.

If the reader's ideas are still fundamentally organised as mine formerly were he thinks men on the edge of the fight, with the prospect before them of very shortly being at grips with the enemy, maintain a sober and a serious front, wearing upon them the look of men who are upborne and inspired by a purpose to acquit themselves steadfastly and well. By the same process of reasoning I take it that the reader, conceding he or she has never been brought face to face with war, pictures men on the march in periods of comparative immunity from immediate peril as singing their way along, with jokes and catchwords flitting back and forth and a general holidaying air pervading the scene presented by the swinging column. Now my observation has been that the exact opposite is commonly the case.

Men on the casual march, say, from one billeting place to another, are apt to push ahead stolidly and for the most part in silence. It is hard work, marching under heavy equipment is, and after a few hours of it the strongest individual in the ranks feels the pangs of weariness in his scissoring legs and along his burdened back. So he bends forward from the hips and he hunches his shoulders and wastes mighty little of his breath in idle persiflage. Only toward the end of the journey, when rest and food are in impending prospect, do his spirits revive to a point where he feels like singing and guying his mates. The thud-thud-thud of the feet upon the highroad, the grunted commands of the officers, and the occasional clatter of metal striking against metal as a man shifts his piece are likely to be the only accompaniments of the hike for miles on end; and there isn't much music really in such sounds as these.

But suppose the same men are moving into action and know whither they are bound. The preliminary nervousness that possesses every normally constituted man at the prospect of facing the deadliest forms of danger now moves these men to hide their true emotions under a masking of gaiety. This gaiety, which largely is assumed at the outset, presently becomes their real mood. Nine men out of ten who pass are indulging in quips and catches. Nine in ten are ready to laugh at trivialities that ordinarily would go unnoticed. One standing by to watch them must diagnose the average expression on the average face as betokening exultation rather than exaltation. The tenth man is quiet and of a thoughtful port. He is forcing himself to appraise the situation before him in its right proportions, and so the infection that fills his comrades passes him by. Yet it is safe to bet on it that the sober one-tenth, in the high hour of the grapple, will contend with just as much gallantry as the nine-tenths can hope to show.

Particularly is the mental slant that I have here sought to describe true in its application to raw troops who have yet to taste of close-up fighting. Seasoned veterans who have weathered the experience before now and who know what it means, and know, too, that they may count upon themselves and their fellows to acquit themselves valorously, are upborne by a certain all-pervading cheerfulness—perhaps as a rule confidence would be a better word than cheerfulness—but they are not quite so noisy, not quite so enthusiastic as the greener hands. At this moment they are not doing very much in the cheering line, though they will yell just as loudly as any when the order is to fix bayonets and charge.

Paradoxically the reaction upon men who have come whole out of the inferno of battling at close quarters affects these two compared classes of soldier-men differently—at least that has been my observation. The unseasoned men, to whom the hell from which they have just emerged has been for them a new kind of hell, are as likely as not almost downcast in their outward demeanour, irritable and peevish in their language. For one thing, they are dog-tired; for another, I would say, a true appreciation of the ordeal through which they have passed is now coming home to them; for still another, the shock of having seen their mates wiped out all about them surely affects the general consciousness of the survivors; and finally, as I appraise their sensations, the calm following the tumult and the struggle leaves them well-nigh numbed. Certainly it frequently leaves them inarticulate almost to dumbness. Give them twenty-four hours for rest and mental adjustment, and the coltishness of youth returns to them in ample measure, especially if there is a victory to their credit.

On the contrasting hand, if you want to witness an exhibition of good cheer at the end of a day of fighting seek for it among the veterans. On a certain day in May when the second of the great German drives was in progress I chanced to be at a spot where a brigade of French infantry—a brigade with a magnificent record made earlier in the war—was thrown into action to reenforce a hard-pressed and decimated British command. Almost without exception the little dusty, rusty poilus went to the fighting in a sort of matter-of-fact methodical silence more impressive to me than loud outbursts could possibly have been. Quietly, swiftly, without lost motion or vain exclamations, but moving all like men intent upon the performance of a difficult and an unpleasant but a highly necessary task, they took up their guns, adjusted their packs of ammunition, set their helmets over their foreheads, and walked with no undue haste but only with an assured and briskened serenity into the awfulness that was beyond the clouds of smoke and dust, just yonder.

That same evening, by a streak of luck, I returned to approximately the same spot at the moment when those who were left of the Frenchmen prepared to bivouac on the edges of the same terrain where all the afternoon they had fought. With the help of some skeleton formations of British companies they had withstood the German onslaught; more than that, they had broken two advancing waves of the gray coats and finally had swept the ripped and riddled legions of the enemy back for a good mile, so that now they held the field as victors. Elsewhere along that fifty-mile front there might be a different story to tell, but here in this small corner of the great canvas of the mighty battle a localised success that was worth while had been achieved by these heroes. Under them now their legs quivered from stark weariness. Some were black like negroes; the stale sweat and the dried dirt and the powder grit had caked them over. Some were red like Indians, where the crusted blood from small unconsidered wounds dyed the skin on their faces and their hands.

Now with the fog of fighting turning grey upon their unwashed bodies they sprawled on the stained and trodden meadow grass alongside the road, looking, with their figures foreshortened by lying, most absurdly like exceedingly dirty small boys who had been playing at soldiering. Yet spent and worn as they were they gibed us as we passed, and with uplifted canteens they toasted us—presumably in the thin Pinard; and they sang songs without number and they uttered spicy Gallic jokes at the expense of the mess cooks for their tardiness in making ready the supper stews. The job of the day was done with and ended; it was a fit time for being merry, and these little men were most exceedingly merry.

Such was the excess of their jollifying that had one not known better one might have suspected that they had been drinking something stronger than the thin wine ration upon which no Frenchman ever gets drunk. I recall one stunted chap who reeled and staggered as he made his way toward our halted car to ask us for news from the eastward. He had stuck into the sooted muzzle of his rifle a sheaf of wild flowers; and reeling and rocking on his heels he sought to embrace us when we offered him cigarettes. He was tipsy all right; but not with liquor—with emotion; the sort of emotion that temporarily befuddles a fighting man who has fought well and who is glad to have finished fighting for the time being, at least. As we left him he was propped upon his short unsteady legs at the roadside singing the song that your poilu always by preference sings when his mood inclines to the blithesome; he sang the Madelon.

Right here, I think, is a good enough time for me to say that in these times the place to hear the Marseillaise hymn played or sung is not France but America. In America one hears it everywhere—the hand organs play it, the theatre orchestras play it, the military bands play it, pretty ladies sing it at patriotic concerts. In France in seven months I have heard it just twice— once in the outskirts of the great battle on March twenty-sixth, just outside of Soissons, when a handful of French soldiers hurrying up to the fight were moved by some passing fancy, which we who heard them could not fathom, to chant a verse or two of the song; and again on Memorial Day, when an American band played it in a French burying ground at a coast town where the graves of three hundred of our own soldiers were decorated.

It may be that the Frenchman has grown wearied of the sound of his national air, or it may be—and this, I think, is the proper explanation— that in this time of stress and suffering for his land the Marseillaise hymn has for him become a thing so high and so holy that he holds it for sacred moments, to be rendered then as the accompaniment for a sacrificial rite of the spirit and of the soul. At any rate it is true that except on the one occasion I have just mentioned I have yet to hear the French soldier in the field sing the Marseillaise hymn. He much prefers his cheerful chansons, and when an American band plays for him it is a jazz tune that most surely may be counted upon to make him cry *"Encore! "*

As illustrative of the difference in temperament between the veteran and the beginner at war I should like to describe what many times I have witnessed as an incident in the streets of Paris. All through the past spring and the early part of the summer the members of the class of 1919 were holding celebrations in commemoration of the fact that they were about to be called to the service. Their emblematic colour for this year is red, and their chosen flower is the poppy, so the youngsters call themselves Coquelicots, which is the French name for the crimson wild poppy that grows everywhere in France. The class of 1918, who went out last year, were Pâquerettes—white daisies; and those of 1917 were Bluets, or cornflowers. Every three years the fancy repeats itself in the same sequence and the same cycle, so that the trinity of the national colours may be preserved.

Almost any hour, day or night, one might see troops of those about to be mobilised—schoolboys of eighteen, apprentice lads, peasant youths, cadets of military academies—parading the avenues. They wore all manner of fantastic garbings, with enormous red neckties and red sashes, and battered high hats banded with red, and with poppies stuck in their buttonholes or festooned in garlands about their necks. And always they were singing and skylarking, marching with fantastic jig steps in grotesque queue formations, and playing pranks upon the pedestrians who got in their way. The sight made an American think of college fraternities conducting outdoor initiations. The scene gave colour and the sparkle of youthful exuberance to a city where the sad sights are commoner than the happy ones.

It was inevitable that in every few rods of their progress the youngsters would encounter soldiers on leave, and then the boys, dropping for a moment their joyousness, would gravely salute the veterans, and the veterans as gravely would return the salute. Then the roisterers would whirl off down the sidewalk waving their exaggerated walking sticks and kicking up their heels as is the way with youth the world over, and the soldiers in their stained patched tunics, and their worn leather housings, and with their worn resolute faces—how often I have seen this little byplay repeated!—would exchange swift expressive glances with one another and smile meaning, sad little smiles, and shake their heads in a sort of passive resignation to the inevitable, before they went trudging on in their heavy, run-down, shabby boots. They knew—these war-worn elders did—what the chosen man children of the generation just emerging from the first stages of its adolescence would very shortly be called upon to face; and so they shook their heads in silent but regretful affirmation of the certain prospect of an added burden of woefulness and suffering for the flowered youth of their stricken land. For these men who had trod the paths of glory that are so flinty and so hard could understand what must lie ahead so much better than those stripling lads to whom the road to war was as yet a shining and a golden highway!

Have you ever seen at the movies a film purporting to show an actual scene in the trenches under hostile fire, wherein the men on guard there all faced, with squinted eyes and scowling brows, across the parapets, fingering their weapons nervously, and rarely or never glanced toward the camera, but seemingly were so absorbed in their ambitions to pot the foeman across the way they had no thought for anything except the tragic undertaking in hand? Then again, have you ever seen another so-called war reel with a similar setting, which brought before you the figures of soldiers who from behind the shelter of the piled-up sandbags grinned self-consciously in the direction of the machine that was recording their forms and their movements for back-home consumption, and who between intervals of loading and firing deported themselves pretty much as any group of sheepishly pleased young men might while under the eye of a photographing machine and who for the moment appeared to be more inspired by a perfectly normal human impulse to show off than by any other thought?

Now I have seen both these varieties of pictures and assuming that the reader has, too, I put to him or her this question: Granting that one of these films was the genuine article, namely, a view of a section of a front-line trench taken at risk of the operator's life; and that the other was a manufactured thing, with carefully rehearsed supers made up as soldiers posing in obedience to a hired director's orders, which one, in the reader's opinion, was the authentic thing and which the bogus?

If I have figured the probable answer aright the probable answer is wrong. The picture in which the soldiers behaved in conformity with the average civilian's notion of the way a soldier does behave under fire—to wit, by being all intent upon the job of shooting, with no regard for any lesser diversions—was the imitation; and the film in which you saw the soldiers crowding forward in the narrow trench way in order to be sure of getting into the focus area—the one where you saw the soldiers grinning toward you and winking and nudging their fellows and generally behaving like curious and embarrassed children—well, that was the genuine article.

For the fact of the matter is that once the novelty of his new environment has worn off—and it does wear off with marvellous speed—the soldier in the front-line trench carries on after identically the same patterns that would govern him under ordinary circumstances. The detail that he is in a place of imminent danger becomes to him of secondary importance. Except for the chance that any moment he may stop a bullet his mode of habit resolves itself back to its familiar elements. He is bored or he is interested by exactly the same things that would bore him or excite him anywhere else. To him the shooting back and forth across the top very soon becomes a more or less tedious part of the daily routine of the trench life, but the intrusion into his corner of a moving-picture man with a camera is a novelty, an event very much out of the ordinary; therefore he pays much more attention to the taking of the picture than to what goes on pretty steadily during practically all of his waking hours.

For added qualities of seeming indifference to externals in the midst of great and stirring exertions, see the artillerymen who serve with the heavies. Generally things are fairly lively among those dainty, darling, death-dealing pets that are called the 75's. Under their camouflaging they look like speckled pups when they do not look like spotted circus ponies. It is a brisksome and a heartening thing to see how fast a crew of Frenchmen can serve a battery of these little pintos, feeding the three-inch shells into the pieces with such celerity that at a distance the reports merge together so one might almost imagine he heard the voice of an overgrown machine gun speaking, instead of the intermingled voices of five separate trouble makers. Near Compiègne one day I watched a battery of 75's at work on the Germans advancing in mass formation, I keeping count of the reports; and the average number of shots per minute per gun was twelve.

But the heavies work more slowly, and their crews have a sluggish look about them as befitting men who do their fighting all at long range and never see the foe; though I suspect the underlying reason to be that they have learned to combine the maximum of efficiency and of accuracy with the minimum of apparent effort and the minimum of apparent enthusiasm. Particularly is this to be said in cases where the gunners have become expert through long practice.

On the Montdidier Front on a gloriously beautiful afternoon of early summer I kept company for two hours with three French batteries of 155's. The guns were ranged in dirt emplacements under a bank alongside a sunken road that meandered out from the main street of a village that was empty except for American and French soldiers. The Germans were four miles away, beyond a ridge of low hills. By climbing to the crest of the nearermost rise and lying there in the rank grass and looking through glasses one could make out the German lines. Without glasses one could mark fairly well where the shells from our side fell. But during the time I stayed there no single man among the artillerymen manifested any desire whatsoever to ascertain the visible effects of his handiwork.

Over the ground telephone an order would come from somewhere or other, miles away. The officer in command of one of the batteries would sing out the order to fire so many rounds at such and such intervals. The angles—the deflections for charge temperature, air temperature, barometer pressure and wind—had all been worked out earlier in the day, and a few corrections for range were required. So all the men had to do was to fire the guns. And that literally was all that they did do.

Not all the explosions in that immediate vicinity were caused by "departs," either. Occasionally there were to be heard the unmistakable whistle and roar and the ultimate crack of an "arrive," for the Germans' counterbatteries did not remain silent under the punishment the French were dealing out. But when an arrive fell anywhere within eye range the men barely turned their heads to see the column of earth and dust and pulverised chalk-rock go geysering up into the air. It was only by chance I found out an enemy shell had fallen that morning among a gun crew stationed near the westerly end of the line of guns, perhaps a quarter of a mile away, and had blown seven men to bits and wounded as many more.

Still, this apathy with regard to the potential consequences of being where an arrive bursts is not confined to the gunners. When one has had opportunity to see how many shells fall without doing any damage to human beings, and to figure out for oneself how many tons of metal it takes to kill a man, one likewise acquires a measure of this same apparent nonchalance.

For sheer sang-froid it would be hard to match those whose work I watched that day. In intervals of activity they lounged under the gun wheels, smoking and playing card games; and when one battery was playing and another temporarily was silent the members of the idle battery paid absolutely no heed to the work of their fellows.

In two hours just one thing and only one thing occurred to jostle them out of their calm. Something mysterious and very grievous befell a half-grown dog, which, having been abandoned or forgotten by his owners, still lived on in the ruins of the town and foraged for scraps among the mess kitchens. Down the road past the guns came the pup, ki-yiing his troubles as he ran; and at the sound of his poignant yelps some of the gunners quit their posts and ran out into the road, and one of them gathered up the poor beastie in his arms and a dozen more clustered about offering the consolation of pats and soothing words to the afflicted thing. Presently under this treatment he forgot what ailed him, and then the men went back to their places, discussing the affair with many gestures and copious speech. Ten German shells plumping down near by would not have created half so much excitement as the woes of one ownerless doggie had created. I said to myself that if the incident was typically French, likewise it was typical of what might be called the war temperament as exemplified among veteran fighters.

I should add, merely to fill out the settings of the scene, that scarcely was there a ten-minute interlude this day in which German observation planes did not scout over our lines or French observation planes did not scout over theirs. Sometimes only a single plane would be visible, but more often the airmen moved in squadron formations. Each time of course that a plane ventured aloft its coursing flight across the heavens would be marked by bursting pompons of downy white or black smoke—white for shrapnel and black for explosive bursts—where the antiaircraft guns of one side or the other took wing shots at the pesky intruder. One time six sky voyagers were up simultaneously. Another time ten, and still another no less than sixteen might be counted at once. But to focus the attention of any of the persons then upon the earth below, an aërial combat between the two groups would have been required, and even this spectacle—which at the first time of witnessing it is almost the most stirring isolated event that military operations have to offer—very soon, with daily repetitions, becomes almost commonplace, as I myself can testify. War itself is too big a thing for one detached detail of it to count in the estimates that one tries to form of the whole thing. It takes a charge in force over the top or something equally vivid and spectacular to whet up the jaded mentality of the onlooker.

CHAPTER XX
THE CALL OF THE CUCKOO

SEEKING for the thrills that experience had taught me would nevertheless probably not be forthcoming anywhere in this so-called quiet sector, I went that same day with a young American officer to a forward post of command, which was another name for a screened pit dug in the scalp of a fair-sized hillock, immediately behind our foremost rifle pits. Sitting here upon the tops of our steel helmets, which the same make fairly good perches to sit on when the ground is muddied, we could look through periscope glasses right into the courtyard of a wrecked château held by the enemy. Upon this spot some of the guns behind us were playing industriously. We could see where the shells struck—now in the garden, now near the shattered outbuildings, now ripping away a slice of the front walls or a segment of the roof of the château itself; and we could see too, after the dust of each hit had somewhat lifted, the small gray figures of Germans scurrying about like startled ants.

A mile away, about, were those Germans, and yet to all intents and purposes they might have been twenty miles away; for as things stood, and with the forces that they had at this point, it would have taken them days or perhaps weeks to bridge the gap between their lines and ours, and it would have taken us as long to get to where they were. For you see both forces had abundance of artillery, but each was holding its front lines with small groups of infantry. To sit there and peer into their defences was like looking into a distant planet peopled by men thinking different thoughts from ours, and swayed by different ambitions and moved by impulses all running counter to those of our breed.

Nevertheless, I must confess that the sensation of crouching in that hole in the ground, spying upon the movements of those dwellers of that other small world, while high above us the shells passed over, shrieking their war-whoops as they travelled from or toward our back lines, very soon lost for me the savour of interest, just as it had lost it a month before when I did the same thing in front of Noyon, or two weeks before near Verdun, or as afterward it was to do when I repeated the experience near Rheims.

So after a bit my companion and I fell to enjoying the beauties of the day. In front of us lay a strip of gentle pasture slope not badly marred by shell craters, and all green except where lovely wide slashes of a bright yellow flower cut across it like rifts of fallen sunshine. The lower reaches of air were filled with the humming of bees, and every minute the skylarks went singing up into the soft skies as though filled with a curiosity to find out what those wailing demons that sped crisscrossing through the heavens might be. Presently from a thicket behind us sounded a bell-like bird note with a sort of melodious cluck in it. I had never heard that note before except when uttered by wooden clocks of presumably Swiss manufacture, but I recognised it for what it was.

"Listen," said my companion: "that's the second time within a week I've heard it. A French liaison officer was with me then, and he said that for three years now the cuckoo had been silent, and he said that the French country people believed that since the cuckoo had begun calling again it was a sign the war would soon be over—that the cuckoo was calling for peace on earth."

"I wonder if he was right," I said.

"Well, he was right so far as he personally was concerned. This war for him was nearly over. Night before last he was riding back to division headquarters in a side car, and a shell dropped on him at a crossroads and he and the driver were killed."

We sat a minute or two longer and nothing was said.

"Well," he said at length, "if you've had enough of this we'll be getting back. It isn't very much of a show, once a fellow gets used to it, and I guess the major will have supper ready for us pretty soon. Ready to go?"

We got up cautiously and put our helmets on the proper ends of us and started back through the shallow communication trench leading to the village.

"Being where you can look right across and down into the German lines makes a fellow wonder," I suggested. "It makes a fellow wonder what those men over yonder are thinking about and what their feelings toward us are, and whether they hate us as deeply as they hate the British'."

"I guess I can figure out what one of them thinks anyhow," he said with a quizzical side-wise glance at me. He flirted over his shoulder with his thumb. "I've got a brother somewhere over yonder ways—if he's alive." He smiled at the look that must have come across my face. "Oh, you needn't suspect me," he went on. "I judge I'm as good an American as you are or any man alive is, even if I do wear a German name. You see I'm a youngest son. I was born in the good old U. S. A. all right enough, but two of my brothers, older than I am, were born in Germany, and they didn't come to

America when the rest of the family migrated. And one of them, last time I heard from him before we got into the mess, was a lieutenant in a Bavarian field battery. Being a German subject I suppose he figures he's only doing his duty, but how he can go on fighting for that swine of a Kaiser beats me. But then, I don't suppose I can understand; I'm an American citizen. Funny world, isn't it?

"Say, listen! That cuckoo is calling again. I wonder if there is anything in the superstition of the French peasants that peace will come this year. Well, so far as I am concerned I don't want it to come until Uncle Sam has finished up this job in the right way. I only hope the next time I hear the cuckoo sing it'll be in the outskirts of Berlin—that is, providing a cuckoo can stand for the outskirts of Berlin."

I reminded him that the cuckoo was a bird that stole other bird's nests— or tried to.

"That being so, I guess Berlin must be full of 'em," said he.

The major's headquarters—he was a major of artillery—was in the chief house of the little town. Curiously enough this was almost the only house in the town that had not been hit, and two days later it was hit, and in the ruins of it a friend of mine, another major, was crushed; but that is a different story, not to be detailed here. It stood—the house, I mean—in a little square courtyard of its own, as most village houses in this part of France do, being flanked on one side by its stable and on the other side by its cow barn and by its chicken houses. There was a high wall to inclose it along the side nearest the street, with rabbit hutches and pigeon cots tucked up under the wall. In the centre of the court was a midden for manure. It had been a cosy little place once. The dwelling was of red brick with a gay tiled roof, and the lesser buildings and the wall were built of stones, as is the French way. Even the rabbit hutches were stone, and the dovecot and the cuddy for the fowls. Now, except for American artillerymen, it was all empty of life. The paved yard was littered with wreckage; the doors of the empty cubicles stood open.

I sat with the major and his adjutant on the doorstep of the cottage waiting for the orderlies to call us in to eat our suppers. Through the lolled gate in the wall an old man, a civilian, entered. He was tall and lean like one of the lombard trees growing in the spoiled vegetable garden at the back of the house, and he was dressed in a long frock coat that was all powdered with a white dust of the roads. He had a grave long face, and we saw that he limped a little as he came across the close toward us. Nearing us he took off his hat and bowed.

"Pardon, 'sieurs," he said in Norman French, "but could I look through this house?"

"No civilians are permitted here now," said the major. "How did you get here?"

"I was given a pass to return," he explained. "Your pardon again, m'sieurs, but I am—I was—the mayor of this town, and this is my house. I mean, it was my house. The Germans came upon us so rapidly we had to leave on but two hours' notice, taking with us very little. Not until to-day could I secure leave to come back. I wished to see what was left of my home—I always had lived here before, you know—and to gather up some of my belongings, if I might."

"Where did you come from?" asked the major.

"From — — — —." He named a town twenty-two miles away.

"And how did you get here?"

"I walked." He lifted his shoulders in an expressive gesture. "There was no other way. And I must walk back to-night. There is no shelter nearer except for soldiers."

He looked past us into the main room of the house. Its floor of tiles was littered with dried mud. A table and three broken chairs that had given way beneath the weight of heavy and careless men were its only furniture now. The window panes had been shattered. It was hard to picture that this once had been a cozy, comfortable room, clean and tidy, smartened with pictures and ornaments upon the walls and with curtains at the casement openings, which now gaped so emptily.

"Not much is left, eh?" said the old man, his face twitching. "Well *c'est la guerre!*"

"I'm afraid your home is rather badly wrecked," said the major. "Since I came here my men have tried to do no more damage to it than they could help, but Algerians were here before us; and the Algerians, as you know, are rough in their habits and sometimes they loot houses. Do you wish to enter? If so, go ahead. And if you are hungry I would be glad to have you stay and eat with us."

The stranger hesitated a moment.

"No, no," he said; "of what use to go in? I have seen enough. And thank you, m'sieur but I do not wish any food."

He bowed once more and turned away from us; but he did not go away directly. He went across the court to his barn and tugged at a door that was half ajar. From within came the grumbled protest of a Yankee gunner lying just inside on a pile of straw, and indignant at being roused from a nap.

The man who owned the barn backed away, making his apologies. He picked up a hay fork that lay upon the dungpile, and near the gate, under the shadow of the wall, he stooped again and picked up a broken clock that some one had tossed out of the house. Then, after one more glance all about the place as though he strove to fix in his mind a picture of it, not as now it was but as once it had been, he stepped through the gate, and with his pitiable salvage tucked under his bony arms he vanished up the road.

When that night I summed up my experiences the memories of the day that stood out clearest in my mind were not of the guns nor the aëroplanes nor the bursting shells nor yet the sight in the German lines, but of the mistreated dog that howled and of the cuckoo that fluted in the thicket and of the old man who had trudged so far, over perilous roads, to look with his eyes for the last time, surely, upon the sorry ruination of his home. And I felt that I, a man whose business it is to see interesting things and afterward to put them down in black and white, was acquiring in some degree the perspective of the soldier, whose mental viewpoint is so foreshortened by the imminent presence of the greater phases of war that he comes after a while to regard the inconsequential, and so looks on the incidental phases of it as of more account than the complexities of its vast, hurrying, overdriven mechanism.

For the point I have been trying, perhaps clumsily, to make clear all along is just this: As a general thing it may be set down that except for those infrequent occasions when there is a charge to be made or a charge to be repelled, or except when some freak of war, new to the trooper's experience, is occurring or has just occurred, he in all essential outer regards is exactly the same person that he was before he went a-soldiering, with nothing about him to distinguish him from what he was then, barring the fact that now he wears a uniform.

Spiritually he may have been transformed; indeed he must have been, but it is a shading of spirituality that but rarely betrays itself in his fashion of speech or in his physical expression or in his behaviour. Doing the most heroic things he nevertheless does them without indulging in any of the heroics with which the fiction of books and the fiction of stagecraft love to invest the display of the finer and the higher emotions of mankind.

Living where death in various guises is ever upon the stalk for him he learns to regard it no more than in civil life he regards the commoner manifestations of a code of civilised procedure that ethically is based upon a plan to safeguard his life and his limb from mischance and ill health. The habit of death becomes to him as commonplace as the habit of life once was. He gets used to the incredible and it turns commonplace. He gets used to the extraordinary, which after it has happened a few times becomes most ordinary. He gets used to being bombed and is bored thereby; gets used to gas alarms and bombardments; to high explosives, spewing shrapnel, and purring bullets; gets used to eating his meals standing up and taking his rest in broken bits. He gets used to all of war's programme—its impossibilities and its contradictions, its splendours, its horrors and its miseries. In short he gets used to living in a world that is turned entirely upside down, with every normal aspect in it capsised and every regular and ordained phase of it standing upon its head.

For a fact it seems to me that in its final analysis the essence of war is merely the knack of getting used to war. And the instantaneous response of the average human being to its monstrous and preposterous aspects is a lesson to prove the elasticity and the infinite adaptability of the human mind. Because people can and do get used to it is the reason why they do not all go mad in the midst of it. Getting used to it—that's the answer. After a while one even gets used to the phenomenon that war rarely or never looks as you would think war should look—and that brings me by a roundabout way back again to the main text of my article.

Troops travelling in numbers across country do not present the majestic panoramic effect that one might expect. This in part, though, is due to the common topography of France. Generally speaking, a given district is so cut up with roads threading the fields that the forces, for convenience in handling, are divided into short columns that move by routes that are practically parallel, toward a common destination. The sight of troops going into camp at night also is disappointing. In France, thickly settled as it is, with villages tucked into every convenient dip between the hills, the men are so rapidly swallowed up in the billeting spaces under house and bam roots that an hour or even half an hour after the march has ended you might traverse a district where, let us say, twenty thousand soldiers are quartered, and unless you know the correct figures the evidence offered to your eyes might deceive you into assuming that not one-tenth of that number were anywhere in the vicinity.

It is this failure of war, when considered as a physical thing, to measure up to its traditional Impressiveness, that fills with despair the soul of the writing man, who craves to put down on paper an adequate conception of it in its entirety. Finally he comes to this: That either he must throw away the delusions he himself nourished and content himself by building together little mosaics with scraps gleaned from the big, untellable, untranslatable enigma that it is, or for the reader's sake must try to conjure up a counterfeit conception, which will correspond with what he knows the average reader's mental vision of the thing to be. In one event he is honest—but disappointing. In the other he is guilty of a willful deceit, but probably turns out copy that is satisfying to his audience. In either event, in his heart he is bound to realise the utter impossibility of depicting war as it is.

It is one of the cumulating paradoxes of the entire paradoxical procedure that the best place to get a reasonably clear and intelligible idea of the swing and scope of a battle is not upon the site of the battle itself, but in a place anywhere from ten to twenty miles behind the battle. Directly at the front the onlooker observes only those small segments of the prevalent hostilities that lie directly under his eyes. He is hedged in and hampered by obstacles; his vision is circumscribed and confined to what may be presented in his immediate vicinity.

Of course there are exceptions to this rule. I am speaking not of every case but of the average case.

A fairish distance back, though, he may to an extent grasp the immensity of the operation. He sees the hammered troops coming out and the fresh troops going in; beholds the movements of munitions and supplies and reserves; observes the handling of the wounded; notes the provisions that are made for a possible advance and the preparations that have been made for a possible retreat. Even so, to the uninitiated eye the scheme appears jumbled, haphazard and altogether confused. It requires a mind acquainted with more than the rudiments of military science to discern purpose in what primarily appears to be so absolutely purposeless. There is nothing of the checkerboard about it; the orderliness of a chess game is lacking. The suggestion is more that of a whirlpool. So it follows that the novice watches only the maelstrom on the surface and rarely can he fathom out the guiding influences that ordain that each twistiwise current moves in its proper channel without impairment or impediment lor any one of the myriad of related activities.

Being a novice he is astonished to note that only infrequently do wounded men act as his fictional reading has led him to believe they would act. To me the most astounding thing about this has been not that wounded men shriek and moan, but that nearly always they are so terribly silent. At the moment of receiving his hurt a man may cry out; often he does. But oftener than not he comes, mute and composed, to the dressing station. The example of certain men who lock their lips and refuse to murmur, no matter how great is their pain, inspires the rest to do likewise. A man who in civil life would make a great pother over a trivial mishap, in service will endure an infinitely worse one without complaint. If war brings out all the vices in some nations it most surely brings out the virtues in others. I hate to think back on the number of freshly wounded men I have seen, but when I do think back on it I am struck by the fact that barring a few who were delirious and some few more who were just emerging into agonised consciousness following the coma shock of a bad injury, I can count upon the fingers of my two hands the total of those who screamed or loudly groaned. Men well along the road to recovery frequently make more troublesome patients than those who have just been brought to the field hospitals; and a man who perhaps has lain for hours with a great hole in his flesh, stoically awaiting his turn under the surgeon's hands, will sometimes, as a convalescent, worry and fret over the prospect of having his hurts redressed.

Among certain races the newly stricken trooper is more apt to be concerned by the fear that he may be incapacitated from getting back into the game than he is about the extent of his wound or the possibility that he may die of it. As an American I am proud to be able to say, speaking as a first-hand witness, that our own race should be notably included in this category. The Irishman who had been shot five times but was morally certain he would recover and return to the war because he thought he knew the fellow who had plugged him has his counterpart without number among the valorous lads from this side of the ocean whose names have appeared on the casualty lists.

CHAPTER XXI
PARADOXES BEHIND THE LINES

WHILE I am on the subject of unusual phases of modern warfare I should like to include just one more thing in the list—and that thing is the suddenness with which in France, and likewise in Belgium, one in going forward passes out of an area of peacefulness into an area of devastation and destruction. Almost invariably the transition is accomplished with a startling abruptness. It is as though a mighty finger had scored a line across the face of the land and said; "On this side of the line life shall go on as it always has gone on. Here men shall plough, and women shall weave, and children shall play, and the ordinary affairs of mankind shall progress with the seasons. On that side there shall be only death and the proofs of death and the promises of yet more deaths. There the fields shall be given over to the raven and the rat; the homes shall be blasted flat, the towns shall be razed and the earth shall be made a charnelhouse and a lazar pit of all that is foul and loathsome and abominable in the sight of God and man."

For emphasis of this sharp contrast you have only to take a motor run up out of a district as yet untouched by war into the scathed zone of past or present combat. By preference I should elect for you that the trip be made through a British sector, because the British have a way of stamping their racial individuality upon an area that they take over—they Anglicise it, so to speak. Besides, a tour through British-held territory partakes of the nature of a flying visit to an ethnological congress, seeing that nearly all the peoples who make up the empire are likely to have representatives here present, engaged in one capacity or another—and that adds interest and colour to the picture.

Let us start, say, from a French market town on a market day. From far away in the north, as we climb into our car with our soldier driver and our officer escort, comes the faint hollow rumble of the great guns; but that has been going on nearly four years now, and in the monotony of it the people who live here have forgotten the threat that is in that distant thundering. Pippin-cheeked women are driving in, perched upon the high seats of two-wheeled hooded carts and bringing with them fowls and garden truck. In the square before the church booths are being set up for the sale of goods. Plump round-eyed children stand to watch us go down the narrow street, which runs between close rows of wattled, gable-ended stone or plaster cottages. Most of the little girls are minding babies; practically all of the little boys wear black pinafores belted in at their chubby waistlines, with soldier cap—always soldier caps—on their heads, and they love to stiffen to attention and salute the occupants of a military automobile.

There are but few men in sight, and these are old men or else they wear uniforms. The houses are tidied and neat; the soil, every tillable inch of it, is in a state of intensive and painstaking cultivation. On all hands vineyards, orchards, pastures and grain fields are spread in squares and parallelograms. The road is bordered on either side by tall fine trees. Chickens, geese and turkeys scuttle away to safety from before the onrushing car, and at the roadside goats and cattle and sheep and sometimes swine are feeding. Each animal or each group of animals has its attendant herder. Horses are tethered outside the hedges where they may crop the free herbage. The landscape is fecund with life and productivity.

It is a splendid road along which we course, wide and smooth and well-kept, and for this the reason is presently made plain. Steam rollers of British manufacture, with soldiers to steer them, constantly roll back and forth over stretches where broken stone has been spread by the repair gangs. These mending crews may be made up of soldiers—French, British, Portuguese or Italians; and then again they may be drafts of German prisoners or members of labour squads drawn from far corners of the world where the British or the French flag flies. Within an hour you will pass turbaned East Indians, Chinamen, Arabs, Nubians, Ceylonese, Senegalese, Maoris, Afridis, Moroccans, Algerians. Their head-dresses are likely to be their own; for the rest they wear the uniforms of the nation that has enlisted or hired them.

Despite this polyglot commingling of types the British influence is upon everything. Military guideposts bearing explicit directions in English stand thick along the wayside, and in the windows of the shops are cruder signs to show that the French proprietors make a specialty of catering to the wants of Britishers. Here is one reading "Eggs and Potato Chips"; there one advertising to whom it may concern, "Washing Done Here." "Post-cards and Souvenirs" is a common legend, and on the fronts of old wine-shops a still commoner one is "Ale and Stout." Rows of beer bottles stand upon the window ledges, with platters of buns and sandwiches flanking them. A "Wet and Dry Canteen" flies a diminutive British flag from its peaky roof.

Evidences of British military activity multiply and re-multiply themselves. Long trains of motor-trucks lumber by like great, grey elephants each with a dusty Tommy for its mahout. A convoy of small, new tanks go wallowing and bumping along bound frontward, and they suggest a herd of behemoths on the move. Their drivers as likely as not are Chinamen who presently will turn their unwieldy charges over to soldier-crews. Officers clatter past on horse-back looking, all of them, as though they had just escaped from the military outfitters; staff-cars whiz through the slower traffic; troops bound for the baths or for the trenches or for rest billets march stolidly up the road or down it as the case may be. Omnibuses from London town, now converted to military usage, are thick in the press. Military policemen are more numerous and more set upon scrutinising your pass than they were a few miles back. And civilians are fewer.

Alongside the highway, settlements of wooden or iron huts increase in number and in proportions. Hospitals, headquarters of various units, bath-houses, punishment compounds, motor stations, supply depots, airdromes, ordnance repair plants, munition warehouses, Y. M. C. A. huts, gas test stations, rest barracks, gasoline depots and all the rest of it show themselves for what they are both by their shapes and by the notice boards which mark them. Here is cluttered all the infinitely complicated machinery of the war-making industry, with its accessories and its adjuncts, its essentials and its incidentals, but so far there is no actual evidence that the rude and disturbing hand of war has actually been laid upon the land. Rather is it a spectacle to make you think of a thousand circus days rolled into one, and mixed in with all this, travelling caravans, gypsy encampments, Wild West shows, horse-fairs, street carnivals and what not.

Of a sudden the picture changes. There are no civilians visible now, no prisoners and no labour-battalions but only soldiers and not so many soldiers either as you encountered just behind you in the intermediate zone because as a general thing, the nearer you come to the actual theatre of hostilities, the fewer soldiers in mass are you apt to see. The soldiers may be near by but they are not to be found until you search for them. They have taken cover in dug-outs and in trenches and in remote billets hidden in handy, sheltered spots in the conformation of the rolling landscape.

Now the vista stretching before you wears a bleak and untenanted look. You notice that the shade trees have disappeared. Instead of living trees there are only jagged stumps of trees or bare, shattered trunks from which the limbs have been sheared away by shell-fire, and to which the bark clings in scrofulous patches. Across the fields go winding, brown bramble-patches of rusted barbed wire. The earth is depressed into hollows and craters, or upthrown into ugly mounds and hillocks. In the wasted and disfigured meadows rank weeds sprout upon the edges of the ragged shellholes. The very earth seems to give off a sour and rancid stink. There is a village ahead of you; it is a village without roofs to its houses, or dwellers within its breached and tottering walls. It is a jumbled nightmare of a ruin. It is as though a tornado had blown a cluster of brick-kilns flat, and then an earthquake had come along and jumbled the fragments into still greater and more utter confusion.

Protruding from the flattened rubble about it, there uprears a crooked, spindle-like pinnacle of tottering masonry. It may have been a corner of the church wall or the town hall. Now it is like a beckoning finger calling to heaven for vengeance. Upon it is set a notice-board to advise you that you are now in the "Alert Zone," which means your gas-respirator must be snuggled up under your chin ready for use and that your steel helmet must be worn upon your head and that you must take such other precautions as may be required.

You ride on then at reduced speed along a camouflaged byway for perhaps fifteen minutes. You come to where once upon a time, before the jack-booted, spike-headed apostles of Kul-tur descended upon this country, was another village standing. This village has been more completely obliterated out of its former image—if such a thing is possible—than its neighbour. It is little else than a red smear in the greyish yellow desolation, where constant bombardment has reduced the bricks of its houses to a powder and then has churned and pestled the powder into the harried earth. There remains for proof of one-time occupancy only the jagged lines of certain foundations and ugly mounds of mingled soil and debris. Up from beneath one of these mess-heaps, emerging like a troglodyte, from a hole which burrows downward to a hidden cellar, there crawls forth a grimed soldier who warns you that neither you nor your car may progress farther except at your dire risk, since this is an outpost position and once you pass from your present dubious shelter you will be in full view and easy target range of Brother Boche. You have advanced to the very forward verge of the battle-line and you didn't know it.

One rather dark night, travelling in an unlighted car, three of us were trying to reach an American brigade headquarters where we expected to sleep. Our particular destination was a hamlet in a forest just behind and slightly east of the main defences of Verdun.

We must have taken the wrong turn at a crossroads, for after going some distance along a rutted cart track through the woods we came to where a deep ditch—at least it seemed to be a deep ditch—had been dug right across the trail from side to side. By throwing on the brakes the chauffeur succeeded in halting the car before its front wheels went over and into the cut. We climbed out to investigate, and then we became aware of an American sentry standing twenty feet beyond us in the aforesaid ditch.

"We are correspondents," said a spokesman among us, "and we are trying to get to General So-and-So's headquarters. Can't we go any farther along this road?"

Being an American this soldier had a sense of humour.

"Not unless you speak German, you can't," he drawled. "The Heinies are dead ahead of you, not two hundred yards from this here trench."

Without once suspecting it we had ridden clear through a sector held by us to the frontline defences alongside the beleaguered city of Verdun.

It's just one paradox after another, is the thing we call war.

CHAPTER XXII
THE TAIL OF THE SNAKE

THE deadlier end of a snake is the head end, where the snake carries its stingers. Since something happened in the Garden of Eden this fact has been a matter of common knowledge, giving to all mankind for all time respect for the snake and fear of him. But what not everybody knows is that before a constrictor can exert his squeezing powers to the uttermost degree he must have a dependable grip for his tail, else those mighty muscles of his are impotent; because a snake, being a physical thing, is subject to the immutable laws of physics. There must be a fulcrum for the lever, always; the coiled spring that is loose at both ends becomes merely a piece of twisted metal; and a constrictor in action is part a living lever and part a living spring. And another thing that not everybody knows is that before a snake with fangs can fling itself forward and bite it must have a purchase for the greater part of its length against some reasonably solid object, such as the earth or a slab of rock.

Now an army might very well be likened to a snake, which sometimes squeezes its enemy by an enveloping movement but more often strikes at him with sudden blows. In the case of our own Army I particularly like the simile of a great snake—a rattlesnake, by preference, since in the first place the rattlesnake is essentially an American institution, and since once before our ancestors fought for their own freedom, much as we now are fighting for the freedom of the world, under a banner that carried the device of a rattler coiled. Moreover, the rattlesnake, which craves only to be let alone and which does not attack save on intrusion or provocation, never quits fighting, once it has started, until it is absolutely no more. You may scotch it and you may bruise and crush and break it, but until you have killed it exceedingly dead and cut it to bits and buried the bits you can never be sure that the job from your standpoint is finished. So for the purpose of introducing the subject in hand a rattlesnake it is and a rattlesnake it shall be to the end of the narrative, the reader kindly consenting—a rattlesnake whose bite is very, very fatal and whose vibrating tail bears a rattle for every star in the flag.

For some months past it has been my very good fortune to watch the rattler's head, snouting its nose forth into the barbed wires and licking out with the fiery tongue of its artillery across the intervening shell holes at Heinie the Hun. Now I have just finished a trip along the body of the snake, stretching and winding through and across France for 800 miles, more or less, to where its tail is wetted by salt water at the coast ports in the south and the east and the southeast. This is giving no information to the enemy, since he knows already that the snake which is the army must have a head at the battleground and a neck in the trenches, and behind the head and the neck a body and a tail, the body being the lines of communication and the tail the primary supply bases.

His own army is in the likeness of a somewhat similar snake; otherwise it could not function. Moreover, things are happening to him, even as these lines are written, that must impress upon his Teutonic consciousness that our snake is functioning from tip to tip. Unless he is blind as well as mad he must realise that he made a serious mistake when he disregarded the injunction of the old Colonials: "Don't Tread On Me."

In common with nearly every other man to whom has been given similar opportunity I have seen hundreds of splendid things at the Front where our people hold for defence or move for attack—heroism, devotion, sacrifice, an unquenchable cheerfulness, and a universal determination that permeates through the ranks from the highest general to the greenest private to put through the job that destiny has committed into our keeping, after the only fashion in which this job properly may be put through.

In the trenches and immediately behind them I thought I had exhausted the average human capacity for thrills of pride, but it has turned out that I hadn't. For back of the Front, back of the line troops and the reserves, back all the way to the tail of the snake, there are things to be seen that in a less spectacular aspect—though some of them are spectacular enough, at that—are as finely typical of American resource and American courage and American capability as any of the sights that daily and hourly duplicate themselves among the guns.

I am sure there still must be quite a number of persons at home who somehow think that once a soldier is armed and trained and set afoot on fighting ground he thereafter becomes a self-sustaining and self-maintaining organism; that either he is providentially provisioned, as the ravens of old fed the prophet, or that he forages for himself, living on the spoils of the country as the train bands and hired mercenaries used to live by loot in the same lands where our troops are now engaged. Or possibly they hazily conceive that the provender and the rest of it, being provided, manage to transport themselves forward to their user. If already we had not had too many unnecessary delegates loose-footing it over France this year I could wish that I might have had along with me on this recent trip a delegation of these unreflecting folk, for they would have beheld, as I did, a greater miracle than the one vouchsafed Elijah, yet a miracle of man's encompassment, and in some measure would have come to understand how a vast American army, three thousand miles from home on foreign shores, is fed and furnished and furbished and refurbished, not at the expense of the dwellers of the soil but to their abundant personal benefit. Finally they would see in its operation the vastest composite job of creation, organisation and construction that has ever been put through, in the space of one year and three months about, by any men that ever toiled anywhere on this footstool of Jehovah.

To me statistics are odious things, and whenever possible I avoid them. Besides, some of the figures I have accumulated in this journey are so incredibly stupendous that knowing them to be true figures I nevertheless hesitate to set them down. By my thinking way adjectives are needed and not numerals to set forth in any small measure a conception of the undertaking that has been accomplished overseas by our people and is still being accomplished with every hour that passes.

Before this war came along Europeans were given to saying that we Americans rarely bragged of producing a beautiful thing or an artistic thing or a thing painstakingly done, but rather were given to advertising that here we had erected the longest bridge and there the tallest building and over yonder the largest railway terminal and down this way the most expensive mansion—that ever was. Perhaps the criticism was justified in peacetimes. Today in the light of what we have done in France these past few months back of the lines it not only is justified but it is multiplied, magnified and glorified. It no longer is a criticism; it is a tribute. When you think of the performance that stands to our credit you must think of it in superlatives, and when you speak of it you must speak in superlatives too. The words all end in "est."

On French soil within twelve months, and in several instances within six months, we have among other things constructed and set going the biggest cold-storage plant, with two exceptions, in the world; the biggest automobile storage depot, excluding one privately owned American concern, in the world; the biggest system of military-equipment warehouses in the world; probably the biggest field bakery in the world; the biggest strictly military seaport base in the world; what will shortly be the biggest military base hospital in the world; the biggest single warehouse for stock provender in the world; the biggest junkshop in the world; the biggest staff training school in the world—three months ago it had more scholars than any university in America ever has had; the biggest locomotive roundhouse under one roof; the biggest gasoline-storage plant; the next to the biggest training camp for aviators, the same being a sort of 'finishing school for men who have already had a degree of instruction elsewhere; the biggest acetylene-gas plant; and half a dozen other biggest things in the world — and we're not good and started yet!

Every week sees the plants we have already constructed being enlarged and amplified; every week sees some new contract getting under way. Every month's end sees any similar period in the building of the Panama Canal made to seem almost a puny and inconsequential achievement by contrast and by comparison with what superbly and triumphantly has gone forward during that month. In military parlance it is called the Service of Supplies. It should be called the Service of the Supremely Impossible Supremely Accomplished. When this war is ended and tourists are permitted to visit foreign parts Americans coming abroad and seeing what has here been done will be prouder of their country and their fellow countrymen than ever they have been.

The Service of Supplies, broadly speaking and in its bearing on operations upon the Continent, begins at tide mark and ends in the front-line trenches, with ramifications and side issues and annexes past counting, but all of them more or less interrelated with the main issues. For example the staff school can hardly be called a part of it, though lying, so to speak, in a whorl of the snake. It is divided into a Base Section, which is that part situate nearest to the coasts; an Intermediate Section, which is what its name implies; and an Advance Section, which extends as close up to the zone of hostilities as is consistent with reasonable safety, the term "reasonable safety" being a relative term in these days of hostile raiding planes. The Base Section is subdivided again into several lesser segments, each centring about a main port.

Broadly described it might be said that any military equipment in its natural course is first unloaded and stored temporarily at the bases. Then it is moved into the Intermediate Section, where it is housed and kept until called for. Thereupon it goes on a third rail journey to the Advance Section, out of the depots of which it is requisitioned and sent ahead again by trucks or wagons, or more commonly by rail, to meet the day-to-day and the week-to-week requirements of the units in the field.

While this is going on all the sundry hundreds of thousands of men engaged on duty along the Service of Supplies must be cared for without impairment to the principal underlying purpose — that of provisioning and arming the fighting man, and providing supplies and equipment for the hospitals and the depots and all the rest of it, world without end. When you sit down to figure how many times the average consignment, of whatsoever nature, is loaded and unloaded and reloaded again even after it has been brought overseas, and how many times it is handled and rehandled, checked in and checked out, accounted for and entered up, and eventually fed out in dribs as fodder for the huge coiling serpent we call an army—you begin to understand why it is that for every 100 men brought across the ocean upward of 50 must be assigned to work in some capacity or another along the communication ways.

For the reader to visit the various departments and sub-departments and subber subdepartments that properly fall within the scope of the Service of Supplies would take of his time at least two weeks. It took that much of my time and I had a fast touring car at my disposal and between stops moved at a cup-racing clip. For the writer to attempt to set down in any comprehensive form the extent of the thing would fill a fat book of many pages. By reason of the limitations of space this article can touch only briefly on the general scheme and only sketchily upon those details that seemed to the present observer most interesting.

For example at one port—and this not yet the busiest one of the ports turned over to us by our allies—we are operating an extensive system of French docks that already were there and with them an even larger system of docks constructed by our Army and now practically completed. Likewise we have here a great camp, as big a camp as many a community at home that calls itself a city, where negro labour battalions are living; two extensive rest camps for troops newly debarked from the transports; enormous freight yards and storage warehouses with still another camp handily near by for the accommodation of the yard gangs and the warehouse gangs; a base hospital that when completed will be the largest military base hospital on earth; a sizable artillery camp where gun crews and ordnance officers take what might be called a post-graduate course to supplement the training they had in the States; a remount station; an ordnance and aviation-storage warehouse; and a motor reception park.

This, remember, is but one of several ports that we practically have taken over for the period of the war. On the land side of a second port are grouped a rest camp, a motor-assembling park, a system of docks inside a basin that is provided with locks, a locomotive-assembling plant, freight yards, warehouses without end, and two base hospitals.

Taking either of these ports for a starting point and moving inland one would probably visit first the headquarters of the Service of Supplies, where also is to be found our main salvage depot for reclaiming all sorts of equipment except motor and air equipment—these go to salvage stations specially provided elsewhere—and not far away an aviation training centre. A little farther along as one travelled up-country he would come to an artillery instruction centre located in a famous French military school; to our engineer training centre and our engineer replacement depots; and thence onward to our air-service production centre with its mammoth plant for assembling, repairing and testing planes and with its camp for its personnel. This would bring one well into the Intermediate Section with its depots, freight yards and warehouses, and with its refrigerating plant, which is the third largest in existence and which shortly will have a twin sister a few miles away. There would be side excursions to the motor supply and spare parts depot, to the main motor repair station, to the locomotive repair shops, to the car shops, to the principal one of our aviation training centres, to the main field bakery, to the gasoline depots, the camouflaging plant and to various lesser activities.

Finally one would land at the Advance Section depots with their complex regulating stations for the proper distribution of the material that has advanced hither by broken stages. And yet when one had journeyed thus far one would merely be at the point of the beginning of the real work of getting the stuff through to the forces without congestion, without unnecessary wastage, without sending up too much or too little but just exactly the proper amounts as needed.

Now then, on top of this please remember that each important camp, each station, each centre has its own water system, its own electric light system, its own police force, its own fire department, its own sanitary squad, its own sewers, its own walks and drives and flower beds, its own emergency hospitals and dispensaries and surgeries, its own Y. M. C. A., its own Red Cross unit, generally its own K. of C. workers and its own Salvation Army squad; as likely as not its own newspaper and its own theatre. Always it has its own separate communal life.

Figure that in a score of places veritable cities have sprung up where last January the wind whistled over stubbled fields and snow-laden pine thickets. Figure that altogether 40,000,000 square feet of covered housing space are required and that more will be required as our expeditionary force continues to expand. Figure that in and out and through all these ramified activities our locomotives draw our cars over several hundred miles of sidings and yard trackage, which Uncle Sam has put down by the sweat of the brow of his excellent sons, supplemented by a copious amount of sweat wrung from the brows of thousands of German prisoners and thousands more of Indo-Chinese labourers imported by the French and loaned to us, and yet thousands more of native French labourers past or under the military age.

Figure that while the work of construction has been going on upon a scope unprecedented in the scheme of human endeavour the men charged with the responsibility for it have had to divide their energies and their man power to the end that the growing Army should not suffer for any lack of essential sustenance while the other jobs went forward toward completion. Figure at the beginning of last winter, nine months ago, scarcely a spadeful of earth had been turned for the foundations anywhere. Figure in with all of this mental pictures of the Children of Israel building the pyramids for old Mister Pharaoh, of Goethals at the Isthmus, of Cæsar's legions networking Europe with those justly celebrated Romanesque roads of his, of the coral insects making an archipelago in nine months instead of stretching the proceeding through millions of years, as is the habit of these friendly little insects; figure in all these things—and if your headache isn't by this time too acute for additional effort without poignant throbbings at the temples you may begin to have a shadowy conception of what has happened along our Service of Supplies over here in France since we really got busy.

So much for the glittering generalities—and Lawsie, how they do glitter with the crusted diamond dust of endeavour and stupendous accomplishment! Now for a few particularly brilliant outcroppings: There is a certain port at present in our hands. For our purposes it is a most important port—one of the most important of all the ports that the French turned over to us. When our engineers set up shop there the port facilities were very much as they had been when the Phoenicians first laid them out, barring some comparatively modern improvements subsequently tacked on by the Roman Emperors and still later by that famous but somewhat disagreeable old lady, Anne of Brittany. There were no steam cranes or electric hoists on the docks, and if there had been they would have been of little value except for ornamental purposes, seeing that by reason of harbourwise limitations ships of draft or of size could not range alongside but must be lightered of their cargoes at their mooring chains out in midchannel anywhere from half a mile to a mile and a half off shore. Moreover, there was but one railroad track running down to the water's edge. Even yet there are no steam cranes in operation; both freight and men must be brought to land in lighters. But mark you what man power plus brains plus necessity has accomplished in the face of those structural obstacles and those mechanical drawbacks.

At the outset it was estimated by experts among our allies that possibly we could land 20,000 troops and 6,000 tons of freight a month at this port— if we kept nonunion hours and hustled. In one day in the early part of the present summer 42,000 American soldiers were debarked and ferried ashore with their portable equipment, and on another day of the same week through one of the original French-built docks—not through the whole row of them, but through one of the row—our stevedores cleared 5,000 tons of freight. Five thousand tons in one day, when those Continental wiseacres had calculated that by straining ourselves and by employing to their utmost all the facilities provided by all the docks in sight we might move 6,000 tons in a month! For this performance and for so frequent duplication of it that now it has become commonplace and matter-of-fact and quite in accordance with expectations, a great share of the credit is due to thousands of brawny black American stevedores drawn from the wharves of Boston, New York and Philadelphia, Galveston, Savannah, New Orleans and Newport News. The victory that we are going to win will not be an all-white victory by any manner of means.

Besides the physical limitations there were certain others, seeming at first well-nigh insurmountable, which our military and civilian executives had to meet and contend with and overcome. I mean the Continental fashion of doing things—a system ponderously slow and infinitely cumbersome. When a job is done according to native requirements over here it is thoroughly done, as you may be quite sure, and it will last for an age; but frequently the preceding age is required to get it done. Europeans almost without exception are thrifty and saving beyond any conceivable standards of ours, but they are prodigals and they are spendthrifts when it comes down to expending what in America we regard as the most precious commodity of all, and that commodity is time. Some of our masters of frenzied finance could wreck a bank in less time than it takes to cash a check in a French one.

Not even the exigencies and the sharp emergencies of wartime conditions can cure a people, however adaptable and sprightly they may be in most regards, of a system of thought and a system of habit that go back as far as they themselves go as a civilised race. Here is a concrete instance serving to show how at this same port that I have been talking about the Continental system came into abrupt collision with the American system and how the American system won out:

The admiral in command of the American naval forces centring at this place received word that on a given day—to wit: three days from the time the news was wirelessed to him—a convoy would bring to harbour transports bearing about 50,000 Yank troopers. It would be the admiral's task to see that the ships promptly were emptied of their passengers and that the passengers were expeditiously and safely put upon solid land. After this had been done it devolved upon the brigadier in command of the land forces to quarter them in a rest camp until such time as they would be dispatched up the line toward the Front.

The great movement of our soldiers overseas, which started in April and which proceeds without noticeable abatement as I write this, was then in midswing; and the rest camps in the neighbourhood were already crowded to their most stretchable limits. Nevertheless the general must provide livable accommodations for approximately 50,000 men somewhere in an already overcrowded area—and he had less than seventy-two hours in which to do it. He got busy; the members of his staff likewise got busy.

That same night he called into conference a functionary of the French Government, in liaison service and detailed to cooperate with the Americans or with the British in just such situations as the one that had now risen. The official in question was zealous in the common cause—as zealous as any man could be—but he could not cure himself of thinking in the terms of the pattern his nation had followed in times of peace.

"I must have a big rest camp ready by this time day after to-morrow," said, in effect, the American. "So I went out this afternoon with my adjutant and some of my other officers and I found it."

Briefly he described a suitable tract four or five miles from the town. Then he went on: "How long do you think it would take for your engineers to furnish me with a fairly complete working survey of that stretch, including boundaries and the general topography with particular regards to drainage and elevations?"

The Frenchman thought a minute, making mental calculations.

"From four to six weeks I should say," he hazarded. "Not sooner than four weeks surely."

"I think I can beat that," said the American.

He turned to his desk phone and called up another office in the same building in which this conference was taking place—the office of his chief engineer officer.

"Blank," he said when he had secured connection, "how long will it take you to give me the survey of that property we went over this afternoon? You were to let me know by this evening."

Back came the answer:

"By working all night, sir, I can hand it to you at noon to-morrow."

"Are you sure I'll get it then?"

"Absolutely sure, sir."

"Good," said the general, and rang off. He faced the Frenchman.

"The survey will be ready at noon tomorrow," he said. "Now, then, I want arrangements made so that construction gangs can take possession of that land in the morning early. They've got a good many thousand tents to set up and some temporary shacks to build, and I'm going to sick 'em on the job at daylight."

"But what you ask is impossible, *mon général*," expostulated the Frenchman. "Days will be required—perhaps weeks. We must follow a regular custom, else there will be legal complications. We must search out the owners of the various parcels of land included in the area and make separate terms with each of them for the use of his land by your people."

"And meanwhile what will those 50,000 soldiers that are due here inside of seventy-two hours be doing?"

The Frenchman shrugged his shoulders. "Very well then," said the American. "Now here's what we must do: I want you please to get in touch, right away, with your Minister of War at Paris and tell him with my compliments that at daylight in the morning I am going to take possession of that tract, and I want the sanction of his department for my authority in taking the step. Afterward we'll settle with the owners of the land for the ground rent and for the proper damages and for all the rest of it. But now—with my compliments—tell the minister we've got to have a little action."

"But to write a letter and send it to Paris even by special courier, and to have it read and to get a reply back, would take three days at the very quickest," the Frenchman replied.

"I'm not asking you to write any letters. I'm asking you to call up the minister on the telephone—now, this minute, from this office, and over this telephone."

"But, my dear general, it is not customary to call a minister of the government on the telephone to discuss anything. There is a procedure for this sort of thing—a tradition, a precedent if you will."

"We'll have to make a new precedent of our own then. Here's the telephone. Suppose you get the minister on the wire and leave the rest to me. I'll do the talking from this end—and I'll take the responsibility."

"But—but, general," faltered the dum-founded Frenchman, "have you thought of the question of water supply? There are no running streams near your proposed site; there are no reservoirs. Of what use for me to do as you wish and run the risk of annoying our Minister of War when you have no water? And of course without water of what use is your camp?"

"Don't let that worry you," said the American. "The water supply has all been arranged for. In fact"—he glanced at his watch—"in fact you might say that already it is being installed."

"But—if you will pardon me—what you say is impossible!"

"Not at all; it's very simple. This town is full of vintners' places and every vintner has—or rather he did have—a lot of those big empty wine casks on hand. Well, I sent two of my officers out this afternoon and bought every empty wine cask in this town. They rounded up 600 of them, and there'll be more coming in from the surrounding country to-morrow morning. I know there will be, because I've got men out scouting for them, and at the price I'm willing to pay I'll have every spare wine cask in this part of France delivered here to me by this time to-morrow. But 600 was enough to start on. I've had 800 of them set up at handy places over my camp site—had it done this evening—and at this moment the other 300 are being loaded upon army trucks—six casks to a truck. To-morrow morning the trucks will begin hauling water to fill the casks now on the ground."

It was as he had said. The minister was called up at night on the telephone, and from him a very willing approval of the unprecedented step in contemplation was secured. The water hauling started at dawn, and so did the tent raising start. The survey was delivered at noon; half an hour later American labour battalions were digging ditches for kitchen drains and latrines, and in accordance with the contour of the chosen spot a makeshift but serviceable sewerage system was being installed. When the troops marched out to their camp in the late afternoon of the second day following, their camp was there waiting for them and their supper was ready.

CHAPTER XXIII
BRICKS WITHOUT STRAW

TAKE any separate project along our line of communication. Pick it out at random. It makes no difference which particular spot you choose; you nevertheless are morally sure to find stationed there a man or a group of men who have learned to laugh at the problem of making bricks without straw. If put to it they could make monuments out of mud pies. Brought face to face with conditions and environments that were entirely new to their own experience, and confronted as they were at the outset by the task of providing essentials right out of the air—essentials that were vitally and immediately needed and that could not be forthcoming from the States for weeks or even months—an executive or an underling invariably would find a way out of the difficulty.

There was pressing need once for a receptacle in which rubber cement could be mixed in small quantities. Neither the local community nor the government stores yielded such a thing and there was no time to send clear back New York or Philadelphia for it. The man who was charged with the responsibility of getting that rubber cement mixed wait on a scouting tour. Somewhere he unearthed probably the only ice-cream freezer in rural Fiance outside of the immediate vicinity of Paris, and he acquired it at the proprietor's valuation and loaded it into his car and hurried back with it to his shop, and ten minutes after he arrived the required cement was being stirred to the proper consistency in the ice-cream freezer.

At the main depot of automobile supplies they needed, right away, springs with which to repair broken-down light cars. As yet an adequate supply of spare parts had not been received from the base, nor was there any likelihood that a supply would be forthcoming at once. The colonel in charge of the depot sent men ranging through the countryside with instructions to buy up stuff that would make springs. They brought him in tons of purchases, and most unlikely looking material it was too—rusted chunks and strips and spirals of metal taken from the underpinnings of French market carts and agricultural implements; but the forces in the machine shops sailed in and converted the lot into automobile springs in no time at all.

This same colonel already had a plant which, exclusive of the value of buildings specially built, represents at this time a national investment of $35,000,000, and the outlay was growing every hour. He used to be the head of a big metal-working establishment at home. As a specialist in his line he joined the Army to help out. Now every month he does a volume of buying that would have made his average year's turnover in times of peace look trifling in comparison. Just before he sailed to take over his present job he ordered $6,000,000 worth of motor parts at one fell swoop, as it were.

Because of the rapidity with which our forces on foreign service multiplied themselves there was a rush order from General Headquarters for more buildings and yet more buildings, at one of our warehouse depots, to provide for storage of perishable foodstuffs in transit from the rear to the Front. Between seven-thirty o'clock in the morning and five o'clock in the evening of a given day a gang of steel riggers accomplished the impossible by rearing and bolting together the steel frame—posts, girders, plates, rafters and crossbeams—for a building measuring 96 feet in width, 24 feet in height and 230 feet in length, the same being merely one of the units of a structure that very soon thereafter was up in the air and that measured 650 feet crosswise and 650 feet lengthwise, with railroad tracks stretching alongside and in between its various segments.

"When we laid out our original plans for this project the French said it would be entirely too large for our uses, no matter how big an army we brought over," remarked to me a young ex-civilian, now wearing a captain's markings on his flannel shirt, who had put through this undertaking. "Our people thought differently and we went ahead, trying to figure as we went along on all future contingencies. The result is that already we are enlarging upon the old specifications as rapidly as possible. Even so the supplies are piling up on us faster than we can store them. Look yonder."

He pointed to a veritable mountain of baled hay—a regular Himalaya of hay—which covered a corner of the field whereon we stood. It towered high above the tops of the trees behind it; it stretched dear to the edge of the woodlands beyond, and it was crowned, as a mountain peak should be, with white; only in this instance the blanket was of canvas instead of snow.

"There are 80,000 tons of American baled hay in that pile," he said, "and in a month from now if the present rate of growth keeps up it will be bigger by a third than it is now. It's quite some job—taking care of this man's army."

In the midriff of the Intermediate Section is a project on which at this writing 10,000 men are at work, and on an air-service field adjoining it 3,000 more men are engaged. Exclusive of material for local construction purposes 500 carloads of strictly military supplies arrive here daily, and approximately 75 carloads a day move out. Later the ratio of outgoing equipment will increase, but the incoming amount is not liable to fall off very much. To house the accumulating mass here and elsewhere in the same zone, including as it does engineers' stores, ordnance stores, fresh meats, salt meats, medical stores, harness, guns and quartermasters' stores, there has been provided or will be provided 4,500,000 square feet of roof-covered space and 10,000,000 square feet of open storage space.

When I came that way the other day miles of the plain had been filled pretty thoroughly with buildings and with side tracks and wagon roads; and, scattered over a tract measuring roughly six miles one way and four miles the other, between 18,000 and 14,000 men were engaged. In January of this year, when a man who now accompanied me had visited the same spot, he said there was one building standing on the area, and that two side tracks were in use; all the rest was a barren stretch of snowdrifts and half-frozen mud and desolation. They were just beginning then to dig the foundations of our main cold-storage plant. It is finished and in operation to-day. Besides being a model plant it is the third largest cold-storage plant in the world, and yet it is to be distinguished from the sixty-odd buildings that surround it only by the fact that it is taller and longer and has more smokestacks on it than any of the rest.

At the principal depot of the Advance Section, where the chief regulating officer is stationed, one of the biggest jobs is to sort out the man provender as it flows in by rail and to fill up each of fifty or sixty track-side warehouses with balanced rations—so much flour, so much salt meat, so much of salt, sugar, lard, canned goods, pepper, vinegar, pickles, and so on, to each building; or else to load a building with balanced man equipment—comprising shoes, socks, underwear, shirts, uniforms and the rest of it down to shoe laces and buttons, the purpose of this arrangement being that when a warehouse is emptied the man who is in charge, even before checking up on the loading gangs, already knows almost to a pound or a stitch just how many rations or how many articles of apparel have gone forward.

In each warehouse the canned tomatoes, the vinegar and the stuff that contains mild acids are stored at the two ends of the building in crosswise barricades that extend to the roof. This disposal was an idea of the officer in control of the arrangement. He explained to us that in case of fire canned stuff bearing a heavy proportion of fluid would burn more slowly than the other foodstuffs, so there would be a better chance of confining the blaze to the building in which it originated and of preventing its spread to adjoining or adjacent buildings, which might be of brick or concrete or stone or sheet metal, but which are more apt to be of frame.

The Glory Of The Coming | 195

A British colonel on a visit of inspection to, our Service of Supplies visited this project on the same day that I came. Radiating admiration and astonishment at every step and at every stop, he accompanied the young first lieutenant who was in personal charge of the warehousing scheme on a tour of his domain, which covered miles. When the round had been completed and the lieutenant had saluted and taken himself away the Britisher said to the chief regulating officer:

"I have never seen anything so perfectly devised as your plan of operation and distribution here. I take it that the young man who escorted me through is one of your great American managing experts. I imagine he must have been borrowed from one of those marvellous mail-order houses of yours, of which I have heard so much. One thing puzzles me though—he must have come here fresh from business pursuits, and yet he bears himself like a trained soldier."

The chief regulating officer smiled a little smile.

"That man," he said, "is an old enlisted man of our little antebellum Regular Army. He didn't win his commission until he came over here. Before that he was a noncom on clerical duty in the quartermaster's department, and before that he was a plain private, and as far as I know he never worked a day for any concern except our own Government since he reached the enlisting age."

In addition to doing what I should say at an offhand guess was the work of ten reasonably active men, the colonel who supervises our Advance Section has found time since he took over his present employment to organise a brass band and a glee dub among his personnel, to map out and stage-manage special entertainments for the men, to entertain visitors who come officially and unofficially, to keep several thousand individuals busy in their working hours and happy in their leisure hours, and at frequent intervals to write for the benefit of his command special bulletins touching on the finer sides of the soldier's duties and the soldier's discipline. He gave me a copy of one of his more recent pronouncements. He called it a memorandum; I called it a classic. It ran as follows:

"1. The salute, in addition to being a soldier's method of greeting, is the gauge by which he shows to the world his proficiency in the profession, his morale and the condition of his discipline.

"2. For me the dial of a soldier's salute has three marks, and I read his salute more accurately than he himself could tell me.

"3. The three gradations are:

(a) I am a soldier; I know my trade or will know it very soon, and I will be a success as a soldier or a civilian, wherever I may be put.

(b) I do not know what I am and do not care, I only do what I am forced to do, and will never be much of a success at anything.

(c) I am a failure and am down and out, sick, homesick and disgruntled. I cannot stand the gaff.

"4. As Americans try to conceal your feelings from our Allies.

"Remember you are just as much fighters here as you would be carrying a pail of food to the fighting line or actually firing a gun.

"Every extra exertion is an addition to the firing line direct.

"Every bit of shirking is robbing the firing line."

"Buck Up!"

For qualities of human interest no joints in the snake's spine, no twists in his manifold convolutions measure up, I think, to the salvage depots. Once upon a time, and not so very long ago, an army in the field threw away what it did not use or what through breakage or stress became unserviceable. That day is gone. In this war the wastage is practically negligible. Our people have learned this lesson from the nations that went into the war before we entered it, but in all modesty I believe, from what I have seen, that we have added some first-rate improvements to the plan in the few months that have been vouchsafed us for experiments and demonstrations. Moreover, to the success of our plans in this regard there have been difficulties that did not confront our Allies to the same extent. For instance our biggest motor-repair depot is housed in what formerly had been a French infantry barracks — a series of buildings that had never been devised for the purposes to which they are now put, and that at first offered many serious problems, mechanical and physical.

In tall brick buildings, under sheds and under tents and out in the open upon the old parade ground a great chain of machine shops, carpenter shops, paint shops, upholstery shops and leather-working shops has been coordinated and is cooperating to attain the maximum of possible production with the minimum of lost energy and lost effort. The scientist who reconstructs a prehistoric monster from a fossilised femur finds here his industrial prototype in the smart American mechanics who build up an ambulance or a motor truck from a fire-blackened, shell-riddled car frame, minus top, minus wheels, minus engine parts. What comes out of one total wreck goes into another that is not quite so totally so. And when a tool is lacking for some intricate job the Yank turns in and makes it himself out of a bit of scrap; and neither he nor his fellows think he has done anything wonderful either. It's just part of the day's work.

The salvage depot for human equipment and for lighter field equipment is established at this writing in what was, not so very long ago, a shop where one of the French railroad lines painted its cars. It began active operations last January with six civilian employees under an officer who four weeks before he landed in France was a business man in Philadelphia. In June it had on its pay rolls nearly 4,000 workers, mainly women and many of them refugees.

When all the floor space available—about 200,000 square feet of it—has been taken over the plant will have a personnel of about 5,000 hands, and it will be possible to do the reclamation work in clothing, shoes, rubber boots and slickers, harness and leather, canvas and webbing, field ranges, mess equipments, stoves, helmets, trenching tools, side arms, rifle slings, picks, shovels and metal gear generally for about 400,000 fighting men, with an estimated saving to Uncle Sam—exclusive of the vast sum saved in tonnage and shipping charges—of about $1,000,000 a month.

At this time 10,000 garments and articles of personal attire are passing through this plant every twenty-four hours, and coming out cleaned, mended, remade or converted to other purposes. A man could spend a week here, I feel certain, and not count his sight-seeing time as wasted. Among the men workers he would find invalided and crippled soldiers of at least six nations—America, Belgium, France, Greece, Serbia and Italy. Among the women workers, who average in pay seven francs a day—big wages for rural France—he would find many women of refinement and education hailing from evacuated districts in northern France and Belgium, whose faces bespeak the terrors and torments through which they have passed in the attempted implanting of the seeds of Kultur upon their homelands. Now they sit all day, driving sewing machines or managing knitting looms alongside their chattering, gossiping sisters of the peasant class.

And every hour in this beehive of industry the man who looked close would come upon things eloquently bespeaking the tragedy or the comedy of war's flotsam and jetsam. Now perhaps it would be a battered German bugle picked up by some souvenir-loving soldier, only to be flung into the camp salvage dump when its finder wearied of carrying it; and now it would be a khaki blouse with a bullet hole in the breast of it and great brown stains, stiff and dry, in its lining. A talking machine in fair order, the half of a tombstone and the full-dress equipment of a captain of Prussian Hussars were among the relics that turned up at the salvage depot in one week.

There is no dump heap behind the converted paint bam, for the very good reason that practically there is nothing to dump. Everything is saved. The salvaged junk comes in by the carload lot from the Front—filthy, crumpled, broken, blood-crusted, verminous, tattered, smelly and smashed. Sorters seize upon it and separate it and classify it according to kind and state of disrepair. Men and women bear it in armloads to sterilisers, where live steam kills the lice and the lice eggs; thence it goes to the cleaning vats, after which it is sorted again and the real job of making something out of what seemed to be worse than nothing at all is undertaken, with experts, mainly Americans, to supervise each forward step in the big contract of renovation, restoration and utilisation.

After the body clothing has been made clean and odourless it is assigned to one of three classes, to wit: (a) Garments needing minor repairs and still sightly and serviceable, which are put in perfect order and reissued to front-line troops; (b) garments not so sightly but still serviceable, which are issued to S O S workers, including stevedores, labourers, railroad engineers, firemen and forestry workers; (c) garments that are not sightly but that will repay repairing. These are dyed green and given to German prisoners of war. Practically no new material is used for repair. Garments that are past salvation in their present shape are cut up to furnish patches. Three garments out of four are reclaimed in one form or another; the fourth one becomes scrap for patchings. Shoes are washed in an acid disinfectant that cleanses the leather without injuring its fabric, and then they are dried and greased before going in to the workers. Shoes that are worth saving are saved to the last one; those past saving are ripped apart and the uppers are cut into shoe strings, while the soles furnish ground-up leather for compositions. Thanks to processes of washing, cleansing and repairing, a salvage average of approximately ninety per cent, is attained in slickers and rubber boots.

Last spring the high military authorities decided to shorten the heavy overcoats worn by our soldiers, so it befalls that the lengths of cloth cut from the skirts of the overcoats are now being fashioned at the salvage plants into uppers for hospital slippers, while old campaign hats furnish the material for the soles. The completed article, very neat in appearance and very comfortable to wear, is turned out here in great numbers. Old tires are cooked down to furnish new heels for rubber boots. Old socks are unravelled for the sake of the wool in them. Tin receptacles that have held gasoline or oil are melted apart, and from their sides and tops disks are fashioned which, being coated with aluminum, become markers for the graves where our dead soldier boys have been buried. Smaller tins are smelted down into lumps and used for a dozen purposes. The solder from the cans is not wasted either. Even the hobnails of worn-down boot soles are saved for future use.

Master of theatrical trick and device that he is, none the less David Belasco could learn lessons at our camouflaging plant. He probably would feel quite at home there, too, seeing that the place has a most distinctive behind-the-scenes atmosphere of its own; it is a sort of overgrown combination of scenery loft, property room, paint shop and fancy-dress costumer's establishment, where men who gave up sizable incomes to serve their country in this new calling work long hours seeking to improve upon the artifices already developed—and succeeding—and to create brand-new ones of their own.

As a branch of military modernism camouflaging is even newer than the trade of scientific salvaging is and offers far larger opportunities for future exploitation. After all there are just so many things and no more that may be done with and to a pair of worn-out rubber boots, but in the other field the only limits are the limits of the designer's individual ingenuity and his individual skill.

We came, under guidance, to a big open-fronted barracks where hundreds of French women and French girls made screenage for road protection and gun emplacements. The materials they worked with were simple enough: rolls of ordinary chicken wire, strips of burlap sacking dyed in four colours—bright green, yellowish green, tawny and brown—and wisps of raffia with which to bind the cloth scraps into the meshes of the wire. For summer use the bright green is used, for early spring and fall the lighter green and the tawny; and for winter the brown and the tawny mingled. For, you see, camouflage has its seasons, too, marching in step with the swing of the year. Viewed close up the completed article looks to be exactly what it is—chicken wire festooned thickly with gaudy rags. But stretch a breadth of it across a dip in the earth and then fling against it a few boughs cut from trees, and at a distance of seventy-five yards no man, however keen-eyed, can say just where the authentic foliage leaves off and the artificial joins on.

For roadsides in special cases there is still another variety of camouflage, done in zebra-like strips of light and dark rags alternating, and this stuff being erected alongside the open highway is very apt indeed to deceive your hostile observer into thinking that what he beholds is merely a play of sunlight and shade upon a sloped flank of earth; and he must venture very perilously near indeed to discern that the seeming pattern of shadows really masks the movements of troops. This deceit has been described often enough, but the sheer art of it takes on added interest when one witnesses its processes and sees how marvellously its effects are brought about.

In an open field used for experimenting and testing was a dump pile dotted thickly with all the nondescript débris that accumulates upon the outer slope of a dug-in defence where soldiers have been—loose clods of earth, bits of chalky stone, shattered stumps, empty beef tins, broken mess gear, discarded boots, smashed helmets, and such like. It was crowned with a frieze of stakes projecting above the top of the trench behind it, and on its crest stood one of those shattered trees, limbless and ragged, that often are to be found upon terrains where the shelling has been brisk.

Here for our benefit a sort of game was staged. First we stationed ourselves sixty feet away from the mound. Immediately five heads appeared above the parapet—heads with shrapnel helmets upon them, and beneath the helmet rims sunburnt faces peering out. The eyes looked this way and that as the heads turned from side to side.

"Please watch closely," said the camouflage officer accompanying us. "And as you watch, remember this: Two of those heads are the heads of men. The three others are dummies mounted on sticks and manipulated from below. Since you have been at the Front you know the use of the dummy—the enemy sniper shoots a hole in it and the men in the pit, by tracing the direction of the bullet through the pierced composition, are able to locate the spot where Mister Sniper is hidden. Now then, try to pick out the real heads from the fake ones."

There were three of us, and we all three of us tried. No two agreed in our guesses and not one of us scored a perfect record; and yet we stood very much nearer than any enemy marksman could ever hope to get. The lifelikeness of the thing was uncanny.

"Next take in the general layout of that spot," said the camouflage expert, with a wave of his hand toward the dump pile. "Looks natural and orthodox, doesn't it? Seems to be just the outer side of a bit of trench work, doesn't it? Well, it isn't. Two of those stakes are what they appear to be— ordinary common stakes. The other two are hollow metal tubes, inside of which trench periscopes are placed. And the tree trunk is faked, too. It is all hollow within—a shell of light tough steel with a ladder inside, and behind that twisted crotch where the limbs are broken off the observer is stationed at this moment watching us through a manufactured knothole. The only genuine thing about that tree trunk is the bark on it—we stripped that off of a beech over in the woods.

"The dump heap isn't on the level either, as you possibly know, since you may have seen such dump piles concealing the sites of observation pits up at the Front. Inside it is all dug out into galleries and on the side facing us it is full of peepholes—seventeen peepholes in all, I think there are. Let's go within fifteen feet of it and see how many of them you can detect."

At a fifteen-foot range it was hard enough for us to make out five of the seventeen peep places. Yet beforehand we understood that each tin can, each curled-up boot, each sizable tuft of withered grass, each swirl of the tree stump—masked a craftily hidden opening shielded with fine netting, through which a man crouching in safety beneath the surface of the earth might study the land in front of him. That innocent-appearing, made-to-order dump pile had the eyes of a spider; but even so, the uniformed invader might have climbed up and across it without once suspecting the truth.

For a final touch the camouflage crew put on their best stunt of all. Five men encased themselves in camouflage suits of greenish-brown canvas which covered them head, feet, body and limbs, and which being decorated with quantities of dried, grasslike stuff sewed on in patches, made them look very much as Fred Stone used to look when he played the Scarecrow Man in "The Wizard of Oz" years ago. Each man carried a rifle, likewise camouflaged. Then we turned our backs while they took position upon a half-bare, half-greened hillock less than a hundred feet from us.

This being done we faced about, and each knowing that five armed men were snuggled there against the bank tried to pick them out from their background. It was hard sledding, so completely had the motionless figures melted into the herbage and the chalky soil. Finally we united in the opinion that we had located three of the five. But we were wrong again. We really had picked out only one of the five. The two other suspected clumps were not men but what they seemed to be—small protrusions in the ragged and irregular turf. Yes, I am sure Mr. Belasco could have spent a fruitful half hour or so there with us.

Thanks to yet another crafty and deceitful artifice of the camouflage outfit it is possible to make the enemy think he is being attacked by raiders advancing in force when as a matter of fact what he beholds approaching him are not files of men but harmless dummies operated by a mechanism that is as simple as simplicity itself. The attack will come from elsewhere while his attention is focused upon the make-believe feint, but just at present there are military reasons why he should not know any of the particulars. It would take the edge of his surprise, even though he is not likely to live to appreciate the surprise once the trick has been pulled.

These details of the whole vast undertaking that I have touched upon here are merely bits that stand out with especial vividness from the recent recollections of a trip every rod of which was freighted with the most compelling interest for any one, and for an American with enduring and constant pride in the achievements of his own countrymen.

There are still other impressions, many of than, big and little, that are going always to stick in my brain—the smell of the crisp brown crusty loaves, mingling with the smell of the wood fires at the bakery where half a million bread rations are cooked and shipped every day, seven days a week; the sight at the motor reception park, where a big proportion of the 60,000 motor vehicles of all sorts that are called for in our programme, as it stands now, can be stored at one time; the miles upon miles of canned goods through which I have passed, with the boxes towering in walls upon either side of me; the cold-storage chamber as big as a cathedral, where a supply of 5,000 tons of fresh meat is kept on hand and ready for use; a cemetery for our people, only a few months old, but lovely already with flowers and grass and neat gravel paths between the mounds; a blacksmith riveting about the left wrists of Chinese labourers their steel identification markers so that there may always be a positive and certain way of knowing just who is who in the gang, since to stupid occidental eyes all Chinamen look alike and except for these little bangles made fast upon the arms of the wearers there would be complications and there might be wilful falsifications in the pay rolls; a spectacled underofficer hailing us in perfect but plaintive English from a group of prisoners mending roads, to say in tones of deep lament that he used to be a dentist in Baltimore but made the mistake of going back to Germany for a visit to his old home just before the war broke out; a Catholic chaplain superintending the beautifying of a row of graves of Mohammedans who had died in our service, and who had been laid away according to the ritual of their own faith in a corner of a burying ground where Christians and Jews are sleeping together; a maimed Belgian soldier with three medals for valour on his shirt front, cobbling shoe soles in the salvage plant; a French waiter boy in a headquarters mess learning to pick out the chords of Dixie Land on an American negro's homemade guitar; a room in the staff school where a former member of the Cabinet of the United States, an ex-Congressman, an ex-police commissioner of New York City and one of the richest men in America, all four of them volunteer officers, sat at their lessons with their spines fish-hooked and their brows knotted; nineteen-year-old Yankee apprentice flyer doing such heart-stopping stunts in a practice plane as I never expect to see equalled by any veteran airman; the funeral, on the same day and at the same time, of one of his mates, who had been killed by a fall upon the field over which this daring youth now cavorted, with the coffin in an ambulance and a flag over the coffin, and behind the ambulance the firing squad, the Red Cross nurses from the local hospital and a company of his fellow cadets marching.

And seeing all these sights and a thousand more like unto them I found myself as I finished my tour along the winding lengths of the great snake we call the Service of Supplies, wondering just who, of all the thousands among the men that labour behind the men behind the guns, deserve of their countrymen the greatest meed of credit—the high salaried executives out of civilian life who dropped careers and comforts and hope of preferment in their professions at home, to give of the genius of their brains to this cause; or the officers of our little old peacetime Army who here serve so gladly and so efficiently upon the poor pay that we give our officers, without hope ever of getting a proper measure of national appreciation for their efforts, since this war is so nearly an anonymous war, where the performances of the individual are swallowed up in the united efforts of the mass; or the skilled railway trainmen volunteering to work on privates' wages for the period of the war; or the plain enlisted man cheerfully, eagerly, enthusiastically toiling here, so far back of the Front, when in his heart he must long to be up there with his fellows where the big guns boom.

CHAPTER XXIV
FROM MY OVERSEAS NOTE-BOOK

BLOWS with a hammer may numb one, but it is the bee-sting that quickens the sensibilities to a realisation of what is afoot. That is why, I suppose, the mighty thing called war is for me always summed up in small, incidental but outstanding phases of it. In its complete aspect it is too vast to be comprehended by any one mind or any thousand minds; but by piecing together the lesser things, one after a while begins in a dim groping fashion to get a concept of the entirety.

When I went up to Ypres, it was not the unutterable desolation and hideousness of what had been once one of the fairest spots on earth that especially impressed me: possibly because Ypres to-day is a horror too terrible and a tragedy too utter for human contemplation save at the risk of losing one's belief in the ultimate wisdom of the cosmic scheme of things. Nor was it the wreck of the great Cloth Hall which even now, with its overthrown walls and its broken lines and its one remaining spindle of ruined tower, manages to retain a suggestion of the matchless beauty which forevermore is gone. Nor yet was it the cemetery, whereon for sheer, degenerate malignity the Germans targeted their heavy guns until they had broached nearly every grave, heaving up the dead to sprawl upon the displaced clods. One becomes, in time, accustomed to the sight of dead soldiers lying where they have fallen, because a soldier accepts the chances of being killed and of being left untombed after he is killed. The dread spectacle he presented is part and parcel of the picture of war. But these men and women and babes that the shells dispossessed from their narrow tenements of mould had died peacefully in their beds away back yonder—and how long ago it seems now!—when the world itself was at peace. They had been shrouded in their funeral vestments; they had been laid away with cross and candle, with Book and prayer; over them slabs of the everlasting granite had been set, and flowers had been planted above them and memorials set up; and they had been left there beneath the kindly loam, cradled for all eternity till Gabriel's Trump should blow.

But when I came there and saw what *Kul-tur* had wrought amongst them—how with exquisite irony the blasts had shattered grave after grave whose stones bore the carved words *Held in Perpetuity* and how grandmothers and grandsires and the pitiable small bones of little children had been flung forth out of the gaping holes and left to moulder in the rags of their cerements where all who passed that way might see them—why, it was a blasphemy and an indecency and a sacrilege which no man, beholding it, could ever, so long as he lived, hope to forget.

And yet, as I just said, it was not the defilement of the cemetery of Ypres which impressed me most when I went up to Ypres. It was the lamp-posts.

Ypres had been studded thick with lampposts; ornamental and decorative standards of wrought iron they were, spaced at intervals of forty yards or so for the length of every street and on both sides of every street. And every single lamp-post in Ypres, as I took the pains to see for myself, had been struck by shells or by flying fragments of shells. Some had been hit once or twice, some had been quite hewn down, some had been twisted into shapeless sworls of tortured metal; not one but was scathed after one mutilating fashion or another.

In other words, during these four years of bombardment so many German shells had descended upon Ypres that no object in it of the thickness of six inches at its base and say, two inches at its top, had escaped being struck. Or putting it another way, had all these shells been fired through a space of hours instead of through a space of years, they would have rained down on the empty town with the thickness and the frequency of drops in a heavy thunder-shower.

Never was the Hun quite so thorough as when he was punishing some helpless thing that could not fight back.

Riding along through France on a Sunday, these times, one is reasonably certain to meet many little girls wearing their white communion frocks, and many Chinamen under umbrellas.

The latter mostly hail from Indo-China. The French imported them in thousands for service in the labour battalions behind the lines. During the week, dressed in nondescript mixtures of native garb and cast-off uniforms, they work at road-mending or at ditch-digging or on truck-loading jobs. On Sundays they dress themselves up in their best clothes and stroll about the country-side. And rain or shine, each one brings along with him his treasured umbrella and carries it unfurled above his proud head. It never is a Chinese umbrella, either, but invariably a cheap black affair of local manufacture. Go into one of the barracks where these yellow men are housed and at the head of each bunk there hangs a black umbrella, which the owner guards as his most darling possession. If he dies I suppose it is buried with him.

Nobody knows here why every Sunday, Chinaman sports an umbrella, unless it be that in his Oriental mind he has decided that possession of such a thing stamps him as a person of travel and culture who, like any true cosmopolitan, is desirous of conforming to the customs of the country to which he has been transported. But a Frenchman, if careless, sometimes leaves his umbrella behind when he goes forth for a promenade; a Chinaman in France, never.

When a ship-load of these chaps lands they are first taken to a blacksmith shop and upon the left wrist of each is securely and permanently fastened a slender steel circlet bearing a token on which is stamped the wearer's name and his number. So long as he is in the employ of the State this little band must stay on his arm. It is the one sure means of identifying him and of preventing payroll duplications.

With the marker dangling at his sleeve-end he makes straightway for a shop and buys himself a black cotton umbrella and from that time forward, wherever he goes, his steel bangle and his umbrella go with him. He cannot part from one and not for worlds would he part from the other.

One Sunday afternoon in a village in the south of France I saw that rarest of sights—a drunken Chinaman. He wiggled and waggled as he walked, and once he sat down very hard, smiling foolishly the while, but he never lost his hold on the handle of his umbrella and when he had picked himself up, the black bulge of it was bobbing tipsily above his tipsy head as he went weaving down the road behind a mile-long procession of his fellows, all marching double file beneath their raised umbrellas.

Whisper—there is current a scandalous rumour touching on these little moon-faced allies of ours. It is said that among them every fourth man, about, isn't a man at all. He's a woman wearing a man's garb and drawing a man's pay; or rather she is, if we are going to keep the genders on straight. But since the women work just as hard as the men do nobody seems to bother about the deceit. They may not have equal suffrage over in Indo-China but the two sexes there seem to have a way of adjusting the industrial problems of the day on a mutually satisfactory basis of understanding.

"Piccadilly Circus. This way to Swan and Edgar's."

The sign-board was the top of a jam box. The upright to which it was nailed was the shell-riddled trunk of a plane tree with one sprig of dried mistletoe clinging in a crotch where limbs had been, like a tuft of dead beard on a mummy's chin. Piccadilly Circus was a roughly-rounded spot at a cross-road where the grey and sticky mud—greyer than any mud you stay-at-homes ever saw; stickier than any mud you ever saw—made a little sea which quaked and shimmered greasily like a quicksand. The way to Swan and Edgar's was down a communication trench with shored sides to it, so that the semi-liquid walls could not cave in, and with duck boards set in it upon spiles for footing, so that men passing through would not be engulfed and drowned in the quagmire beneath.

So much for the immediate setting. The adjacent surroundings were of a pattern to match the chosen sample. All about on every side for miles on end, was a hell of grey mud, here up-reared into ridges and there depressed into holes; and the ridges heaved up to meet a skyline of the same sad colour as themselves, and the holes were like the stale dead craters of a stale dead moon.

Elsewhere in the land, spring had come weeks before, but here the only green was the green of the skum on the grey water in the bottoms of the shell-fissures; the only living things were the ravens that cawed over the wasted landscape, and the great, fat, torpid rats with mud glued in their whiskers and their scaled tails caked with mud, that scuttled in and out of the long-abandoned German pill-boxes or through holes in the rusted iron sides of three dismantled British tanks. For lines of trees there were up-ended wrecks of motor trucks and ambulances; for the hum of bees, was the hum of an occasional sniper's bullet; for the tap of the wood-pecker, was the rat-tat of machine guns marking time for a skirmish miles away; for growing crops, in these once fecund and prolific stretches of the Flanders flat-lands, there were eighty-thousand unburied dead, all encysted in the mud except where the gouging shells had uprooted them out of the loblolly. And from far up on the rise toward Passchen-daele came the dull regurgitations of the big guns, as though the war had sickened of its own horrors and was retching in its nausea.

What now was here must, in a measure, always be here. For surely no husbandman would dare ever to drive his ploughshare through a field which had become a stinking corruption; where in every furrow he would inevitably turn up mortal awfulness, and where any moment his steel might strike against one of the countless unexploded shells which fill the earth like horrid plums in a yet more horrid pudding.

You couldn't give this desolation a name; our language yields no word to fit it, no adjective to cap it. Yet right here in the stark and rotten middle of it a British Tommy had stopped to have his little joke. Was he downhearted? No! And so to prove he wasn't, —that his spirits were high and that his racial gift of humour was unimpaired, he stuck up a sign of sprawled lettering and it said:

"Piccadilly Circus. This way to Swan and Edgar's."

Mister Kaiser, you might have known, if your mental processes hadn't been stuck on skew-wise, forty ways for Sunday, that you could never break through an army of good sports who make jokes at death and coin gibes at what might well drive less hardy souls to madness.

Mighty few men outwardly conform to the rôles they actually fill in life. I am not speaking of drum-majors in bands or tattooed men in side-shows or floor-walkers in department stores. Such parties are picked for their jobs because, physically, they live up to the popular conception; perhaps I should say the popular demand. I am speaking of the run of the species. A successful poet is very apt to look like an unsuccessful paper-hanger and I have known a paper-hanger who was the spittin' image of a free versifier.

I think, though, of two men I have met over here who were designed by nature and by environment to typify exactly what they are. One is Haig and the other is Pershing. Either would make the perfect model for a statue to portray the common notion of a field-marshal. General Sir Douglas Haig is a picture, drawn to scale, of the kind of British general that the novelists love to describe; in mannerism, in figure, in size, in bearing, in colouring and expression, he is all of that. And by the same tokens Pershing in every imaginable particular is the typical American fighting-man. Incidentally I might add that these two men are two of the handsomest and most splendid martial figures I have ever met. They say Haig is the best-dressed officer in the British army and that is saying a good deal, considering that the officers of the British army are the best dressed officers of any army.

Pershing has the poise and port of a West Point cadet; has a cadet's waist-line and shoulder-lines, too. A man may keep a youthful face but in the curves of his back is where nearly always he betrays his age. Look at Pershing's back without knowing who he was and you would put him down as an athlete in his early twenties.

I have taken lunch with General Sir Douglas Haig, and his staff, including his Presbyterian chaplain who is an inevitable member of the commander's official family, and I have dined with General Pershing and his staff, as Pershing's guest. When you break bread with a man at his table you get a better chance to appraise him than you would be likely to get did you casually meet him elsewhere. From each headquarters I brought away the settled conviction that I had been in the company of one of the staunchest, most dependable, most capable personalities to whom authority and power were ever entrusted. Different as they were in speech and in gesture, from each there radiated a certain thing which the other likewise possessed and expressed without knowing that he expressed it—a sense of a stupendous, unremitting responsibility, gladly accepted and well discharged; an appreciation of having in his hands a job to do, the tools for the doing of which are human beings, and in the doing of which, should he make a mistake, the error will be charged up against him in figures of human life.

Always I shall remember one outstanding sentence which Haig uttered and one which Pershing uttered. Curiously enough, each was addressing himself to the same subject, to wit: the American soldier. Haig said:

"The spirit of the American soldier as I have seen him over here since your country entered the war, is splendid. When he first came I was struck by his good humour, his unfailing cheerfulness, his modesty, and most of all by his eager, earnest desire to learn the business of war as speedily and as thoroughly as possible. Now as a British commander, I am very, very glad of the opportunity to fight alongside of him—so glad, that I do not find the words offhand, to express the depth of my confidence in the steadfastness and the intelligence and the courage he is every day displaying."

Pershing said:

"When I think, as I do constantly think, of the behaviour of our men fighting here in a foreign land; of the disciplined cheerfulness with which they have faced discomforts, of the constant determination with which they have confronted difficulties, and of the splendid dash with which they have met the enemy in battle, I cannot speak what is in my mind because my emotions of gratitude are so great they keep me from speaking of these things."

At a French railway station any day one sees weeping women but they do not weep until after the trains which carry their men-folk back to the trenches have gone. To this rule I have never seen an exception.

A soldier who has finished his leave—a *permissionaire* the French call him—comes to the station, returning to his duties at the Front. It may be he is a staff officer gorgeous in gold lace. It may be he is a recruit of this year's class with the fleece of adolescence still upon his cheeks but with the grave assurance of a veteran in his gait. Or it may be that he is a grizzled territorial bent forward by one of those enormous packs which his sort always tote about with them; and to me this last one of the three presents the most heart-moving spectacle of any. Nearly always he looks so tired and his uniform is so stained and so worn and so wrinkled! I mean to make no cheap gibe at the expense of a nation which has fine-tooth-combed her land for man, power to stand the drain of four years of war when I say that according to my observations the back-line reserves of France in 1918 are a million middle-aged men whose feet hurt them.

Be he staff officer though, or beardless youth or fifty-year-old rear-guard it is certain that his women-folk will accompany him to the station to tell him farewell. He has had his week at home. By to-night he will be back again at the Front, in the mud and the filth and the cold and the wet. By to-morrow he may be dead. But there is never a tear shed at parting. He kisses his wife or his mother or his sister or all of them; he hugs to his breast his babies, if he has babies. Then he climbs aboard a car which already is crowded with others like him, and as the train draws away the women run down the platform alongside the train, smiling and blowing kisses at him and waving their hands and shouting good-byes and bidding him to do this or that or the other thing.

And then, when the train has disappeared they drop down where they are and cry their hearts out. I have witnessed this spectacle a thousand times, I am sure, and always the sight of it renews my admiration for the women of what I veritably believe to be the most patient and the most steadfast race of beings on the face of the globe.

In early June, I went up to where the first division of ours to be sent into the British lines for its seasoning under fire was bedded down in billets hard by the Flanders border; and there I saw a curious thing. There were Canadians near at hand, and Australians and New Zealanders and one might naturally suppose the Yankee lads would by preference fraternise with these soldiers from the Dominions and the Colonies who in speech, in mode of life and in habit of thought were really their brothers under the skin.

Not at all. In many cases, if not in a majority of cases, that came under my notice I found Americans chumming with London Cockneys, trading tobacco for cheese; prunes for jam, cigarettes for captured souvenirs; guying the Londoners because they drank tea in the afternoons and being guyed because they themselves wanted coffee in the mornings.

The phenomenon I figured out to my own satisfaction according to this process of deduction: First, that the American and the Cockney had discovered that jointly they shared the same gorgeous sense of humour, albeit expressed in dissimilar ways; second, that each had found out the other was full of sporting instincts, which made another tie between them; and third and perhaps most cogent reason of all, that whatever the Yankee might say, using his own slang to say it, sounded unutterably funny in the Cockney's ear, and what the Cockney said on any subject, in his dialect, was as good as a vaudeville show to the Yankee.

Personally I do not believe it was the Anglo-Saxon strain calling to the Anglo-Saxon strain, because the American was as likely to be of Italian or

Irish or Jewish or Teutonic or Slavic antecedents as he was to be of pure English ancestry. I am sure it was not the common use by both of the same language—with variations on the part of either. But I am sure that it was the joyous prospect of getting free and unlimited entertainment out of the conversations of a new pal.

Anyway our soldiers are cementing us together with a cement that will bind the English-speaking races in a union which can never be sundered, I am sure of that much.

The madness which descended upon our enemies when they started this war would appear to have taken a turn where it commonly manifests itself in acts of stark degeneracy. Every day I am hearing tales which prove the truth of this. If there was only one such story coming to light now and then we might figure the terrible thing as proof of the nastiness of an individual pervert manifesting itself; but where the evidence piles up in a constantly accumulating mass it makes out a case so complete one is bound to conclude that a demoniacal rottenness is running through their ranks, affecting officer and men alike. For the sake of the good name of mankind in general one strives not to accept all these tales but the bulk of them must be true.

A young tank-officer of ours whom I knew before the war in New York, where he was a rising lawyer, and whom I knew to be truthful, tells me that an honest appearing British non-com in turn, told him that a week or two ago the Britishers having cleaned up a nest of enemy machine guns, sent a detail out to bury the dead. The squad had buried two Germans, then they came upon the body of one of their own men who had fallen in the fighting two days earlier when the Britishers made their first attack upon the Germans only to be forced back and then to come again with better success. The sergeant who stood sponsor for the narrative declared that as he bent over the dead Englishman to unfasten the identification tag from the wrist, he saw that something was fastened to the dead man's arm and that this something was partly hidden beneath the body. Becoming instantly suspicious, he warned the other men to stand back and then kneeling down and feeling about cautiously, he found a bomb so devised that a slight jar would set it off. Before they fell back, the surviving Germans had attached this devilish thing to a corpse with the benevolent intent of blowing to bits the first man among the victors who should undertake to move the poor clay with intent to give it decent burial.

Our men have been warned against gathering up German helmets and German rifles in places from which the enemy has retired, because such souvenirs have a way of blowing up in the finders' hands by reason of the explosive grenades that have been attached to them and hidden beneath them with the cap so arranged that a tug at the wired-on connection will set off the charge; but this crowning atrocity shows they are making improvements in their system. From sawing down fruit trees, from shoveling filth in the drinking wells, from wantonly destroying the villages which for years have sheltered them, from laying waste the lands which they are being forced now to surrender back into the hands of their rightful proprietors, the ingenious Hun has progressed in his military education to where he makes dead men serve his purposes. Personally, I have heard of but one act to match this one. An American trooper entered a half-wrecked hamlet which the retreating Germans had just evacuated, and on going into a villager's house, saw a china doll lying upon a cupboard shelf, and saw that, hitched to the doll, was one of these touchy hand-bombs. Now, it is only reasonable to assume the German who planned this surprise went upon the assumption that the doll would be the prized possession of some French child and that when the family who owned the house found their way back to it, the child would run first of all to recover her treasured dollie and picking it up would be killed or mangled, thereby scoring one more triumph, if a small one, for Vaterland and Kaiser.

To a dressing station behind our front lines up beyond St. Mihiel— so I am reliably informed—our stretcher-bearers brought two wounded prisoners and laid them down. One of the pair was a Prussian captain with a hole in his breast; the other a weedy boy-private with a shattered leg. There were two surgeons at work here—a Frenchman and an American.

As the Frenchman bent over the captain, in the joy of service forgetting for the moment that the man lying before him was his enemy and filled only with a desire to save life and relieve human agony, the Prussian who seemingly had been unconscious, opened his eyes in recognition. Thereupon the surgeon, making ready to strip away the first-aid dressings from the punctured chest, spoke to his patient in French saying he trusted the captain did not suffer great pain. The reply Was Prussianesque. The wounded man cleared his throat and spat full in the Frenchman's face.

I hope I am not blood-thirsty, but I am happy to be able to relate a satisfactory sequel. The Frenchman, who must have been a gentleman as well as a soldier, stood true to the creed of an honourable and merciful calling. He merely put up his hand and without a word wiped the spittle from his face which had grown white as death under the strain of enduring the insult. But an American stretcher-bearer who had witnessed the act, snatched up a rifle from a heap of captured accoutrements near the door of the dugout and brought the butt of it down, full force, across the hateful, gloating mouth of the Prussian.

For contrast, mark the behaviour of the boy-soldier who also had just been borne in. It was the American surgeon who took the private's case in hand. Now this American surgeon was of pure German descent and bore a German name and he spoke well the tongue of his ancestors. So naturally he addressed the groaning lad in German.

Between gasps of pain, the lad told his interrogator that he was a Saxon, that his age was eighteen and that he had been in service at the Front for nearly a year. Even in the midst of his suffering he showed pleasure at finding among his captors a man who knew and could use the only language which he himself knew. Noting this, the surgeon continued to address the youngster as he made ready to do to the mangled limb what was needful to be done.

As his skilled fingers touched the wound, some sub-conscious instinct quickened perhaps by the fact that he had just employed the mother-speech of his parents set him to whistling between his teeth a song he had known as a child. And that song was *Die Wackt am Rhein*.

Under his ministering hands the young Saxon twitched and jerked. Perhaps he thought the surgeon meant to gloat over him, captured and maimed for life as he was; perhaps it was another emotion which prompted him to cry out in a half-strangled shriek:

"Don't whistle that song—don't!"

"I am sorry," said the American, "I did not mean to hurt your feelings. I thought you might like to hear it—that it might soothe you."

"Like to hear it? Never!" panted the lad. "I hate it—I hate it—I hate it!"

"Surely though you love your country and your Emperor, don't you?" pressed the American, anxious to fathom the psychology of the prisoner's nature.

"I love my country—yes," answered the boy, "but as to the Kaiser, to him I would do this—" And he drew a finger across his throat with a quick, sharp stroke.

I am putting down this scrap of narrative in a room in a hotel that is two hundred years old, in the heart of a wonderful old Norman city and while I am writing it, twenty miles away, in front of Montdidier, they are giving my friend the kind of funeral he asked for.

I call him my friend, although I never saw him until four weeks ago. He was a man you would want for your friend. Physically and every other way, he was the sort of man that Richard Harding Davis used to love to describe in his stories about soldiers of fortune. He seemed to have stepped right out of the pages of one of Davis's books—he was tall and straight and slender, as handsome a man as ever I looked at and a soldier in every inch of him. The other officers of the regiment admired him but his men, as I have reason to know, worshipped him—and that, in the final appraisals, is the test of an officer and a gentleman in any army.

I met him on the day when I rode up into Picardy to attach myself bag and baggage—one bag and not much baggage—to a foot-regiment of our old regular army, then moving into the battle-lines to take over a sector from the French. He had a Danish name and his father, I believe, was a Dane; but he was born in a Western state nearly forty years ago. In the Spanish war he was a kid private; saw service as a non-com in the Philippine mess; tried civil life afterwards and couldn't endure it; went to Central America and took a hand in some tinpot revolution or other; came home again and was in business for a year or so, which was as long as his adventurous soul could stand a stand-still life; then moved across the line into the Canadian Northwest and got a job in the Royal Mounted Police. In 1914, when the war broke, he volunteered in a Canadian battalion as a private. On our entrance into the conflict he was a major of the Dominion Forces.

He resigned this commission forthwith, hurried back to the States and joined up at the first recruiting office he saw after he reached New York. And now when I met him, he had his majority in an American regiment which has a long and a most honourable record behind it.

During this past month I saw a good deal of him. So far as I could judge, he had one, and just one, bit of affectation about him—if you could call it that. He wore always the British trench helmet that he had worn in the Canadian forces and he liked to finger the gap in its brim where a bit of shrapnel chipped it as he climbed up Vimy Ridge, and he liked to tell about that day of Vimy so glorious and so tragic for the valorous whelps of the British lion who hail from our own side of the blue water. He had another small vanity too, as I now understand—a vanity which to-day is being gratified.

Six days ago I left the regiment to spend a day and a night with a battery of five-inch guns just west of Montdidier. As I was starting off he hailed me and we made an engagement for a dinner together here in this town where the food is very, very good, said dinner to take place "sometime soon." He was standing in the road as I rode away and when I looked back out of the car he waved his hand at me.

The village where I stayed for that night and the following day, formed a hinge in the line that our forward forces had taken over. It was within two miles of the German trenches and within three or four miles of some of their heavy batteries. Through the night I slept at battalion headquarters, in the only house in the town which up until then had escaped serious damage from German gunfire.

Coming back again to my regiment—as I shall call it—on the second day following, I learned that almost immediately after my departure the batteries I left in and near this village had been ordered to take up a prepared position in a patch of woods a mile farther in the rear and that my friend's battalion had gone up to hold the town and to act as a reserve unit there until its turn should come to relieve part of another infantry regiment in the trenches proper. So I knew that in all probability he now was domiciled in the cottage where I had slept the night previous. As it turned out my guess was right—that was where he was. Three days ago I borrowed a side-car and ran on down here where I could get in touch with the divisional censor and file some of the copy I have been grinding out lately.

Yesterday afternoon in the main square I bumped into the adjutant of my regiment and with him, one of the French liaison officers attached to the regiment.

"Hello," I said, "what brings you two down here?"

"We came to get some flowers for the funeral to-morrow," the adjutant told me.

"Whose funeral?" I asked.

When they told me whose funeral, I was stunned for a moment. From them I learned when my friend died and how. And this, then, is the story of it:

Night before last he and his battalion liaison officer, a Frenchman of course, and his battalion adjutant were eating supper in that same small red brick house which had sheltered me for a night. The Germans had been punishing the place at long distance; now there was a lull in the bombardment, but just as the three of them finished their meal, the enemy reopened fire. Almost at once a shell fell in the courtyard before the house and another demolished a stone stable in the orchard behind it. All three hurried down into an improvised bomb-proof shelter in the cellar.

"You fellows stay here," said the major when they had reached the foot of the stairs. "I left my cigars and a couple of letters from home upstairs in the kitchen. I'll go up and get them and be back again with you in a minute."

Thirty seconds later, to the accompaniment of a great rending crash, the building caved in. Wreckage cascaded down the cellar stairs but the floor rafters above their heads stood the jar and the two who were below got off with bruises and scratches. They made their way up through the debris. A six-inch shell had come through the roof, blowing down two sides of the kitchen, and under the shattered walls the Major was lying, helpless and crushed.

They hauled him out. He was conscious but badly hurt, as they could tell. The adjutant ran to a dug-out on the other side of the village and brought back with him the regimental surgeon. It didn't take the surgeon long to make his examination.

To the others he whispered that there was no hope—the Major's spine was broken. But because he dreaded to break the word to the victim he essayed a bit of excusable deceit.

"Major," he said, bending over the figure stretched out upon the floor, "you've got it pretty badly, but I guess we'll pull you through. Only you'd better let me give you a little jab of dope in your arm—you may begin to suffer as soon as the numbness of the shock wears off."

My friend, so they told me, looked up in the surgeon's face with a whimsical grin.

"Doc," he said, "your intentions are good; but there comes a time when you mustn't try to fool a pal. And you can't fool me—I know. I know I've got mine and I know I can't last much longer. I'm dead from the hips down already. And never mind about giving me any dope. There are several things I want to say and I want my head clear while I'm saying them."

He told them the names and addresses of his nearest relatives—a brother and a sister, and he gave directions for the disposal of his kit and of his belongings. He didn't have very much to leave—professional soldiers rarely do have very much to leave.

After a bit he said: "I've only one regret. I'm passing out with the uniform of an American soldier on my back and that's the way I always hoped 'twould be with me, but I'm sorry I didn't get mine as I went over the top with these boys of ours behind me. Still, a man can't have everything— can he?—and I've had my share of the good things of this world."

He began to sink and once they thought he was gone; but he opened his eyes and spoke again:

"Boys," he said, "take a tip from me who knows: this thing of dying is nothing to worry about. There's no pain and there's no fear. Why, dying is the easiest thing I've ever done in all my life. You'll find that out for yourselves when your time comes. So cheer up and don't look so glum because I just happen to be the one that's leaving first."

The end came within five minutes after this. Just before he passed, the liaison officer who was kneeling on the floor holding one of the dying man's hands between his two hands, felt a pressure from the cold fingers that he clasped and saw a flicker of desire in the eyes that were beginning to glaze over with a film. He bent his head close down and in the ghost of a ghost of a whisper, the farewell message of his friend and mine came to him between gasps.

"Listen," the Major whispered, "Old Blank,"—naming the regimental chaplain—"has pulled off a lot of slouchy funerals in this outfit. Tell him, for me, to give me a good swell one, won't you?"

He went then, with the smile of his little conceit still upon his lips.

That was why the two men whom I met here yesterday rode in to get flowers and wreaths. They told me the Colonel was going to have the regimental band out for the services to-day too, and that a brigadier-general and a major-general of our army would be present with their staffs and that a French general would be present with his staff. So I judge they are giving my friend what he wanted—a good swell one.

The France to which tourists will come after the war will not be the France which peacetime visitors knew. I am not speaking so much of the ruined cities and the razed towns, each a mute witness now to thoroughness as exemplified according to the orthodox tenets of Kul-tur. For the most part these never can be restored to their former semblances—Hunnish efficiency did its damned work too well for the evil badness of it ever to be undone. Indeed I was told no longer ago than last week, when I went through Arras, dodging for shelter from ruin-heap to ruin-heap between gusts of shelling from the German batteries, that it is the intention of the French government to leave untouched and untidied certain areas of wanton devastation, so future generations of men looking upon these hell's quarter-sections, will have before their eyes fit samples of the finished handicraft of the Hun. I am sure this must be true of Arras because in the vicinity of the cathedral—I mean the place where the cathedral was once—signs are stuck up in rubble-piles or fastened to upstanding bits of splintered walls forbidding visitors to remove souvenirs or to alter the present appearance of things in any way whatsoever. I sincerely trust the French do carry out this purpose. Then in the years to come, when Americans come here and behold this spot, once one of the most beautiful in all Europe and now one of the foulest and most hideous, they may be cured of any lingering inclination to trust a people in whose veins there may linger a single trace of the taints of Kaiserism and militarism. However, I dare say that by then our present enemies will have been purged clean of the blight that now is in their blood.

When I say that the France of the future will never be the France which once was a shrine for lovers of beauty to worship at—which was all one great altar dedicated to loveliness—I am thinking particularly of the rural districts and not of the communities. I base my belief upon the very reasonable supposition that after the armies are withdrawn or disbanded—or, as in the case of our foes, killed off or captured or driven back,—the peasants in their task of making the devastated regions fit once more for human habitation, will turn to the material most plentifully at hand and that of which the quickest use can be made. This means then, that instead of rebuilding with masonry and cement and plaster after the ancient modes, they will employ the salvage of military constructions. And by that same sign it means that ugly characterless wooden buildings with roofs of corrugated iron, and all slab-sided and angular and hopelessly plain, will replace the quaint gabled houses that are gone—and gone forever; and that where the picturesque stone fences ran zig-zagging across the faces of the meadows, and likewise where the centuries-old, plastered walls rose about byre and midden and stable-yard, will instead be stretched lines of barbed wire, nailed to wooden posts.

The stuff will be there—in incredible quantities—and it will be cheap and it will be available for immediate use, once the forces of the Allies have scattered. It is only natural to assume therefore that the thrifty country-folk and the citizens of the villages will take it over. For a fact in certain instances they are already doing so. Just the other day, up near the Flanders border in the British-held territory, I saw a half grown boy wriggling through a maze of rusted wire along an abandoned defence line, like Brer Rabbit through the historic brier-patch; and when I drew nearer, curious to know what sort of game he played all alone here in a land where every game except the great game of war is out of fashion, I saw that he was tearing down the strands of the wire, and through the interpreter he told me he was going to enclose his mother's garden with the stuff. Think of a French garden fenced in after the style of a Nebraska ranch yard. Also I have taken note that the peasants are removing the plank shorings from the sides of old, disused trenches and with the boards thus secured are knocking up barns and chicken-sheds and even makeshift dwellings.

Assuredly it will never be the old France, physically. But spiritually, the new France, wearing the scars of her sacrifice as the Redeemer of Mankind wore the nail-marks of His crucifixion, will be a vision of glory before the eyes of men forevermore. I like this simile as I set it down in my note-book. And I mean no irreverence as I liken the barbed wire to the Crown of Thorns and think of two cross-pieces of ugly wood out of a barrack or a rest-billet as being erected into the shape of The Cross.

When the military policemen first came upon him in the Gare du Nord he made a picture worth looking at. For he stood above six-feet-two in his soleless and broken brogans, and he was as black as a coal-hole at twelve o'clock at night during a total eclipse of the moon and he was as broad across between the shoulders as the back of a hack. He wore a khaki shirt, a pair of ragged, blue overalls and an ancient campaign hat. He didn't appear to be going anywhere in particular; he was just standing there.

Now the M. P.9 have a little scheme for trapping deserters and malingerers. They edge close up behind a suspect and then one of them snaps out "Shun!" in the tones of a drill-officer. If the fellow really is a truant from service, force of habit and the shock of surprise together make him come to attention and then he's a gone gosling, marching off the calaboose with steel jewelry on both his wrists.

But when this pair slipped nearer and nearer until they could touch the big darky, and one of them barked the command right in his ear, he merely turned his head and without straightening his languid form inquired politely;

"Speakin' to me, Boss?"

Nevertheless, to be on the safe side, one of them asked for his papers.

"Whut kinder papers?"

"Your military papers—your pass—something to identify you by."

"W'y, Boss," he asked, "does you need papers to go round wid yere in Sant Nazare?" "This ain't St. Nazare," they told him. "This is Paris."

"Paris? My Lawd! Den dat 'splains it."

"Explains what?" They were getting cross with him.

"'Splains w'y I couldn't fine all dem niggers dey tole me wuz in Sant Nazare. Here I been in Paris all dis time—ever since early dis maw-nin'—an' I didn't know it. No wonner I couldn't locate dem big wharf-boats an' dem niggers."

"Never mind that now—I just asked you where're your papers?"

"Papers? Me? Huh, Boss, I ain't got no more papers 'n a ha'nt. Effen you needs papers to git about on, you gen'elmen better tek me an' lock me up right now, 'ka'se I tells you, p'intedly, I ain't got nary paper to my name."

"That's precisely what we aim to do. Come on, you."

They took him to number ten Rue St. Anne where our provost-marshal in Paris has his headquarters and there the tale came out. I got it first hand from the captain of the Intelligence Department who examined him and I know I got it straight, because the captain was a monologist on the Big Time before he signed up for the war, and he has both the knack of narrative and the gift of dialects. Then later I myself saw the central figure in the comedy and interviewed him. In a way of speaking, I think his adventure was the most remarkable of any I have heard of on this side of the ocean—and I have heard my share. How a big lubberly American negro with absolutely nothing on his person to vouch for him or his purposes, could travel half way across a country where no one else may stir a mile without a pocket full of passes and *vises* and credentials; and how, lacking any knowledge of the language, he managed to do what he did do—but I am anticipating.

It was at ten Rue St. Anne that my friend the ex-vaudevillian took him in hand with the intention of conferring the third degree. For quite a spell the interrogator couldn't make up his mind whether he dealt with the most guileless human being on French soil or with a shrewd black fugitive hiding his real self behind a mask of innocence. After he had made sure the prisoner was what he seemed to be, the intelligence officer kept on at him for the fun of the thing.

Batting his eyes as the questions pelted at him, the giant made straightforward answers. His name was Watterson Towers; his age was summers 'round twenty-fo' or twenty-five, he didn't perzactly 'member w'ich; he was born and fotched up in Bowlin' Green, Kintucky, and at the time of his coming to France he resided at number thirty-fo', East Pittsburgh.

"Number thirty-four what?" asked the inquisitor.

"Naw suh, not no thirty-fo' nothin'—jes' plain thirty-fo'."

"But what street is it on?"

"'Tain't on no strett, Boss."

"What do you mean—no street?"

"Boss, wuz you ever in East Pittsburgh? Well suh, den does you 'member dat string of little houses dat stands in a row right 'longside de railroad tracks ez you comes into town f'um de fur side? 'Taint no street, it's jes' only houses. Well suh, I lives in de thirty-fo'th one."

"I see. How did you get here?"

"Me? I rid, mostly."

"Rode on what?"

"Rid part de time on a ship an' part de time on de steam-cyars but fust an' last I done a mighty heap of walkin', also."

Further questioning elicited from Watterson Towers these salient facts: He had taken a job which carried him from East Pittsburgh to New York and left him stranded there. He had heard about the draft. He knew that sooner or later the draft would catch him and send him off to France where he would be expected to fight Germans, so he decided that before this could happen, he would visit France on his own hook, and as a civilian bystander, a private observer, so to speak, would view some of the operation of war at first-hand, with a view to deciding whether he cared enough for it as a sport, to take a hand in it voluntarily.

He had smuggled himself aboard a transport—Heaven alone knew how!—and fortified with a bag of ginger-snaps he had remained hidden away in a cargo-hold until the ship sailed. Two days out from land a new and very painful sickness overcame the stowaway and he made his way up on deck for air. There he had been caught and had been sent to the galley to work his passage across. When he had progressed thus far, his cross-examiner broke in. "What was the name of the ship?"

"Boss, I plum' disremembers, but it muster been de bigges' ship dey is. W'y suh, dey wuz 'most six-hund'ed folks on dat ship, an' I had to wash up after ever' las' one of 'em. W'ite folks suttinly teks a lot of dishes w'en dey eats—I'll tell de world dat."

"Well, where did the ship land?—do you know that much?"

"Boss, hit wuz some place wid a outlandish name an' dat's all I kin tell you. I never wuz no hand fur 'memberin' reg'lar names let alone dese yere jabber kind of words lak dese yere French folks talks wid."

"What happened when you came ashore?"

"W'y, suh, dey let me off de ship an' a w'ite man on de wharf-boat he tells me I'se landed right spang in France an' he axes me does I want a job of wuk an' I tells him 'Naw suh, not yit.' I tells him I'se aimin' to travel round an' see de country an' de war 'fore I settles down to anythin'. Den 'nother w'ite man dat's standin' dere he tells me dey's a lot of my colour in a place called Sant Nazare an' I 'cides I'll go dere an' 'sociate aw'ile wid dem niggers. So I changed my money an' I—"

"I thought you said you didn't have any money when you started?"

"I didn't, Boss, but de w'ite folks on de ship dey taken up a c'lection fur me, account of me washin' all dem dishes so nice an' clean. It come to twenty dollahs. So I changes it into dese yere francs. De man give me twenty francs fur my twenty dollahs—didn't charge me no interes' a-tall, but jes' traded even; an' den I sets out to find dis yere Sant Nazare place. Dat wuz two days ago an' I been mov-in' stiddy ever sense."

"How did you know what train to take?"

"I didn't. I jes' went to de depot an' I dim' abo'd de fus' train I sees dat look lak she might be fixin' to go sommers. An' after 'w'ile one of dese Frenchies come 'round to me whar I wuz settin' sin' he jabber somethin' at me an' I tell him plain ez I kin, whar I wants to go an' is dis de right train? An' den he jabber some mo' an' I keep on tellin' him an' after 'w'ile he jes th'ow up both hands, lak dis, an' go on off an' leave me be in peace. W'ich dat very same thing happen to me ever' time I git on a train an' I done been on three or fo' 'fore I gits to dis place, dis mawnin'.

"My way wuz to stay by de train t'well she stop an' don't start no mo' an! den I'd git off an' walk round lookin' for de big wharf-boats where de w'ite man tole me dem niggers would be wukkin', but not no place I went did I see ary wharf-boats, so I jes' kept a-movin' t'well I got yere, lak I'm tellin' it to you, an' I says to myself den, 'Dis sutt'inly must be Sant Nazare—it's shore big enough to be, anyway.' But I walked 'bout ten miles an' I couldn't find no wharf-boats an' no niggers neither, scusin' some Frenchified niggers all dressed up lak Misty Shriners, an' dey couldn't talk our way of talkin'. I seen plenty of our soldiers but I wuz'n' aimin' to be pesterin 'round wid no soldiers 'till I'd done seen de war. So finally I sees a big place dat look lak it mout be 'nother depot, an' I went on in there an' wuz fixn' to tek de next train out, w'en dem two soldier-men of your'n wid de bands on dere arms dey come up to me an' dey run me in. An' yere I is."

It was explained to Watterson Towers that, to avoid complications he had better enter the army forthwith and very promptly he agreed. Travel, seemingly, was beginning to pall on him. Then to spin out his gorgeous humour of the interview, the intelligence officer put one more question and when he told me the answer I agreed with him the reward had been worth the effort.

"Now, Watterson," he said, "what kind of a regiment would you prefer to join—an all-white regiment or an all-black regiment or a mixed regiment, part black and part white? You can 'take your choice—so speak up."

"Boss," said Watterson, "it don't make no dif'ence a-tall to me w'ich kind of a regiment 'tis—jes' so it's got a band!"

One's war-time experiences is crowded with constant surprises. For five months, off and on, I have been living on the fourth floor of one of the largest and most noted of Paris hotels, and not until to-day did I find out that two floors of the building have all along been in possession of the government for hospital purposes. The patients, mainly wounded men who have been invalided back from the trenches are brought by night and carried in through a rear entrance, which opens on a barred and guarded alley-way. The guests never see them and they never come in contact with the guests.

Under my feet all these weeks hundreds of disabled fighting-men have been getting better or getting worse, recovering or dying, and I would never have guessed their presence had it not been for the chance remark of a government official who is connected with one of the bureaus having charge of the *blessés*.

I learn now that the same thing is true of several other prominent hotels, but so carefully is the business carried on and so skillfully do the authorities hide their secret that I am sure not one guest in a thousand ever stumbles upon the fact.

When I was writing a tale about one visit of several which I paid to the old Luneville sectors where our buddies, in the spring of this year, first left their tooth-marks on the Heinies, I forgot to tell of an incident that occurred on the last day of our stay up there as the guests of a regiment of the Rainbows.

Martin Green and I had just returned from a four-hour tramp through some of our trenches. It was long after the hour for the mid-day meal when we got back, weary and mud-coated, to regimental headquarters in a knocked-about village. But the colonel's cook obligingly dished up some provender for us and for the young intelligence officer who had been our guide that day. Just as we were finishing the last round of flap-jacks with molasses, the Germans began shelling the battered town so we adjourned to the nearest dug-out, which was the next door cellar, that had been thickened as to its roof with sand-bags and loose earth and strips of railroad iron. Down there we came upon several others who had taken shelter, including one of the majors.

"When were you fellows figuring on starting back to your own billet?" he inquired. "Sometime this afternoon, wasn't it?"

"Yes," said Green, "we had counted on leaving here about three o'clock. But I guess we'll be delayed, if the Germans keep up their strafing. Neither of us fancies trying to make a break out of here while the bombardment is going on, and I don't suppose our chauffeur would be so very enthusiastic over the prospect, either. I only hope the Germans let up on the fireworks display before dark. It's forty-odd miles to where we're going and the thought of riding that distance after nightfall over these torn-up roads with no lights burning on our car and the road full of supply trains coming up to the front, does not strike me as a particularly alluring prospect."

"Don't worry," said the Major with a grin which proved he was holding back something. "You can get away from here in—well, let's see—." He glanced at the watch on his wrist. "In just one hour and three-quarters, or to be exact, in one hour and forty-six minutes from now, you can be on your way. It's now 2:15. At precisely one minute past four you can climb into your car and beat it from here and if you hurry you'll be home in ample time for dinner."

"You talk as though you were in the confidence of these Germans," quoth Green.

"In a way of speaking, I am," said the Major. "I've been here for eight days now, and every day since I arrived, promptly at 2 p. M. those batteries over yonder open up on this place and all hands go underground. The shelling continues—in the ratio of one shell every two minutes—until four o'clock sharp. Then it stops, and until two o'clock the next day, things around here are nice and quiet and healthy. So don't get chesty and think this show was put on especially on your account, because it wasn't: it's in accordance with the regular programme. Therefore, judging to-day's matinee by past performances, I would say that at one minute past four you chaps can be on your way with absolutely nothing to worry about except the chances of a puncture."

"Funny birds—these Germans," exclaimed one of us, still half in doubt as to whether the Major joked.

"Funny birds is right," he said, "and then some. We've got it doped out after this fashion: The officer in command of the German battery just over the hill from where you were to-day probably has instructions to shoot so many rounds a day into us. So in order to simplify the matter he, being a true German, starts at two and quits at four, when he has used up his supply of ammunition for the day. Now that we're wise to his routine we don't take any chances, but withdraw ourselves from society during the two hours of the day when he is enjoying his customary afternoon hate. Old George J. Methodical we call him. You fellows still don't quite believe me, eh? Well, wait and see whether I'm right."

We waited and we saw, and he was right.

Somewhere over our heads a charge of shrapnel or of high explosive exploded every two minutes until precisely four o'clock. Sharp on the hour the shells quit falling and before the dust had settled after the farewell blast we were gathering up our dunnage for the departure. As we sped out of the huddle of shattered cottages and struck the open road there was a half-mile stretch ahead of us and while we traversed it we were within easy range and plain view of the Germans. But no one took a wing shot at us as we whizzed across the open space.

After we slid down over the crest into the protection of the wooded valley below, I remembered an old story—the story of the peddler who invaded a ten-floor office building in New York and made his way to the top floor before one of the hall attendants found him. The attendant kicked the peddler down one flight of stairs to the ninth floor and there another man fell upon him and kicked him down another flight to the eighth floor where a third man took him in hand and kicked him a flight and so he progressed until he had been kicked down ten flights by ten different men and had landed upon the sidewalk a bruised and battered wreck, with the fragments of his wares scattered about him. He sat up on the pavement then and in tones of deep admiration remarked: "Mein Gott, vot a berfect system!"

In the original version of the tale the peddler was Yiddish. But I'm certain now that he was German and that he went back to the Vaterland after the war broke out and became the commander of a battery of five-inch guns on the old Luneville front.

On the day before Decoration Day of this year of 1917 I was in a seaport town on the northeastern coast of France which our people had taken over as a supply base. The general in command of our local forces said to me as we sat in his headquarters at dinner that evening; "I wish you'd get up early in the morning and go for a little ride with me out to the cemetery. You'll be going back there later in the day, of course, for the services but I want you to see something that you probably won't be able to see after nine or ten o'clock."

"What is it?" I asked.

"Never mind now," he answered. "To tell you in advance doesn't suit my purposes. But will you be ready to go with me in my car at seven o'clock?"

"Yes, sir. I will."

I should say? it was about half-past seven when we rode in at the gates of the cemetery and made for the section which, by consent of the French, had been set apart as a burial place for our people. For considerably more than a year now, dating from the time I write this down, a good many thousands of Americans have been stationed in or near this port, and many, many times that number have passed through it. So quite naturally, though it is hundreds of miles from any of the past or present battle fronts, we have had numerous deaths there from accident or from disease or from other causes.

We rounded a turn in the winding road and there before us stretched the graves of our dead boys, soldiers and sailors, marines and members of labor battalions; whites and blacks and yellow men, Jews and Gentiles, Catholics, Protestants and Mohammedans—for there were four followers of the faith of Islam taking their last sleep here in this consecrated ground—row upon row of them, each marked, except in the case of the Mohammedans, by a plain white cross bearing in black letters the name, the age, the rank and the date of death of him who slept there at the foot of the cross.

Just beyond the topmost line of crosses stood the temporary wooden platform dressed with bunting and flags, where an American admiral and an American brigadier, a group of French officers headed by a major-general, a distinguished French civic official, and three chaplains representing three creeds were to unite at noon in an hour of devotion and tribute to the memories of these three-hundred-and-odd men of ours who had made the greatest of all human sacrifices.

But it was not the sight of the rows of graves and the lines of crosses nor the peculiar devices uprearing slantwise at head and foot of the graves of the four Musselmans nor yet the brave play of tri-coloured bunting upon the sides and front of the platform yonder which caught my attention. For at that hour the whole place was alive with the shapes of French people—mostly of women in black but with a fair sprinkling of shapes of old men and of children among them. All these figures were busy at a certain task—and that task was the decorating of the graves of Americans.

As we left the car to walk through the plot I found myself taking off my cap and I kept it off all the while I was there. For even before I had been told the full story of what went on there I knew I stood in the presence of a most high and holy thing and so I went bare-headed as I would in any sanctuary.

We walked all through this God's acre of ours, the general and I. Some of the women who laboured therein were old and bent, some were young but all of them wore black gowns. Some plainly had been recruited from the well-to-do and the wealthy elements of the resident population; more though, were poor folk and many evidently were peasants who, one guessed, lived in villages or on farms near to the city. Here would be a grave that was heaped high with those designs of stiff, bright-hued immortelles which the French put upon the graves of their own dead. Here would be a grave that was marked with wreaths of simple field flowers or with the great lovely white and pink roses which grow so luxuriantly on this coast. Here would be merely great sheaves of loose blossoms; there a grave upon which the flowers had been scattered broadcast, until the whole mound was covered with the fragrant dewy offerings; and there, again, I saw where fingers patently unaccustomed to such employment had fashioned the long-stemmed roses into wreaths and crosses and even into forms of shields.

Grass grew rich and lush upon all the graves. White sea-shells marked the sides of them and edged the narrow gravelled walks. We came to where there were two newly made graves; their occupants had been buried there only a day or so before as one might tell by the marks in the trodden turf, but a carpeting of sods cut from a lawn somewhere had been so skillfully pieced together upon the mounds that the raw clods of clay beneath were quite covered up and hidden from sight, so that only the seams in the green coverlids distinguished these two graves from graves which were older than they by weeks or months.

Alongside every grave, nearly, knelt a woman alone, or else a woman with children aiding her as she disposed her showing of flowers and wreaths to the best advantage. The old men were putting the paths in order, raking the gravel down smoothly and straightening the borderings of shells. There were no soldiers among the men; all were civilians, and for the most part humble-appearing civilians, clad in shabby garments. But I marked two old gentlemen wearing the great black neckerchiefs and the flowing broadcloth coats of ceremonial days, who seemed as deeply intent as any in what to them must have been an unusual labour. Coming to each individual worker or each group of workers the general would halt and formally salute in answer to the gently murmured greetings which constantly marked our passage through the burying-ground. When we had made the rounds we sat down upon the edge of the flag-dressed platform and he proceeded to explain what I already had begun to reason out for myself. Only, of course I did not know, until he told me, how it all had started.

"It has been a good many months now," he said, "since we dug the first grave here. But on the day of the funeral a delegation of the most influential residents came to me to say the people of the town desired to adopt our dead. I asked just what exactly was meant by this and then the spokesman explained.

"'General,' he said to me, 'there is scarcely a family in this place that has not given one or more of its members to die for France. In most cases these dead of ours sleep on battlefields far away from us, perhaps in unmarked, unknown graves. This is true of all the parts of our country but particularly is it true of this town, which is so remote from the scenes of actual fighting. So in the case of this brave American who is to-day to be buried here among us, we ask that a French family be permitted formally to undertake the care of his grave, exactly as though it were the grave of their own flesh-and-blood who fell as this American has fallen, for France and for freedom. In the case of each American who may hereafter be buried here we crave the same privilege. We promise you that for so long as these Americans shall rest here in our land, their graves will be as our graves and will be tended as we would tend the graves of our own sons.

"'We desire that the name of each family thus adopting a grave may be registered, so that should the adults die, the children of the next generation as a sacred charge, may carry on the obligation which is now to be laid upon their parents and which is to be transmitted down as a legacy to all who bear their name. We would make sure that no matter how long your fallen braves rest in the soil of France, their graves will not be neglected or forgotten.

"'We wish to do this thing for more reasons than one: We wish to do it because thereby we may express in our own poor way the gratitude we feel for America. We wish to do it because of the thought that some stricken mother across the seas in America will perhaps feel a measure of consolation in knowing that the grave of her boy will always be made beautiful by the hands of a Frenchwoman whose home, also, has been desolated. And finally we wish to do it because we know it will bring peace to the hearts of our French women to feel they have a right to put French flowers upon the graves of your dead since they can never hope, most of them, to be able to perform that same office for their heroic dead.'"

The general stopped and cleared his voice which had grown a bit husky. Then he resumed:

"So that was how the thing came about, and that explains what you see here now. You see, the French have no day which exactly corresponds in its spiritual significance to our Decoration Day and our Memorial Day. All Souls' Day, which is religious, rather than patriotic in its purport, is their nearest approach to it. But weeks ago, before the services contemplated for to-day were even announced, the word somehow spread among the townspeople. To my own knowledge some of these poor women have been denying themselves the actual necessities of life in order to be able to make as fine a showing for the graves which they have adopted as any of the wealthier sponsors could make.

"Don't think, though, that these graves are not well kept at all times. Any day, at any hour, you can come here and you will find anywhere from ten to fifty women down on their knees smoothing the turf and freshening the flowers which they constantly keep upon the graves. But I knew that at daylight this morning all or nearly all of them would be here doing their work before the crowds began to arrive for the services, and I wanted you to see them at it, in the hope that you might write something about the sight for our people at home to read. If it helps them better to understand what is in the hearts of the French you and I may both count our time as having been well spent."

He stood up looking across the cemetery, all bathed and burnished as it was in the soft rich sunshine.

"God," he said under his breath, "how I am learning to love these people!"

So I have here set down the tale and to it I have to add a sequel. Decoration Day was months ago and now I learn that the custom which originated in this coast town is spreading through the country; that in many villages and towns where Americans are buried, French women whose sons or husbands or fathers or brothers have been killed, are taking over the care of the graves of the Americans, bestowing upon them the same loving offices which they would visit, if they could, upon the graves of their own men-folk.

It was one of those days which will live always in my memory—my feet wouldn't let me forget it even if my brain wanted to—when I had to walk to keep up. The available forces offered by Pershing to the French and British at the time of the great spring push of the Germans were moving up across Picardy. I, as one of the correspondents assigned each to a separate regiment, had set out at dawn to foot it for fifteen miles across country at the tail of the headquarters company. This happened to be a day, of which there were several, when neither a side-car, a riding-horse, or a seat in an ambulance or a baggage-wagon was available, and when the colonel's automobile was so crowded with the colonel and his driver and his adjutant and his French liaison officer and all their baggage, there was no room in it for me. That painful period of my martial adventures has elsewhere in these writings been described at greater or less length.

I was hoofing it over the flinty highway, trying to favour my blisters, when I heard a hail behind me. I turned around and there was an angel from Heaven, temporarily disguised as a Y. M. C. A. worker, sitting at the wheel of a big auto-truck with the sign of the red triangle on its sides.

"Could you use a little ride?" he inquired, grinning through the dust clouds as he drew up alongside and halted.

Could I use a little ride! For fear he might change his mind or something, I boarded him over a front wheel before I began expressing my eternal gratitude.

This ceremony being over, he told me who he was, and I told him who I was, and after that we became friends for life. He was a minister from a city in southern California but he didn't look it now, what with a four-days' growth of stubbly red whiskers on his weatherbeaten chops and grease spots on his service uniform. He had given up a good salary and he had left behind him a wife and three children—I am sure about the wife and I'm pretty sure there were three children, or two anyhow—to come over here and at the age of forty-four or thereabouts to run a perambulating canteen for the boys. There are a lot more like him in France, serving with the "Y" or the K. of C.'s or the Salvation Army or the Red Cross and as a rule they assay about nineteen-hundred and ninety-nine pounds of true gold to the ton.

"Willing to earn your passage, ain't you?" he inquired when the introductions were concluded. "Well then, climb into the back of my bus and stand by to get busy, heaving out the cargo."

I looked then and saw his truck was loaded to the gunwales with boxes of California oranges.

"What the-?" I began, in surprise.

"Go on and say it," he urged. "Don't hang back just because I'm a parson by trade. Trailing around with this man's army, I'm used to hearing cuss words. Quite a jag of freight, isn't it? Some good fellow out in my state shipped a train-load of oranges across with the request that they be distributed among the boys, free gratis for nothing, and it's my present job to catch up with this division and give part of the stuff away. I lit out from Paris before daylight this morning and here I am. But I can't steer this wagon and pass out the truck at the same time so if you'll go aft and do the Walter Johnson, I'll play Bobby Waltour here at this end and between us we can spread the light and keep right on moving at the same time."

Before we ran out of oranges, which was about three o'clock in the afternoon just as we rolled into the village where the headquarters company and the colonel and his staff—and incidentally I—were to be billeted for the night, I had a sore arm to keep company with my sore feet. All day this had been our procedure: As we ranged up behind a column of marching troops my new pal, the red-haired dominie, would yell out "Who wants a nice, juicy orange, fellows?" and then as we rolled on by I would fling out the fruit, trying to make sure that every man got one orange and that no man got more than one.

I threw oranges to men afoot, to men on wagons and on guns, to men and officers on horseback and to men perched upon ambulances and wagons. My throwing was faulty but the catching approximated perfection.

An arm would fly up and the flying orange would find a home in the deftly cupped palm of the band at the far end of the arm. The news travelled ahead of us, somehow, and whole companies would be lined up as we arrived, to get their share.

A few minutes before the finish of the trip came, we caught up with a couple of French battalions. Neither of us remembered the French word for orange, but that made no difference. His whoop of announcement and my first fling in the direction of a trudging Poilu, were as signals to all the rest and up went their paws. Their intentions were good, but I don't think I ever in all my life witnessed such a display of miscellaneous muffing, and I used to see some pretty raw fielding back at Paducah in the days of the old Kitty League. As the scorers would say, there was an error for nearly every chance. Among the Americans not one orange in ten had been dropped; among the Frenchmen not one in ten was safely held.

"Get the answer, don't you?" inquired the preacher-driver as we left the trudging Frenchmen behind and hurried ahead to connect with a khaki-clad outfit just defiling out of a crossway into the main road a quarter of a mile ahead of us.

"Sure," I answered, "the Yanks make traps of their paws but the Frenchmen make baskets of theirs. The orange stays in the trap but it rolls out of a butter-fingered basket."

"Yes," he said, "but the real cause goes deeper down than that. Baseball — that's the answer. Probably every American in France played baseball when he was a kid, or else he still plays it. No Frenchman ever knew anything about baseball until we came over here last year and introduced it into the country. The average Frenchman looks on a sporting event as a spectacle, but the average American, at some time or other in his life, has been an active participant in his national sport and the lessons we learn as children we never entirely forget even though lack of practice may make us rusty."

Which, of course, was quite true. Likewise, I think it is the underlying reason for the fact that our boys are the best hand-grenade tossers among the Allies.'

We certainly are creatures of habit. Because somebody, a century or so behind us, speaking with that air of authority which usually accompanies the voicing of a perfectly wrong premise, stated that all Irishmen were natural wits and that no Englishman, could see a joke, the world accepted the assertion as a verity. Never was a greater libel perpetrated upon either race. It has been my observation that the Irish at heart are a melancholy breed.

Certain it is that no people have produced more first-rate humourists and more first-rate comedians than the English. Witness the British output of humour in this war; witness Bairnsfather and those satirical verses on war topics that have been running in *Punch* lately. I'm mostly Celt myself — North of Scotland and South of Ireland, with some Welsh and a little English mixed up in my strain — and I feel myself qualified to speak on these matters.

Another common delusion among outsiders and particularly among Americans is that Englishmen are stolid unimaginative creatures who fail to show their feelings in moments of stress because they haven't any great flow of feelings to show. Now, as a general proposition, I think it may be figured that a Frenchman on becoming sentimental will give free vent to the thoughts that are in his heart; that an American will try to hide his emotions under a mask of levity and that an Englishman, expressing after a somewhat different pattern the racial embarrassment which he shares with the American, will seek to appear outwardly indifferent, incidentally becoming more or less inarticulate. The Frenchman takes no shame to himself that he weeps or sings in public; the Yankee is apt to laugh very loudly; the Englishman will be mute and will exhibit slight confusion which by some might be mistaken for mental awkwardness. But there are exceptions to all rules. In so far as the rule pertains to the Britisher, I am thinking of two exceptions. To one of these instances I was an eye-witness; the other incident was told to me by a man who had been present when it occurred. He said he was passing through Charing Cross station one night when he saw two Canadian subalterns emerging from one of the refreshment booths. Both of them had been wounded. One had his right arm in a sling and limped as he walked. The other was that most pitiable spectacle which this war can offer — a young man blinded. Across his eyes was drawn a white cloth band and he moved with the uncertain fumbling gait of one upon whom this affliction has newly come. With his uninjured arm the lame youth was steering his companion. The two boys — for they were only boys, my informant said — halted in an arched exitway to put on their top-coats before stepping out into the drizzle. The crippled officer released his hold upon his friend's elbow to shrug his own garment up upon his shoulders. The second *blessé* was making a sorry job at finding the armholes of his coat, when an elderly officer with the badges of a major-general upon his shoulders and a breast loaded with decorations, stepped up and with the words, "Let me help you, please," held the coat in the proper position while deftly he guided the blind boy's limbs into the sleeve openings.

All in a second the unexpected denouément came. The youngster reached in his pocket, then felt for the hand of his volunteer who had come to his assistance. "Thank you very much," he said. And there in the palm of the astonished general lay a shilling.

The other lieutenant hobbled to his comrade's side. He may have meant to whisper, but in his distress he fairly shouted it out: "You've just handed a tip to a major-general!" Horrified, the blind boy spun about on his heels to apologise.

"I'm so sorry, sir," he gasped. "I—I thought it was a porter, of course. I beg your pardon, a thousand times, sir. I hope you'll forgive me—you know, I can't see any more, sir." And with that he held out his hand to take back the miserable coin.

The splendid-looking old man put both his hands upon the lad's shoulders. His ruddy face was quivering and the tears were running down his cheeks.

"Please don't, please don't," he gulped, almost incoherently. "I want to keep your shilling, if you don't mind. Why God bless you, my boy, I want to keep it always. I wouldn't take a thousand pounds for it."

And then falling back one pace he saluted the lad with all the reverence he would have accorded his commander-in-chief or his king.

Here is the other thing, the one of which I speak as having first-hand knowledge. Three of us, returning by automobile from a visit to the Verdun massif, took a detour in order to call upon our friends the blithe young Britishers who made up Night Bombing Squadron No. ——. They were a great outfit, representing as they did, every corner of the Empire; but the pick of the lot, to my way of thinking, were Big Bill and the Young-'Un, both captains and both seasoned pilots of big Handley-Page bombing planes. As I think I have remarked somewhere else in these pages, the average age of this crowd was somewhere around twenty-two.

This fine spring night we arrived at their headquarters opportunely for there was to be a raiding expedition to the Rhine Valley. First though, there was a good dinner at which we were unexpected but nonetheless welcome guests. Catch a lot of English lads letting a little thing like the prospect of a four hundred mile air jaunt into Germany and back interfere with their dinner.

Just before the long, lazy twilight greyed away, to be succeeded by the silver radiance of the moonlight, all hands started for the hangars a mile or two away across on the other side of the patch of woods which surrounded the camp. Upon the running-boards of our car we carried an overflow of six or eight airmen; the rest walked. Clinging alongside me where I rode in the front seat, was a tall, slender boy—a captain for all his youth—whom I shall call Wilkins, which wasn't his name but is near enough to it. He was the minstrel of the squadron; could play on half a dozen instruments, including the piano, and sing Cockney ballads with a lovely nasal whine.

At the field our added passengers dropped off and each ran to superintend the soldier crews as they went over the planes, tuning them up. After a little while the signal for departure came. One after another thirteen machines got away, each bearing its pilot and its gunner-ob-server and with its freight of great bombs dangling from its undersides as it rose and went soaring away toward the northeast, making a wonderful picture, if in rising, it chanced to cut across the white white disk of a splendid full moon which had just pushed itself clear of the wooded mountainside.

Next day about noon-time our route again brought us within ten miles of the squadron's camp and we decided to turn aside that way for an hour or so and learn the results of the raid. Sprawled about the big living-room of their community house in the birch forest, we found a score or more of our late hosts.

"Well, what sort of a show did you put on last night?" one of us inquired as we entered.

"Oh, a priceless show," came the answer from one. "We gave the dear old Boche a sultry evenin' and make no ruddy error about it. Spilt our little pills all over Mannheim and Treves. Scored a lot of direct hits too, as well as one might judge while comin' away in more or less of a hurry."

"It was rippin' fun while it lasted," put in another. "We didn't get back though until nearly four o'clock this mornin'. It left me feel-in' rather seedy—I must have my beauty sleep or I'm no good for the whole day." Behind his hand he yawned.

Now ordinarily, the next question would have been framed with a view to finding out whether all the bombers had safely returned; but the airman's code of ethics forbade. It was perfectly proper to inquire regarding the effects of a raid into hostile territory but the outsider must refrain from seeking information regarding any losses on the part of the raiders until one of them volunteered the news of his own accord.

But there was no rule against our silently counting noses and this we did, industriously. As nearly as I could make out there were, of those whom we knew had participated in the expedition, five or six missing from the assembled company; but then of course the absentees might be asleep in their quarters.

It struck the three of us, and in my own case I know the impression deepened as the minutes passed, that for all their kindly hospitality and all their solicitude that we should feel at home, there was a common depression prevalent among them. Some, we thought betrayed their feelings by a silence not habitual among these high-spirited youths.. Some seemed abstracted and some just a trifle irritable. And when this one or that described the bombing of the enemy towns which had been their particular targets I was sure I detected something forced about the enthusiasm he out into his speech.

Presently there befell one of those awkward little silences which inevitably occur in any gathering where the spirit of things is a bit forced and strained. It was broken by a lanky twenty-year-old flyer.

"Hm—" he began, clearing his throat and striving to make his tone casual, "you know, Wilkins and his observer didn't get back." That was all—no details of how his two mates had gone rocketing down somewhere behind the German lines probably to instant death. In these few words he stated the bald fact of it and then he looked away, suddenly and unduly interested in the movements of somebody passing by one of the open windows.

On my right hand sat that winning little chap whom his mates called the Young-'Un. The Young-'Un was lighting a pipe.

"Beastly annoyin'," he grunted between puffs at the stem of his briar-root, "losin' Wilkins. As a matter of fact he was the only decent pianist we had. Rotten luck and all that sort of thing to lose our pianist, eh what?" Coming from the Young-'Un, with his gentle smile and his soft whimsical drawl, the last remark seemed so utterly unsympathetic, so callous, so cold-blooded, that the shock of what he said left me mute. It left my two companions mute, too.

I turned in my chair and looked at the Young-'Un. He seemed to have trouble getting his pipe going. His two hands were cupped over the bowl, making a mask for his face. By reason of his hands I could not see much of his face but I could see this much—that his chin was trembling, that the big muscles in his throat were twitching and jumping and that though he winked his eyes as fast as he could, he couldn't wink fast enough to keep the big tears from leaking out and running down his cheeks.

Because he was an experienced airman it was a part of his professional code to make no pother over the loss of a fellow-flier by the hazard of chance which every one of them dared as a part of his daily life. Because he was an Englishman, he felt shame that he should show any emotion. But because his heart was broken he cried behind the cover of his hands.

Shells and bombs are forever doing freakish things. The effects of their tantrums set one to thinking of the conduct of cyclones and earthquakes. For example:

In Bar-le-Duc, which most Americans used to think of, not as a city but as a kind of jelly, I saw when we passed through there the other day, where a bomb dropped by a German airraider did a curious bit of damage. I reckon people who believe in omens and portents would call it significant. Just off the railroad station in a little paved square stands a monument put up by popular subscription to the men of this town who died for their country in 1870-71. Upon one face of the granite shaft, being the one which looks inward toward the town, are two bronze figures of heroic size. The lowermost figure is that of a dying boy-soldier, with one hand pressed to his breast and the other holding fast to his musket. The other figure—that of a winged angel typifying the spirit of France—is hovering above him with a palm branch extended over his drooping head.

The bomb, descending from on high, must have grazed the face of the monument. A great hole in the pavement shows where it exploded. One flying fragment sheared away the fingers and thumbs of the dying soldier's hand so that the bronze musket was tom out of his grasp and flung upon the earth. Some one picked up the musket and laid it at the base of the marble but the hand sticks out into space empty and mutilated.

I dare say a German might interpret this as meaning France would be left crippled, disarmed and mangled. But to me I read it as a sign to show that France, the conqueror, and not the conquered, will be one of the nations that are to take the lead in bringing about universal peace and universal disarmament, once Germany has been cused of what ails her.

I saw them when they first landed at Camp Upton—furtive, frightened, slew-footed, slackshouldered, underfed, apprehensive—a huddle of unhappy aliens speaking in alien tongues; knowing little of the cause for which they must fight and possibly caring less.

I saw them again three months later when the snow of the dreadful winter of 1917-18 was piling high about their wooden barracks down there on wind-swept Long Island. The stoop was beginning to come out of their spines, the shamble out of their gait. They had learned to hold their heads up, had learned to look every man in the eye and tell him to go elsewhere with a capital H. They knew now that discipline was not punishment and that the salute was not a mark of servility but an evidence of mutual self-respect as between officer and man. They wore their uniforms with pride. The flag meant something to them and the war meant something to them. Three short hard months of training had transformed them from a rabble into soldier-stuff; from a street-mob into the makings of an army; from strangers into Americans.

After nine months I have seen them once more in France. For swagger, for snap, for smartness in the drill and for cockiness in the billet; for good humour on the march and for dash and spunk and deviltry in the fighting into which just now they have been sent, our army can show no better soldiers and no more gallant spirits than the lads who mainly make up the rank and file of this particular division.

They are the foreign-born Jews and Italians and Slavs of New York's East Side, that were called up for service in the first draft.

No wonder the mother who didn't raise her boy to be a soldier has become an extinct species back home.